THE

SUMMER

HOUSE

THE
SUMMER
HOUSE

A Tradition of Leisure

Amy Willard Cross

HarperPerennial
HarperCollins*PublishersLtd*

Grateful acknowledgement is made for permission to reprint from the following: "The Long-legged House" from *Recollected Essays 1965-1980*, copyright © 1981 by Wendell Berry, published by North Point Press and reprinted by permission of Farrar, Strauss & Giroux, Inc. *Keeping Faith* by Jimmy Carter, copyright © 1982 by Jimmy Carter. Reprinted with permission of Bantam Books. *A God Within* by René Dubos, reprinted with permission of Charles Scribner's Sons, an imprint of Macmillan Publishing Company, copyright © 1972 René Dubos. *A Sand County Almanac* by Aldo Leopold, copyright © 1949 Aldo Leopold, published by Oxford University Press. *Crossing to Safety* by Wallace Stegner, copyright © 1987 by Wallace Stegner, published by Random House. "Once More to the Lake," from *One Man's Meat* by E.B. White, copyright © 1942 by E.B. White, published by Harper & Row.

First Edition

Illustrations by Tracey Eve Winton

Canadian Cataloguing in Publication Data

Cross, Amy Willard, 1960-
  The summer house: a tradition of leisure

ISBN 0-00-637889-7

1. Vacation homes - History. 2. Vacations - History.
I. Title.

HD7289.2.C76 1992   643'.2   C92-093933-3

92 93 94 95 96 ❖ RRD 5 4 3 2 1

for the studio and the riverhouse
and the people who built them

ACKNOWLEDGMENTS

Many people have helped me with this adventure into summer, but I would not have traveled very far without Patrick. I am fortunate to have had his house, his insights, his bracing and trussing, and his companionship while speeding around the landscape of summer. To each of the Crosses, I offer my heartfelt thanks for constantly lending me a hand, and then holding mine—for their enthusiasm, encouragement and criticism. I am indebted to my editor Barbara Berson, who saw the book when it was no more than an apparition, for her utter reasonableness, guidance and patience. In addition, I have benefitted from Deborah Viets' incisive comments and improvements. My thanks also go to Daphne Hart and Helen Heller for their early support, Tracey Winton for her drawings, Lorraine Johnson for her suggestion and Robert Donnelly of Panasonic who processed my work into computer form. I am grateful to all those who offered me hospitality along the way, especially the ladies of Castine and all the Youngs of Sans Souci. Most of all, I want to thank the countless people who shared with me their thoughts about summer.

CONTENTS

INTRODUCTION

When I arrive at the studio on Friday nights, I fling open the door and cast my eyes about all the familiar things, left like a play stopped in midscene. Even before taking off my coat, I go to the sink and turn on the tap, let it run and fill a glass with cold mineral water, drink it down and fill another. That water, with its copper and calcium, is the taste of home. I crave it; nothing else can quench my thirst. I've tried to import this flavor to town in a plastic jug, but like delicate wine after a rough trip, the water dulls and flattens. So I return to the studio as often as possible to drink my fill of that water, the woods and the man who built the place.

The studio sits high in the woods like a treehouse, bordered on three sides by beeches, oaks and ironwoods, its windows looking into the boughs. I had lived and worked there day in and day out for two years. It was a home like any other, where there was always something to do—like washing the dishes or taking down screens. I earned my bread there, in a corner set aside for commerce, furnished with a phone, a light and a machine.

Then I moved into the city—as did my files and equipment—and what was once a house turned into a cottage. It's been transformed into a carefree sanctuary wholeheartedly dedicated to pleasure. Lunches become picnics and the simplest dinners feel like parties. Free to do whatever pleases me, I read, walk in the woods or just daydream in a pool of winter sunlight. I can stay up late, sleep late or even nap in the afternoon because the day declares its own rhythm. Going there feels like taking off tight clothes; even though elastic leaves marks on the skin, the memory of tightness quickly fades. I can stretch out and get comfortable. Like a child who's climbed into a tree fort, I feel I'm out of reach, out of sight, hidden away. Nobody much comes to visit: I don't ask them. Hardly anyone calls, so the telephone loses its usual menace.

Like a treehouse, the studio is but one room. Such a simple dwelling houses—rather demands—a simple life. There are no walls to hide bad moods. There are no closets for collecting things. No dressers store unworn clothes. No desk. No television tantalizes. The kitchen, consisting of a hot plate and portable oven, doesn't stand for complicated food. Not a hardship, doing without gives me time to do.

Even though the bulk of my possessions live in the city, this remains home. It's the place I imagine while writhing in the dentist's chair. It's the place I want to come home to when rumpled by the rigors of traveling. Because it doesn't house "real" life, the studio has the warmth of homecoming, without the worries. There's no junk mail to open, no messages to return.

The layers of droning engines and voices stacked on top of each other in town get peeled back to reveal the world's true silence. From this lookout, I can watch over all the goings-on. I sit on the balcony at summer dusks, waiting for the red-tailed hawk to swoop down and get his dinner by the stream, and I stay, watching this universe close down for the night, until mosquitoes chase me to the other side of the screens.

Although it wasn't originally intended as one, the studio is my summer house. By summer house I mean a house occupied on weekends and vacations that is filled with as much pleasure and as much warmth as summer itself. Of course, *cottage*, *cabin* or *camp* mean the same thing, but ultimately the name is less important than how it's thought about—how it's approached. To someone unfamiliar with the story of my desk and its move, my studio would not appear to be a cottage at all, since it sits on the cusp of countryside and suburbia, far from the usual summer playgrounds. Nevertheless, it is a cottage by virtue of its nonfunctional function. No longer an office, or even a mailing address, the studio has since been invested with other meaning.

If moving a desk can transform shelter into fantasy, changing how I thought about, lived in and used a place reveals just how abstract a destination a summer house is. Not real estate, it is more a state of mind that can be packed and moved about—to any woods or seaside. And many of us travel through life with this memory of a perfect place waiting for our return.

In a sense, I've always gone to the studio; it has simply taken on different forms. For every place I have lived, there has been an opposite place I've escaped to—in reaction to the first. For every city, there has been a countryside; although I've never been a naturalist, athlete or particularly outdoorsy, I, too, have had cravings for quiet mornings and views into the vanishing point. I've never bought, built or even rented a pleasure house, but these places have always appeared graciously before me, and have been shared or loaned. While mired in the smog of Los Angeles, I escaped to a geodesic dome in the Topanga Mountains, dry as drought. Another time I went to a house at Malibu, to visit a friend who made me throw my troubles out to sea—with big gestures—over the balcony. Long before that, I spent childhood summers on an island with a few dozen houses, the island connected to the world only by an erratic seven-car ferry. Folding into itself, the family did things together until the *I* melted into the *we*. My parents later moved that beach house—although not literally—to a riverside bay closer to their house, recreating an enclave of family, that becomes the family home during assorted holidays and weekends. Leaving a bathing suit and sneakers in the closet there gives me tenancy, and somehow guarantees my return home.

The notion that a cottage is an *idea*—a movable concept—made me want to examine the summer house, not as a Thorstein Veblen or another serious social critic, but as someone who knows and experiences it and who succumbs to its romanticism as well. The summer house is often romanticized and sentimentalized, but it's rarely examined. Usually, we're in such a rush to pack and finally *get there* that few of us stop to think about the meaning behind the migration. Once there, reclining in a bath of fresh air, we rightfully luxiuriate in sensation, taking second or third helpings without counting. It is as Henry James said, "When you wander about in Arcadia, you ask as few questions as possible." As much as I have appreciated my brief stays in Arcadia, I did have questions. What made James compare a corner of New Hampshire to that mythic bucolic paradise? What makes Arcadia? Why do we go there, and why would we leave?

But the answers were long in coming. There's a drawer full of handy phrases to describe these houses that we pull out when needed, and I've heard them all: heaven on earth, Shangri-la, Brigadoon, an oasis, a private Eden, home away from home, our chance to get away from it all, a place to relax and unwind, a little piece of paradise. I wanted to get beyond that wall of easy phrases and clichés, to go beyond raptures about paradise to find out why we consider these places, as Wallace Stegner did, the headquarters of happiness.

On the surface, the entire topic of getaway houses seems like undiscovered terrain, as though something so obvious does not merit serious attention. An unenlightened librarian once laughed right into the telephone in response to my search for material on summer houses. Gradually, though, as on a treasure hunt, each cryptic clue led me to another hidden under a piece of driftwood, and then another, as I got closer, and eventually discovered something—such as a diary of summer pleasures from the 1850s.

High up on library shelves, I found crumbling books that had preserved summer life, like dried Queen Anne's lace between the pages. I was astonished to find what a rich history these houses had in North America, how deeply they left their mark on, and at the same time reflected, our culture. There was quite a cultural cache; writers, thinkers and others had left behind records of their experience. It turned out that a substantial written tradition accompanied our escapes, starting of course with the Roman poets vaguely recalled from high school classrooms, those writers who come to life once read in English. One of the earliest summer wildernesses in North America, the Adirondack Mountains of New York, have camped out permanently in the cultural imagination. Of course, the oldest summer territories had the richest written traditions upon which I could draw—and did. I found myself fascinated by others' accounts of their summer houses. Each house had its own story, yet each story reinforced and enriched the picture that was starting to take shape.

Searching for this newfound Arcadia, I wandered around the Adirondacks, the Blue Ridge, the Finger Lakes and Thousand Islands, canoed on Ontario lakes and Georgian Bay, cycled around Nantucket and Martha's Vineyard and drove along the Maine coast, visiting whatever places I could, talking to hundreds of people sitting in the shade of their verandas. I traveled by telephone to yet farther places. Rifling deeper into that drawer, sorting out the jumbled top layer of well-worn phrases, revealed artifacts, evidence of Arcadia's value: a reunion photograph in which an entire family wears bathing suits and matching T-shirts; a stiff moth carcass of a rare species; a poem by a grandchild, expressed in tentative handwriting, photocopied and sent around. There was something bigger at play here. Summer places may appear to be fantasies, but they connect us with real things. More than just places to spend vacations, they allow us to put ourselves back together there. Actually, these houses hold up a mirror to our culture's needs, so looking at that reflection—taking a tour through the cottage—tells much about ourselves and our longings.

When talking about their summer places, these modern-day Arcadians would tell me such and such lake, or town, or beach, or mountain was the most beautiful, the most private, the most wild— simply their favorite place in the world. They would declare I must either write about it, being the best cottage in the world, or that I shouldn't, because that would just bring more people around who would ruin their idyll. I wish I could have visited all of those places, talked to people from every little summer hamlet from lakes in the middle to seashores on the very eastern tip. But I went where I was invited, and in the end it doesn't matter. Whether it's the Laurentians, Skeleton Lake or Southeast Harbor, the experience is universal. Whether it's fresh or saltwater, pines or palms, the details may differ, but the essence of the summer house remains the same.

My subject is not the castles of Newport or great country estates imitating the English nobility. Rather, it is the little bungalow, the house made from a kit snuggled into a lakeside clearing, the family farm transformed into a weekend retreat, the studio in the woods. As insignificant as that modest vacation house may seem, it contains secrets—about us, about our times.

le petit Trianon

1. THE IDEA OF THE IDYLL

On the hand that makes up the Finger Lakes, Keuka represents the pinkie, deformed by an accident of a glacial nature. It has no universities, no cities, no famous golf course at its tip, like the more shapely digits formed by Seneca and Cayuga lakes. Steep hills covered with a trellis of vineyards fall right to the shore of Keuka Lake, which is outlined by the asphalt aura of Highway 54.

All along that curving asphalt ribbon, there are houses—vacation houses, summer houses, mobile homes, cabins and cottages. The older farmhouses sit above the highway, but vacation houses have been squeezed onto the ribbon of shoreline between the highway and the lake. There's hardly a piece of shoreline that hasn't been built on. In addition to all the cabins, there are bed-and-breakfasts and collections of housekeeping cabins, rented by the week. Mobile homes, decorated with a skirt of latticework and a garden, are lined up neatly in communities overlooking the lake. These are the accessible villas of our age—fifty feet of lakeshore with a cottage.

Like a city fountain, Keuka Lake is a place to splash and play in; for the people who come here from upstate New York and southern Ontario on weekends and vacations, Keuka Lake is heaven on earth, the center of the world. This is vacation life, where there's liberty to wear little or no clothes and pursue happiness in the outdoors.

Although most of the vacation houses have been built in the past fifty years, people have been coming to Keuka Lake since the 1880s by trains and steamers. Down the road, the well-to-do from Hammondsport and Bath built themselves lakefront cottages, less than ten miles from their winter houses. It stayed much the same until after World War II, when the lakeshore was carved up like the top tier of a wedding cake, a tidbit for everyone's pillow, all for the dream of ultimate leisure. In the 1950s, a cottage on the lake cost some $10,000. Claiming a share in the dream, vacationers converted old waterside ice houses and grape-packing sheds into cottages, or improvised—like the streamlined trailer covered by a plywood carport. Since much of Keuka Lake is not blessed with a broad sweeping beach, most cottages are built on steep, hilly lots; each cottage deals with the terrain differently, modifying the shoreline and creating an individual, perfect landscape of leisure. Some pile up landfill and modified sheet pilings to create more lawn; others substitute a deck promontory for the perfunctory bright green blanket; and some import enough sand to create their own little beaches.

Although snug to the road, these cabins dug into the slope are camouflaged by a fence of trees. Only mailboxes—decorated with begonias or white wooden geese—signal the presence of a cottage. When viewed from the water, each cottage seems much the same; patios and decks cluttered with chairs overlook the lake and docks mark each residence as clearly as a mailbox. Closed to the road, the cottages bare all to the lakeside: sliding glass doors and huge plates of glass cut into each facade, and fill the void with a view of the water. That water, claimed to be the purest around, is what seduces people from the city.

If they're not boating, trolling or swimming in the lake, Keuka's weekenders are looking at it. They gaze at the lake's mesmerizing silhouette, and the fascinating traffic of fishing trawlers, canoes, waterskiers and motorboats taking the family out for a ride. This lake is a culture of boats, where complicated dockside hoists lift the hulls protectively out of the water. Even though the houses are packed together as close as eggs in a carton, cottagers don't see their neighbors; instead, they see the open horizon before them. At dusk, they sit outside on folding lawn chairs, looking out as the sunset throws its mirror image into the water. In the daytime, they align themselves perfectly with the sun's angle like a shadow painted by the arm of a sundial. As the afternoon progresses, the lawn chairs subtly adjust to the sun's movement.

At the bottom of the lake, in the village of Hammondsport, I saw an unlikely, but perhaps the consummate, summer house, reduced to the very core of its meaning—living outdoors and basking in leisure. It has no foundations, but floats on pontoons. It has no lawn or beach, but a deck of plastic grass, cordoned off by rope. It has no guesthouse, but a small box trailer that pops into a tent, which is parked in the center. This ten-by-twelve-foot raft moored at the city docks is outfitted with an outboard motor, but mainly it stays put. The raft has more in common with the houseboats of Kashmir, where British officers spent hot Indian summer, than with the speedboats traveling Keuka Lake. This is a place of leisure for a couple who live in a little town halfway up the hillside. They drive down to spend weekend afternoons on the lake at this do-it-yourself vacation house, reclining on folding chaise longues, resting, reading, sunning, puttering about and doing as little as possible.

With very little, this family reproduced the ideal of the summer house—reduced to its very best and shorn of its encumbrances. Without the bother of maintenance, they have another place to escape to. Without high taxes on waterfront property, they can share in the water and its pleasures.

Although not as well known as Muskoka or Murray Bay, thousands of pleasure communities like Keuka Lake exist. All along the millions of miles of lakeshore in this country, bungalows, trailers and cabins huddle closely together, as close as they can to a cooling body of water.

Without porches and croquet lawns, that raft may not conform to the conventional idea of a summer house. Nevertheless, that home-made houseboat counts as one by virtue of its nonfunctional function, as do all the motor homes lined up in the parks overlooking Keuka Lake, and the grape-packing sheds turned into weekend hide-aways. As modest as they all are, those little lakeshore escapes are what F. Scott Fitzgerald dubbed "inessential houses" when describing Long Island estates in *The Great Gatsby*. Defined not by location, architectural style or size, a summer house—or cottage—represents a *psychological* destination. A house becomes a cottage when it provides refuge from a wearying world. Summer houses are places of forgetting, where the demands and routines of normal life recede from memory. (When spelled as one word, however, a summerhouse is a gazebo in the garden.) Not merely shelter, but shelter from the storm, these refuges manifest themselves in vastly different disguises, from rafts to castles. Whether it's called a studio, summer home, lodge, cabin, beach house, retreat, camp, condo, dacha or vacation house, a cottage is inhabited in the summer, or on weekends, or during deep snows when skiing and tobogganing compensate for perpetually gray winter months. The point is not *when* it's used, but *how*. Whether it's visited once a year or once a week, a cottage exists for *pleasure*, not to fulfill any real need or specific function. The French make that very clear, calling some of these places *maisons de plaisance*—literally "houses of pleasure." There, we city dwellers throw ourselves into the pursuit of pleasures unavailable in town: the outdoors, simple living, families, boating, long leisurely lunches with uncounted glasses of wine or just doing whatever we please.

That floating deck is one very personal idea of escape. Different things to different people, cottages come in hundreds of varieties. If houses express our personalities, cottages shout our innermost longings; they are the shelter equivalent of lingerie, where we can build fantasies and live out dreams.

Everyone retains his or her own particular, personal idea of what a cottage should be. Some people escape to apartments at the beach furnished in painted wicker. Others may envision a rambling gingerbreaded farmhouse with lots of bedrooms for guests, rather than a solitary shack. Some people may spend many happy years building their own log cabin off the main road in the mountains. The idea of the cottage takes many forms, from farmlike to fancy. Although worlds away from homemade barges and lakeside wooden bungalows, even Marie-Antoinette's Petit Trianon counts as a cottage, for despite its extravagance and superficiality, it offered pleasure and escape. *Chacun à son goût.*

Lavished on her by her ill-fated husband, Louis XVI, the Petit Trianon hides in a corner of the sprawling Parc de Versailles, just a stone's throw from the palace. At this eight-room house, outfitted with shabby furniture left by previous occupants, Marie-Antoinette indulged her heart's desire: not to be queen for a day. She would spend an afternoon or a month at the Trianon, escaping oppressive court rituals and sometimes court itself, where, she complained, even family life became a performance. At the Trianon, she explained, "I hold no court there, I live like a private person." Visiting courtiers did not need to stand at attention when the queen entered a room, which seemed remarkably casual at the time. Like a movie star at the supermarket, Marie-Antoinette sought a few moments of relative normalcy. She longed for some privacy after living in a palace surrounded by ladies of honor and ladies of the bedchamber. As the Trianon had but one bedroom, no ladies could stay overnight. Nor could gentlemen, for that room's single bed presumably discouraged connubial company.

Besides providing a convenient escape from the drudgery of queendom, Le Petit Trianon was what we'd call "a good time." Dressed in simple muslin gowns and straw hats, the queen let down her hair. She frolicked on swings, lolled in the grass, fished and played hide-and-seek just like the white-haired maidens depicted in the paintings of Boucher and Watteau. In a misunderstood attempt to rediscover nature, she built gardens and the Hameau—the hamlet, a rustic little dwelling located away from the Trianon. The Hameau's garden intended to duplicate *all* of creation—complete with lakes, mountains, faux brook and fauna from around the globe. The infamous hamlet, with its dovecots and dungheaps, duplicated a peasant village—albeit a sanitized one. To complete this eighteenth-century theme park, shepherdesses and peasants toiled for the queen's amusement. Apparently, Marie-Antoinette loved watching cow-milking, although, *chez elle*, the milk flowed into a Sèvres porcelain bowl. With so many fun things to do, she could easily forget the heavy burden of the crown—until, of course, the head that carried it was cut off.

As grand as Le Petit Trianon may seem, it fulfilled the same need for sanctuary as the cottages and cabins surrounding Keuka Lake—perhaps too well. There, the queen forgot her troubles and those of France, misusing the beleaguered treasury to do so. Her increasingly frequent retreats may have even hastened her downfall.

A Snapshot History of the Summer House

Some historians make mention of farms maintained by wealthy Athenians, still others point to Egyptian places of escape as the beginning of cottages. It is certain that the institution of retreats evolved just about as soon as did cities, dating back to the mother of modern cities, Rome. Wealthy Romans sought refuge at country villas that operated as income-producing farms, or at the seaside house, called *villa maritima*. They established watering holes such as Cumae and Baie—classical versions of Muskoka or Chester, Nova Scotia. Roman writers Horace, Pliny and Martial wrote poetically and prolifically about their country places. Horace's patron even bestowed on the poet his Sabine Farm, complete with slaves and overseer. During the late Renaissance, French royalty and aristo- crats went to Loire châteaux such as Chambord and Chenonceaux Venetians hired Palladio to build them country villas in the Veneto or along the Brenta Canal in the sixteenth century. In seven- teenth- and eighteenth-century China, the rulers of the Qing dynasty spent the summer months at Chengde, near Mongolia, at the "Mountain Manor for Escaping the Summer Heat," where they received envoys. English aristocrats, however, inverted the idea of rural escapes; they lived in their country houses year-round, making short forays into the city to do business and catch a few ses- sions of Parliament. Some also maintained a separate and addi- tional country house, a "hunting box" from which they pursued various game.

The villa tradition surfaced in Canada as early as 1780, when Governor Frederick Haldimand built a house by Montmorency Falls outside Quebec City. Called Montmorency House, it was a villa of Palladian design, complete with verandas and pavilions. Soon, the city's elite followed him, building their own country houses. Gover- nor General Sydenham is said to have had a summer place on Toronto Island as far back as 1839. English officers maintained "hunting and fishing boxes" on Rice Lake in the 1850s. The elite built summer places in lake towns such as Cobourg, Grimsby and Niagara-on-the-Lake.

By the 1870s and 1880s, summer watering holes multiplied, as North Americans traveled farther afield. Steamers opened up Lake Muskoka in the 1860s, and trains took Montrealers as far as St. Andrews, New Brunswick, in the 1890s. As much as these technologies opened up new territories for summer, artists did as well. Thomas Cole painted the Catskills in the 1840s. After visiting Maine's Mt. Desert Island in the late 1840s, Frederick Church is credited with creating that island's popularity after exhibiting a painting, *Fog Off Mt. Desert Island*, back in New York. Historian Hans Huth developed a perceptive theory about the development of summer colonies; discriminating people such as writers, artists and professors spend time at a place of beautiful natural scenery, spread word of the place through paintings and prose, encouraging visitors to come and experience that beauty. Eventually, so many visitors come that the place becomes a crowded version of its former self, and the exclusive crowd either tries to deter the crowds, or colonizes another pristine spot. The pattern happened over and over at Newport, Mt. Desert and points beyond.

In the last two decades of the nineteenth century, resorts flourished, as did the huge so-called cottages erected by the movers and shakers of the Gilded Age. This was ultimate leisure for the leisure class. Yet, not only robber barons built their second castles; an 1865 book on country residences noted that "prosperous merchants, professional men, bankers, and wealthy citizens" were enjoying summer idylls at country houses. The aristocratic villa had trickled down the upper and middle classes in this booming and prosperous era. The Gilded Age was also such for the summer house. And the very appealing idea of leaving the city to live a quieter, simpler, cleaner life in nature captivated the cultural imagination in a grand way. It became *the* thing to do. The 1874 *Guide to Summer Resorts in Wisconsin, Minnesota & Michigan* explained, "A summer Holiday Excursion has become a necessity of modern life. Divines preach it and practice it faithfully, Physicians insist upon it, and experience teaches it." During this era, magazines such as the *Century* or *Harper's Monthly* regularly published dispatches from the land of summer. Novels such as W. D. Howells's *Landlord at Lion's Head* and Edith Wharton's *The House of Mirth* were set against a backdrop of summer places.

Summer houses experienced a stunning renaissance during the past century. As more people lived in cities, more people wanted to leave them. It seems that as soon as farmers' citified descendants were liberated from the drudgery of farming, they longed for bucolic vistas and pastoral pleasures without the drudgery of chores or crops. From out of the grime, crime and chaos of contemporary cities, summer colonies rose up like Venus from the shell. Suddenly, people could reach hard-to-get-to places. Fast transport, in the form of railroads and steamers, plentiful land and big bucks contributed to the explosion of summer houses. Even faster transport later turned summer residences into weekend houses. As the pace of life quickened, people needed a way of slowing down. As more and more people experienced the luxury of a vacation, they needed some place to spend it. And so the second house, the cottage as we know it, was born.

Slowly, as summer places became an accepted part of life for many urban people, this fascination evaporated. During the 1930s, people had more important things to do with their money, and in the 1940s few people had the gas to get there.

In the 1950s, the next gilded age, cottages experienced a renaissance, thanks to highways, the prefabricated housing industry and all-round postwar affluence. A man who spent summers at Minnesota's Ottertail Lake remembers fishing at a nearby pristine lake in the 1940s; within ten years, the lakeshore was solidly ringed with little wooden cabins. During the booming 1980s, the vacation house prospered once more, and decorating magazines profiled these ever more sophisticated getaway houses.

The summer house rises and falls with cycles of economic prosperity. This inessential institution prospers in good times like a tree pushing out a fat growth ring after plenty of rain and sun. With each burst of wealth, the summer house economy pyramid expands to let more and more people into the dream.

Despite these cycles, one thing doesn't change. In good times or bad, people have always wanted to leave the city for a country idyll. Only the rationale behind these escapes has changed with the times.

Reasons for Leaving

The Decameron tells how people fled the city and its plague for the safety of a country villa. For centuries, sweltering cities have bred sickness: cholera, malaria, typhus and the down-to-earth summer complaint caused from sweating mayonnaise and unrefrigerated foodstuffs. These were all very good reasons to leave. A blaze of cholera in Quebec sent residents up to Cap-à-l'Aigle on the St. Lawrence for the first time. After a yellow-fever epidemic in Talla-hassee, Florida, in the 1840s, the gentry traveled four miles south to a summer town called Bel Air located in the flat pine woods—complete with Episcopal church. Even in the early part of the twentieth century, parents sent their children to the country to get them away from the dreaded infantile paralysis. Ironically, Franklin Delano Roosevelt fell ill with that sickness while at his family's twenty-room cottage on Campobello Island, New Brunswick, to which he never returned thereafter, choosing instead the health-giving waters of Warm Springs, Georgia, where he built a cottage. At the Asheville, North Carolina, sanatorium where tubercular patients—called "lungers" by the locals—used to recuperate, their families would rent cottages for the duration of treatment. Asheville also became known as a nice place for healthy people to visit: after all, George Washington Vanderbilt chose that mountain town as the site of America's most extravagant country house, the Biltmore. Southerners still spend the hot months in those hills.

Not just an escape from disease but a quest for better health also prompted people to leave the city. Indeed, the continent's very first resorts were springs. In the European tradition of Bath and Baden, North Americans took the waters, hoping to cure a variety of ailments by drinking and bathing in liquid loaded with minerals. Indeed, a doctor started the first hotel on Block Island off Rhode Island, which he named Hygeia for the Greek goddess of health. Stafford Springs, Connecticut, Saratoga Springs, New York, Sulphur Springs, Virginia, were all established in the late eighteenth century. St. Catharines, Ontario, was also a place to go for "taking the waters."

The countryside itself promised to heal the sick. *The New York Weekly Tribune* reported in 1853 on the salutary effects of Mackinac Island, Michigan: "The cold transparent waters the pure bracing air—the delicious white fish and trout, possess a strengthening, life-renewing efficacy, and give the enervated system of the invalid, new strength and healthful action." A Nantucket brochure from the 1870s boasted that invalids could put on twenty-five to forty pounds a season, and that the local population lived seventy to one hundred years. Resorts of the time also vaunted the quality of their ozone—which was somehow connected to good health. After all, good air, like the resinous atmosphere of pine woods such as those of the Adirondacks, was thought to cure consumptives. Following that regimen, poor New York immigrants suffering from "workers' disease" recuperated at Catskill boarding houses in the first decades of this century. Getting away from the city made sick people better, and staying in the city could make them sick.

In the United States, country houses also offered relief from a hot climate. A desire for not just better but *less* weather prompted people to pack up and move house. In the early 1800s, the planters around Charleston, South Carolina, traveled to higher ground, away from the muggy swamps, where they lived in "mosquito" houses raised off the ground for protection against those insects. And they straightforwardly named their summer headquarters Summerville. In the early days of swampy Washington, D.C., people actually traveled less than ten miles to reach higher ground in the northwest quadrant of the city. Before air conditioning, the seaside offered breezes and the mountains refreshed with cooler air. Resorts seduced travelers with promises of "dryness and uniformity of temperature"—like the constancy of the thermostat. Coastal Georgians went into the Black Mountains, as did many Carolinians and Virginians. The cool temperatures of Maine and the Maritimes better suited the copious layers of clothing endemic to the late nineteenth and early twentieth century. (In even hotter India, officers of the Raj ascended to hill stations from where they ruled the empire during the excruciatingly hot months.)

Besides heat and humidity, pollen was the other scourge of summer weather. St. Andrews, New Brunswick, where the Canadian Pacific Railway and many Montrealers went, was claimed to be a hay-fever-free zone, as were parts of Maine and Michigan. Some hotel circulars from about 1890 even promised relief to people suffering from rosecold, an allergy that seems since to have disappeared, perhaps vanquished for good at those resorts.

Although air conditioning cools off the concrete jungle, antihistamines offer hay-fever relief, and vaccines and vitamins assure us resistance to disease, we still travel to these same seaside towns and mountain resorts seeking the same pleasure and escape earlier summer folk found—but for different reasons. For example, the 1937 edition of *Building in Canada* offered economic arguments for summer shelter: it actually *saves* money to close the winter house, and eventually saves on vacation costs. After all, the reasoning went, "No one can tell you, 'your cabin has failed and your principal is lost.'" That kind of dollars-and-cents attitude was, and is still, a popular rationale for a summer house: it will cost less than years of hotel bills; its value increases the more it's used; it can provide rental income, be sold at a profit and become a retirement residence. Financial language makes it seem necessary and prudent to maintain another house somewhere else, even when one already has a house. Calling it an investment in the good life makes it sound less frivolous. In that utilitarian vein, artists may say they need a cottage for inspiration, parents may say they need to get children away from the television. The rationale people have for going doesn't seem nearly as important as the fact that, summer after summer, they go.

Today we seek a change of climate that transcends humidity and barometric fluctuations. Torontonians and New Yorkers go to their places in the country for the same reasons the Romans did. They seek the special but powerful atmospheric conditions of their summer houses. They crave mists of quiet, rains of calm and tempests of togetherness; in other words, the perfect climate. Finding it for a few weeks gives us the strength to weather the storm.

Summer Migrations

Migration is a natural rhythm. Countless creatures move in concert with the seasons, traveling between the same places year after year. Butterflies, birds, whales, moose, bats, turtles and even snakes move from one home territory to another. Fish return to spawning grounds after years of swimming the open seas. Grouse and quail climb up and down mountains in an annual pattern. All travel in search of plentiful food supplies, healthy mates or nesting grounds where they birth and nurse their young. Besides roaming to feed or breed, they leave when food is scarce or the climate is harsh. Some African elephants flee sheltered forests because of bothersome humidity and insects in the rainy season. Some birds fly to unreachable places where they can moult, safe from predators. Without the help of calendars or travel agents, generation after generation completes the same voyage, scheduling their departure by the subtle changes in light or jumps in temperature that announce the seasons.

Following animal peregrinations, people once moved in harmony with the seasons. Before white settlers invaded, tribes of the North American plains inhabited earth lodges during the winter, leaving cultivated fields to hunt buffalo come summer. They followed the buffalo across the great plains; living in tepees, they moved from camp to camp, planting their tents in a familiar circle. (Indeed, cottagers in Lipps and Alice Beach in Saskatchewan often find stone rings for tepees by their summer lakes, where the natives had probably camped in summer.) The Micmac of the East Coast and other tribes hunted in the woods during winter, and lived off the fruits of the sea at the coast, at spots where the European settlers eventually built shingled cottages. Even after domesticating animals, people followed their rhythmic migrations. Laplanders still herd the reindeer through Arctic Finland. And so shepherds wandered with their herds in search of greener and greener pastures. Winter. Spring. Summer. Fall.

Now, we migrate to summer houses in highway-shaped formations, fleeing the heat and tyranny of cities, escaping the sameness of suburbs. Unlike the directed paths of butterflies and birds, our migratory paths radiate from the city in all directions. We land at every point on the compass. We travel to the mountains, the lake, the sea, the country, the river, seeking what might be a summer without end, as we pack up our notion of home and take it on the road. Living in cities, people are divorced from seasons. No running of the salmon or harvest marks them. Only the ever-obvious crocus or back-to-school sales announce the year's progress. Food supplies remain constant; bountiful supermarket harvests produce strawberries, lettuce and tomatoes in the dead of winter. This migration to the summer house is in fact one of the few things that marks the seasons for people distanced from their four-beat rhythm.

As daylight lingers past the dinner hour, we long to load the car and follow the herd of automobiles—to summer nesting grounds. It starts with a family filling the car with foodstuffs and the paraphernalia of fun, before embarking on the annual, or weekly, journey.

With a canoe strapped to the roof, or a boat trailing behind, the car follows a route seemingly embedded in genetic memory, which includes stopping for a bite to eat along the way. Once we're past the point of no return, what was forgotten is remembered, and the summer migration happens just as it always has.

Flocks of people leave the cities on these well-worn flyways. Just about every metropolis has colonized its own summer nesting ground within driving distance. And so, like the patriarchs of the Old Testament, Ottawa begat the Gatineaux, Laurentians and Rideau Lakes. New York begat the Hamptons and the Catskills. Red Deer begat Sylvan and Gull lakes. Boston begat Cape Cod and the Berkshires. Washington begat Rehobeth. Chicago begat the Harbor Counties along Lake Michigan. Vancouver begat the Gulf Islands— the same chain that Seattlites call the San Juans. When colonies become crowded, summer people move on in search of open terri- tory, just as flocks divide when food supplies shrink. As fall fore- shadows its arrival with dwindling insect populations, summer migrants flock once more and travel in the opposite direction.

Like the opposable thumb, migration is an adaptation for survival. Unlike animals, humans aren't lured from their hunting grounds to find mates or an abundant food supply. A mixture of abstract instincts incite us to migrate from the city, as crucial as food or mating to survival—psychological survival. Even though ours has been a rooted agricultural society for millennia, that migratory urge still lives within us. Frustrated nomads confined to shrinking terri- tory, and no longer equipped with both winter and summer tents, we crave a *change*. So vacations are a kind of institutionalized nomadism; moving from one home to another provides the comfort of pacing or rocking, back and forth, across the countryside.

Looking onto the ribbon of traffic eking slowly northward on Toronto's Highway 11, or other well-traveled migratory routes, recalls the common determination of hardy salmon swimming, fighting upstream, past fishermen and through dams' turbines, in an effort to return at whatever cost. The trip may be unpleasant, the stay at the cottage may not live up to its promise, the whole family may complain; yet they will return next year. The homing instinct prevails. All told, these migrational instincts are so strong that we submit to high waterfront taxes, endure tedious drives and tolerate the bane of second-home maintenance in exchange for a few days at the cottage. Some people forgo adventures in exotic locations, instead repeating the same summer they've had every year since childhood. It's a curious compulsion.

The Institution of Idleness

In North America, the summer house has been a vital institution since the very beginning. In Canada, where there are millions of miles of lakeshore, just about every vacation includes a stay at a house on the water. Summer houses have brought us the Muskoka (aka Adirondack) chair, prefabricated house kits and the shingle style, not to mention the hammock. Thanks to a castle in the Thousand Islands, we have been blessed with a salad dressing of that name and mysterious viscosity. Back in the 1930s, Eaton's even produced a catalog for "cabins and summer cottages" that sold everything from blankets and canoes to coffee and vegetables and offered delivery within two hundred miles of Toronto. Summer pleasure has even contributed to culture: the beaches of Rhode Island spawned the Provincetown Players and their winter Playhouse, which still stands in Greenwich Village. And Dr. MacCallum's West Wind Island cottage in Go Home Bay, refuge to Group of Seven artists, contributed several masterpieces and murals that now hang in the National Gallery in Ottawa.

To cottage counts as a verb in some circles of society in Ontario. And of course, to summer means a person maintains a certain residence during the hot months. (Some people even winter, but autumn or spring are seasons for staying put.) Even governments support vacation houses—or rather taxpayers do. In the late nineteenth century, the Turkish, British and Australian embassies moved from Washington to Bar Harbor, Maine. The U.S. Forest Service aggressively marketed leases for cabin lots in the 1920s. The Canadian government has maintained a prime minister's summer residence on Harrington Lake since 1959, as well as other places on the now-cursed Meech Lake, in hopes that politicians might benefit from exposure to nature. Prime Minister Mackenzie King made a gift of Kingsmere, his summer place in Gatineau Park near Ottawa, to the people of Canada, to thank them for permitting him to serve. Like denim, the summer house is part of our national fabric. And like denim, it has traveled several social classes away from its origins, and become democratized in affluent industrial societies. No longer a luxury available only to the royal or richly rich, cottages are within the reach of many. Just like any current electronic product, their cost has spiraled downward until many could afford the benefits of a summer spent outside the city. After World World II, people of the middle class could afford a getaway place, and in the past forty years, vacation houses have grown like mushrooms after a fall rain. Today, the summer house mystique flourishes in countries living in the lap of luxury—places such as Scandinavia, Western Europe, England, Australia, Canada, the United States and even parts of Eastern Europe where laps aren't so luxurious. Getting away from it all has practically evolved into a basic right.

To make sure that getting away remains within everyone's reach, the summer house experience is packaged in many forms, to suit all tastes and pocketbooks: large rambling lake houses; timeshares overlooking a beach or boardwalk; parkside motels with housekeeping cabins; and resort condominiums. On the shores of Lake Michigan in New Buffalo, there's even something called a "dockominium." According to the U.S. Internal Revenue Service, houseboats count as secondary residences, with all the accompanying interests and tax deductions. At the turn of the century, they were quite common in Seattle and San Francisco. Summer shares, or group houses on the beach, make the summer-house experience possible for single young professionals, and a group of fire fighters own a house jointly on Elk Lake in Oregon. So essential is the experience that it's made available to those unable to afford to rent their own: Martha's Vineyard has a Camp Jabberwocky for disabled children. Some companies maintain retreats for their employees, such as the 3M Corporation's duck-shooting cabin on Lake Christina in Minnesota. That idea of employee places is not unique to 3M; before Bear Run became Frank Lloyd Wright's Fallingwater, it was a camp for employees of the Kaufmann's store. There's another option: those who can't buy or rent a summer Shangri-la can drive one—the recreational vehicle.

The RV represents the cottage's lowest common denominator. Behind the wheel of a movable cottage, be it a pick-up-cum-king-cab or a twenty-foot Winnebago, RVs hit the road and venture into national parks in search of Eden. Trailers can park in a sylvan setting complete with trout pond and swimming pool for a few hundred bucks a summer, where they join hundreds of other trailers outfitted with folding porches, plastic fences and picnic tables. With the right attitude, an RV equals a weekend condominium. Or so says a woman with a family of five and what her children call "the big bus." Unlike renting a house, there's no planning involved with a mobile condominium. The family takes up residence wherever or whenever—even on the spur of the moment. A rootless summer house can look onto Lake Huron one week and Lake Erie the next. It's easy to leave if a beach becomes too crowded. Best of all, these mobile cottages are as changeable as chameleons. A self-contained residence holding the family in its cozy embrace, this RV also becomes an instant guesthouse—a metallic outbuilding to another cottage. At someone else's country place, the RV can park, share the view and get an easement to the water. The proud owner of that weekend condominium explains, "We're the perfect guests—we have everything right there; we've got our own towels, our own bathroom, our own beds." It's Home Sweet Second Home.

Villa Values

The ideal of the villa has reseeded itself over and over on willowy riverbanks, hilltops and ocean shores. It has grown across the countryside, just as purple loosestrife has invaded marshes with its deceptively pretty flowers. All over the world, millions and millions of people own, operate, maintain and rent second houses. In the past twenty years, vacation houses have been breeding at very high rates. There are millions of vacation houses scattered all over North America. Add to that all the rentals, timeshares and houseguests, and you realize that going to a beach house or weekend farm is an experience many of us share. What is behind the newest blossoming of this very particular form of vacation?

Is the cottage explosion just another example of conspicuous consumption? Since Roman times, a house in the country marked status and measured climbs up the social ladder. Observing grand villas at the seashore, Horace wrote, "Thou at the threshold of death art contracting for marble pavements and building houses without thought of the grave, and art fain to thrust back further the shore of the sea that breaks on Baie, not rich enough to thy taste with the coast-line of the mainland."

Ironically, the people who live in the city's "best neighborhoods" are those who possess the luxury of a second house. When second-home owners already have access to perfectly livable living quarters, such duplication seems like another case of overconsumption by societies that already devour most of what the world produces. When there are so many without sufficient shelter, a second home seems like a decadent luxury.

While this lust for second-home ownership could be explained by the recent feeding frenzy of prosperity, I suspect it goes deeper than that. Certainly, more people have acquired what was once the rich man's play villa because it shouts wealth, but condominiums, RVs and prefab cottages have proliferated because we *need* them. While not as vital as post offices and legal codes to the functioning of society at large, cottages fulfill a nontangible function as clearly as an umbrella keeps off rain and a fire chases cold.

The second-home phenomenon is symptomatic of a malaise; in troubled societies they multiply. Shortly after 1968 when the Russians invaded Czechoslovakia, cottage culture flourished there. Twenty years later, the *Washington Post* reported that most Czechs had access to some kind of cottage. Of course, a higher standard of living, freeing of land and government policy contributed to the explosion, but during those repressive years of occupation, the call of the cottage was stronger than the call to work. Czechs often left the city on Thursday morning to put in a weekend of work at the cottage—making the paid work week shorter than the restorative weekend puttering. They have a saying there: "A Czech's first job is his cottage, and his second job is the one he takes to pay for the cottage."

In that country, as in this one, the second house works like a safety valve, where people let off that increasing steam before they boil over—a well-oiled metaphor tooled from a mechanistic society. So those who count the money, treat the sick, make the widgets can recover sufficiently from that pressure to continue counting, treating and making for the rest of the year. The summer house's explosive popularity signals dissatifaction with life, and a craving for a better one. It reveals how standard of living and quality of life do not always come together.

Summer houses provide an antidote to real life. And the stronger the sickness, the stronger and longer the dose required. This is why so many New Yorkers, Parisians and Londoners need to leave those intense cities every four and a half days, not just once a year on summer vacations. On the West Coast, where cities are surrounded by big-scale nature and plenty of public land, not many people have vacation houses; they don't need them to escape the city; hiking, skiiing and the ocean are within a short drive.

The summer house provides what's missing from daily life. It's a place where children can play outside freely. Away from the putrid night glow surrounding cities, you can see stars again. You can breathe the air, you can drink the water. You can talk to people you encounter walking down the street. You can let down your guard, unlock the door, shout if you want to. You can spend your day outside in the sun, in the shade, in the open air. You can hear real, penetrating quiet. You can see the full expanse of a sunset or sunrise, unobstructed. You can dry your laundry in the open, fresh and sun-drenched air. You can read by daylight. These are not really luxuries, but necessities that full-time urban people manage to do without. Going away corrects our imbalances like a vitamin shot after a long period of malnutrition.

After some two thousand years, the Roman villa has evolved into the cottage. The columns, the courtyard and the olive groves have been torn down and replaced with shingles and a front porch. Today's cottage is rarely surrounded by an estate or working farm. Rather, it is but a simple structure, within reach of many. Of course, the elite or recently arrived still build monuments to social mobility in the countryside, like the marble palaces Horace lamented at Baie. Some shades of Rome have survived in today's version of villas, but in other respects, it's very much an institution of the moment, molded and shaped to our culture's very current needs. Whether in Czechoslovakia, Quebec or Connecticut, the cottage is a significant phenomenon, an institution whose popularity reveals much about the conditions of the times.

Second houses transcend physical shelter. Materially, they may be "inessential," but these houses are essential to peace of mind; they shelter our psyches and house our unsaid longings. Back in 1856, while visiting Saratoga, George Curtis, suspecting greater meaning behind summer leisure, wrote: "It is not all dress and dancing. Like every aspect of life, and like most persons, it has a hint of something high and poetic." Not just a good time, cottages are good for us—in the manner of cold baths, fresh vegetables and physical exercise. In fact, summer houses are probably the only dwellings outfitted with a philosophical agenda. As James Ackerman points

out in his remarkable book *The Villa*, the country retreat has historically been imbued with moral and ideological values. It's a utopia
where values missing in the city are found. Today's retreats share
many of those values.

What are the ideological values of today's escape houses?
Nature, family, retreat and simplicity are the four posts on which
this very primitive structure sits, solidly and permanently. Those
four essentials are lacking in modern life, and so we find them for a
time at the cottage. Some pillars may bear more weight than the
others, some houses may be held up by more pillars, but that basic
structure sustains just about every summer house.

Because we are distanced from the very earth that supports us,
because we dance to the merciless beat of the work ethic, because
families are disjointed and ill-acquainted, because modern life is so
complicated, we need cottages. We need them in order to connect—with nature, with the self, with family and a simpler life. An
institution like any other, the cottage has developed its own culture,
its own particular building form and its own world of experience, all
of which reflect and reinforce the four pillars that support it. Wherever it is, the summer house is built in nature, reduced to the essentials, screened from the mundane and filled with family.

the shack

2. LIVING ON THE EDGE OF NATURE

"There are two spiritual dangers in not owning a farm. One is the danger of supposing that breakfast comes from the grocery, and the other that heat comes from the furnace," wrote Aldo Leopold. He himself had such a place, and called it the shack. It began as a hunting cabin during Wisconsin's first bow-and-arrow deer season, became Aldo Leopold's weekend farm and was finally immortalized in a book, *A Sand County*

Almanac—a masterpiece of nature writing that has been called the environmentalist's holy writ.

A Sand County Almanac was the culmination of Leopold's life-long naturalist's career. He began it as a boy, birding along the Iowa banks of the Mississippi where rafts of logs floated down from Wisconsin as the northern forests were emptied, and continued his explorations in those northern woods. Every summer, his family traveled to a cottage in Les Cheneaux Islands in Lake Huron, a pilgrimage that was ostensibly a hay-fever cure for his mother. He hunted with his father, who had codified his own sportsman's ethics, and would only allow his son to shoot a bird on the wing. The young Leopold made daily tramps in the surrounding countryside to observe wildlife and flora—a practice that he continued back East at prep school.

After graduating from the new forestry school at Yale, he became one of the country's first to practice that new science, then based in utilitarian conservation—seeing nature as an economic resource. Leopold worked for the U.S. Forest Service in New Mexico's Sangre de Cristos and San Juan mountains, administering predator control programs, and lobbied for game conservation early in his career. After a transfer to Wisconsin, he found himself in the U.S. Forest Products Laboratory pushing paper, counting trees. During his lifetime, he had the privilege of traveling through some of the last truly wild, unknown places of the United States, yet his lifelong naturalist's education culminated at his farm in central Wisconsin—where he studied under the tutelage of his dog, Flick, whose nose and instincts were admittedly superior to his own.

During the dust-bowl era, Aldo Leopold bought an abandoned farm in Wisconsin's so-called sand counties, from which he derived the fictionalized name Sand County for his book. Settlers had badly treated the area; prairie grasses had been killed off by crops; scanty topsoil had all but drifted away, and its marshes were drained to the point that peat fires often raged uncontrollably. The sad state of that sandy soil had finally discouraged farmers from continuing with the ongoing and fruitless struggle to wrest some kind of living from land whose bushel yield decreased year by year. At first Leopold leased it for $10, then he bought up the surrounding 120 acres, wanting, like so many of us, to own the land he walked. The owner was glad to have money for it, without any more back-breaking work. The place wasn't particularly scenic, or healthful; the farmhouse had burned, the island across the way had been cleared and the marsh nearby had also burned.

Leopold acquainted himself with this one single ecosystem as intimately as did the rabbits, whom he described as being able to negotiate a quarter of a mile of his property until reaching the safety of a woodpile. That same homestead, so cruel to the family that created it from scrub and wood, acted generously toward Leopold, whose demands were simpler. He merely wanted a weekend place to hunt, to walk, to cut his own wood and to watch the world around him. He didn't ask the land for his livelihood, or even his winter vegetables. Leopold, his wife and five children kept the place simple. They lived in the sole building left on the property, a chicken shack with a clay floor and unadorned plank walls. Plain straw filled out the mattresses. They drew water from a pump outside the door. They cooked in the hearth, filling a Dutch oven with dinner. The place's only claim to grandeur was the name of its outhouse, "the Parthenon."

Leopold drove down to the sand counties most weekends with the determination of a churchgoer. Apparently, he was so anxious to get to the farm on Friday afternoons that he'd sit waiting in the car until the family joined him. Once at the shack, the Leopolds got to work. A man who publicly preached his doctrines of the conservation ethic and wildlife preservation, Leopold practiced them on his own property. After fixing up their house, the Leopolds began repairing the land that had been so mistreated, working together as a family just as the homesteaders had done. A partner with the land, Leopold set out to restore the place to its ecological integrity.

The Leopolds' first act was to plant a patch for wildlife to graze on. Then they began a prairie restoration experiment, coaxing back

that magnificient ecosystem—an experiment that Leopold also conducted at the University of Wisconsin, where he taught. Every year,
the forester-turned-professor planted thousands of red, white and
Norway pines, of which only a few would survive the various
assaults from droughts, rabbits and other dangers felt by tiny nurs-
ery-bred pines let loose into the wild. The Leopold family—which
added two more noted ecologists to the conservation movement—
also built birdhouses. Leopold banded some of the birds who came
to visit, and kept track of how far they wandered in winter. His
powers of observation increased with each year as he read the signs
of wildlife on the snowy slate; like Thoreau at Walden Pond, he
kept meticulous notes of when the sorghum sprouted, how many
geese flew overhead and how the seedlings fared. Students from his
classes at the university came for field trips to observe their professor's weekend ecological experiments.

These 120 acres, which had been chewed and spit out so care-
lessly, helped give shape to Leopold's philosophy. In *A Companion to
A Sand County Almanac*, Susan Flader states that buying the farm
instigated in Leopold a different relationship with the land, as his
direct participation deepened his ecological, ethical and aesthetic
appreciation of it. He soon started to believe in preserving species
that were not game, but species pure and simple that had a right to
continue. At the farm, he practiced and refined his idea of "the land
ethic"—that land had to be regarded as more than property, as an
entity to which we belong. His ethic demands that humans exercise
ethical restraints in our complicated relationship with nature.

Ultimately, his weekends and wanderings in Sauk County gave
shape to *A Sand County Almanac*. His stories of the birds, animal
tracks and trees of the farm become parables, intimate illustrations
of the ecological points discussed more philosophically later in the
book. In one essay, he notes the diseases attacking his trees, and
shows how each tree's decay or demise contributed to the forest as a
whole, by making a habitat for another life, shading a grouse or
hiding a coon from a hunter, thus revealing the intertwining and

cyclical truths of the natural world, which are as connected and interwoven as threads running through cloth. Looking at the detail—120 acres of central Wisconsin—explained the whole.

At the sand county farm, Leopold became a partner with the land. He learned it and learned from it. The sand farm became his territory to control, patrol and protect. The farm was a practicum lab, where he put his theories into practice. Instead of taking from the land, squeezing crops out of the sandy soil, Leopold restored the sick farm—improved it, regenerated, preserved it. Most important, he left it healthier than he found it. Cutting that small square from the larger abstract quilt of nature changed the way Leopold thought about nature itself. The personal replaced the theoretical. Later, he said he bought the farm to try to discover why its first cultivators didn't just leave after their failures; he wanted to experience their strong sense of place that kept them on such barren land. And he did.

Few of us will compose an environmental holy writ while visiting our weekend houses, yet like Leopold, we hone our own relationship to nature and develop our own land ethic. We have a patch of ground to know. Even if we don't grow our own wheat or chop our own wood, a weekend farm points us in the direction of where the wheat and the wood come from. Like Leopold, each of us finds and defines our own relationship to one particular place—be it a farm on a Wisconsin river or a patch of grass-covered dunes in Nag's Head. Suddenly, nature is no mere abstract ideal, but a composition of flooding rivers, migrating birds and prairie grasses—one very real place well known and cared for.

Natural Relations

Nature is the raison d'être of the summer house. Indeed, we refer to the place by its setting in nature: the beach house, mountain cabin, country place, lake cottage or river house. After all, the beach, mountain, countryside, lake or river is what attracts us. Water is the element of nature that attracts us most. Like the arrowhead plant, summer houses seem to need wet roots, and plant themselves by oceans, streams, lakes, rivers, bays and even canals. Come summer, masses of people all over the world travel to the water, to bathe, to sail or to float in its liquid embrace.

Reunion, communion with nature, is the point. Fishing, hunting or gardening connect people to the natural world, as do sojourns at summer houses. Fishermen wait at secret spots, anchored, just *being* there for hours, attuned to and perceiving the slightest sign of life. Hunters walk through the woods and fields, looking for sign of their game, their tracks, their scat; they learn about their prey. Gardeners make a fertile partnership with nature, coaxing life out of seeds, watching the miracle of sun and soil on a little germ of a flower. So, too, cottages institutionalize nature for people native to concrete and clipped lawns. Like honeymoon motels, they're places to consummate the relationship.

Ever since the Romans, people have left the city to live amid nature. All that's changed is how cultures relate to living amid nature. In fact, a culture's relationship and attitude toward nature are revealed through its summer houses. At their retreats, Romans preferred nature improved by human hands—pastoral scenes of cultivated fields and grazed meadows that recalled their noble agrarian past. Cato, an early writer on villas, thought they should face south at the foot of a mountain, near the sea or river, with vineyards, woods and forests nearby. At Pliny's Tuscan villa, formal gardens radiated out from the house; boxwoods were cut into topiaries, flowers spelled out his wife's name and in the center of one garden was a representation of wild nature, according to art historian James Ackerman. Surrounding this manicured domain were fields and meadows planted with trees, a view of which Pliny admired; ". . . it looks more like a beautiful landscape painting than the real thing . . ." Not willing to venture into nature, Pliny was content to fish from a couch.

In the New World, puritanical notions of the evils of wilderness still thrived, and excursions into nature were intended primarily to mine and extract nature's healthful properties. Early-nineteenth-century resorts stayed close to springs and the sea for their healthy atmosphere. In these places, drinking in a natural setting was literal; visitors drank up to twenty-eight glasses of the curative waters daily. *Lotus Eating: A Summer Book*, by George Curtis, described the nature of a day and the day's nature appreciation at Saratoga Springs in 1856. "We rise and breakfast at any time. Then we chat a little and bowl till noon . . ." The noon hour drew visitors to the parlor for polka; after that, women went shopping and men to the bath—or springs. After the dinner hour, the band played on the lawn as the people promenaded on the piazza or walked in the court, looking over each other's dress and manners. At five, the carriages arrived and all traveled into the country. "There is but one drive: every body goes to the lake"—an expedition into nature the author compared to "stepping out on summer evening from the glaring ball-room upon the cool and still piazza"—nothing more than a change of scene, a bit of fresh air.

The resort Summerville, South Carolina, has a motto, *Sacra Pinus Esto*—"the pine is sacred." Not a literal representation of God, the tree was sacred medicine. In the mid-nineteenth century, the resinous forest air and pines were seen to be health-giving, and so essential to that summer town that the residents incorporated in 1847 to save the pines from being cut to make way for the incoming railroad. Although Summerville is practically a Charleston suburb and tubercular complaints have all but disappeared, it remains a misdemeanor to destroy any tree over a specific size.

As the country opened up and the frontiers pushed west, nine-teenth-century summer vacationers also traveled farther afield. According to George Woodward's *Country Homes* of 1865, "But for some years past . . . instead of confining themselves to their former resorts, they now seek the upper country . . ." As society became increasingly industrialized, the need to find solace in nature spread to more people. Still, nature was admired at a distance. In the Berkshires, summer folk compared their views like models of cars. Visitors to Catskills hotels didn't penetrate far into the mountain scenery, preferring to stroll landscaped paths or admire the sublime views from rustic gazebos and verandas crowded with wicker chairs and swaying rockers. Then, as real wilderness fell to the saw, the homestead and the range, it ceased to frighten—and began to inspire North Americans to conduct pilgrimages to the wilderness.

In 1858, at painter W. J. Stillman's instigation, Ralph Waldo Emerson, scientist Louis Agassiz, James Russell Lowell and seven others camped out at Long Lake in the Adirondacks. Scholars credit this historic holiday, called the Philosophers Camp, with changing the nature of summer migrations, or at least presaging it. For several weeks they painted, explored, fished and hunted in the woods. And the idea of a wilderness vacation caught on. By 1870, camping was all the rage, thanks to books like Reverend William Murray's *Adventures in the Wilderness; or Camp Life in the Adirondacks* of 1869, which combined the miraculous tale of a consumptive's cure and the transcendental idea of finding God in nature. Similar books, such as *Camps and Tramps* and *The Modern Babes in the Woods, or Summerings in the Wilderness*, offered glowing accounts of the woodsman experience along with plenty of practical advice on such things as packing, where to find guides and so on. The author of *Camps and Tramps*, Judd Northrup, traveled beyond romantic views of nature into transcendental communion: "The forest of the Adirondacks blesses its worshippers who come with reverent love to its wooded shrines and placid lakes and changeful streams and sends them forth again rich in the good gifts it holds for the forest loving in heart."

Nature itself, as wild and unkempt as possible, was seen as the ideal summer companion. Suddenly, summer visitors wanted a more direct relationship with nature, and ventured into the landscape rather than just looking at it. Country houses moved deeper into the countryside, becoming cabins in the woods. Canoes and sailboats brought visitors deeper into the landscape. Some thirty years after painter Thomas Cole visited Mt. Desert Island in the 1840s, a writer for *Harper's Magazine* remarked how Bar Harbor visitors took nature walks of up to fifteen miles in the hills. Around the same time, poet Celia Thaxter filled albums with dried seaweed specimens. W. D. Howells's turn-of-the-century novel, *Landlord at Lion's Head*, describes how summer colonists went on nature tramps in the White Mountains with a local farmer who educated them in the local flora, and even kept a few specimens tucked in his hatband. Nowadays, that relationship becomes even more direct as we plow through the waves on Windsurfers, ski through the woods or canoe down rapids, getting as close as we can.

The Nature of Summer

Often, the nature of summer houses is not wilderness, but a tamed and shaped landscape. These clusters of summer living are more like glorified suburbs, a densely vegetated residential park with expansive views, where the landscaping separating the houses seems haphazard. Much summer nature resembles E. B. White's description of the place where he summered as a child: a lake set down in the middle of farming country, which was ringed with cottages all around its shoreline.

Many resort areas where we reconnect with nature have already been denatured once, if not more. Farms once covered Martha's Vineyard, Block Island and even some islands of Maine. (Tybee Island near Savannah was a quarantine station for sick slaves who were later buried there.) The beautiful landscapes of Muskoka were exhausted by overly intensive farming and logging; when people first started camping there, log jams still ran through nearby waters. And Blue Hill, Maine, was lumbered, mined for copper, quarried for granite (which later became part of the New York Stock Exchange building) before coming to thrive as a chic summer village. Once the land has been exhausted—every resource extracted, any minerals, iron, lumber, clay and stone mined, harvested or quarried—it is fit only for recreation.

When the early campers of the Adirondacks hunted, fished and hiked into this three-million-acre parcel of New York State ordained in its Constitution in the 1890s as "forever wild," its tangled wildness had already been combed by logging companies, and farms struggled here and there in the rocky landscape. Today's woods are often second- or third-growth forests. The Ontario, Michigan and New England woods have been logged at least once; the leftovers—roads and infrastructure—are tossed to city people as scraps. Indeed, the first lodges in Ontario's Algonquin Park occupied old logging camps. Commerce paid for those roads into nature, which otherwise might not have been built. Just as Aldo Leopold adopted an overworked sandy farm, summer people, whether they realize it or not, often experience nature on hand-me-down landscapes, land that is no longer wanted, land that can no longer pay its way—if lakes proved to possess any practical purpose would they be the fountains of pleasure we make them?

Henry James observed this recycling mechanism at work while staying near the White Mountains of New Hampshire where summer people—including his brother, William—had settled in the mid-nineteenth century. "Written over the great New Hampshire region at least, and stamped, in particular, in the shadow of the admirable high-perched cone of Chocorua . . . everywhere legible was the hard little historic record of agricultural failure and defeat . . . a stout experiment had been tried, had broken down." No amount of good intention could make crops from rocks.

Although they impeded cultivation, those rocks and haphazard boulders looked like rugged and beautiful geology to cultivated eyes. Henry James saw "the disinherited, the impracticable land throwing itself, as for a finer argument, on the non-rural, the intensely urban class, and the class in question throwing itself upon the land for reasons of its own." As frustrated farmers and tired fishermen vacate the countryside, city people quickly fill it up with cottages and their dreams of wild nature. On Nantucket Island, resort promoters once tried adding to the natural bounty by introducing game in the form of grouse and rabbit. It was an attempt to "re-nature" the landscape, to give it life.

Besides being recycled, summer nature is often illusory, the result of artifice. Wild scenes of nature are cultivated for the pleasure of its visitors. Marie-Antoinette had a garden duplicating all of nature. At the imperial summer palaces in Chengde, a complex of gardens represents seventy-two different kinds of natural scenery around China. Similarly, the U.S. Army Corps of Engineers cuts reservoirs into the earth, filling them with water like a backyard pool, drawing urbanites into their illusion of natural water by renaming reservoirs lakes. Finding nature—or the refreshing nature of water—wherever they can, Midwesterners build cottages on the banks of man-made lakes.

In the middle of Michigan, there's a lake where Saginaw lumber barons spent summers beginning in the 1870s. Although they logged all around the lake, denuding the landscape, they left a collar of old-growth white and red pines one-eighth of a mile wide surrounding it. Amid forests shorn like Samson, they kept the illusion of pristine nature on land they intended to use, so they could wrap their arms around a trunk aged a few hundred years. That curtain of foliage shuts out human marks on the landscape, pulling itself closed over any signs of technology, letting only greenish light shine through the gap.

Without formal gardens or Cartesian parterres, it may seem that summer landscapes are unpruned, left to their natural state. In fact, we weed and cut back new growth just as in any garden. In his Maine town, W. D. Howells asserted that the summer visitors left nature untouched, not wanting to "affront her"—it's a common, yet mostly inaccurate, conceit. Wildflowers may grow in place of perennial borders, but the landscapes are still planned and planted like any garden.

We shape the seemingly natural landscape, play with it, improve, change it, enhance its picturesque qualities. It's as though nature itself needs a helping human hand—to become more natural, to please us. It is cultivated to suit our purpose. Shorelines are taken up and down like hems, filled with sand or rock; trees are culled to liberate a deckside view. I even heard of someone who blasted free a peninsula to make it into an island, creating a shortcut for traveling canoes. Developers at Fire Island often flattened the dunes to give cottagers a better view over their porch, but losing those natural storm fences let many hurricanes sweep cottages away. In the Adirondacks, I've seen people landscape their view of the Gothics, placing boulders in the foreground to give depth and pruning birch to let more of the mountains show through.

Leaving a landscape as it was found almost seems unnatural. Mackenzie King described how he rehabilitated the land surrounding his summer house. "It was a joy of joys to see the larger vista opened up and the fine stretches of lawns. The weeds of course were much in evidence but they will be cleared off in time." Into that vista, he planted stone ruins—one of which was made from stones salvaged from the first Parliament building—in the manner of eighteenth-century English landscape gardens. One ruin was lyrically named Window on the Forest. (Interestingly, he fumed at the locals' woodcutting in the forest for fuel, changing the landscape for practical rather than aesthetic reasons.) "There is no joy comparable to that of redeeming the waste places, making the desert to blossom like the rose whether it be in the wilds of nature or in the vagaries of human nature."

Wild nature is made even wilder. Well ahead of her time, Frances Kinsley Hutchinson in the 1920s planned a sanctuary for native Wisconsin birds and flora amid the virgin forests at her Lake Superior summer home. Still, the place had to fit her idea of sanctuary for wildlife. Her book, *Wychwood: The History of an Idea*, tells about carving a place for her house and garden from the dense forest. She said she wanted the house "to look like a house dropped down in the woods rather by chance." But chance had little to do with anything. Following a surveyor's advice, she lined the house to the shore, let out the hem of the shoreline, had the channel deepened and carted out 30,000 loads of mud used to bring the terrace fifteen feet above the level of the lake. Hutchinson modeled the new shore on the one nearby and placed "pebbles and sand and rocks in irregular outline." Within these seventy-two acres, she planted shrubs to attract birds, and added 217 wildflowers. (There was also human sanctuary in the plan: a soft, safe green lawn and formal gardens on the inland side of the house, designed by the Olmsted brothers, made a transition between forest and house.) Hutchinson herself landscaped the wildlife sanctuary, culling trees and planting indigenous species where she deemed best. "How much the success of a country place lies in its willingness to submit to Nature's whims!" However, submitting to those whims seems almost beyond human nature, as though to do so would make us feel out of place, as though there would be no room for us otherwise.

When returning to his Kentucky river camp every spring, writer Wendell Berry writes, he would chop tree sprouts, prune branches and mow the wild grass, elderberries and nettles. "It was some instinctive love of wildness that would always bring me back here, but it was by the instincts of a farmer that I established myself." Until those weeds were clipped, the camp was not "imaginable." Doing made it come into being. As much as we love a place, we love to change it. It seems that we need to make a mark on the landscape, a kind of brand of belonging that establishes rights beyond that of a squatter. Planting a meadow, piling up a beach, pruning a tree, making an island out of what was once a pennisula—this is a way to write a lease into the landscape.

Whether the nature of a place is recycled or not, illusory or not, cultivated or not matters little. What matters are nature's metaphors that come through. When Emerson wrote, "Within these plantations of God, a decorum and sanctity reign . . . In the woods, we return to reason and faith," he apparently discovered those truths not in wild woods, but in the shade of Concord Common—a manicured village green. In those populated stretches of Long Island Hamptons, the splash of the Sound and constantly shifting dunes constitute nature. Although tamed, even that landscape reveals the truths, the processes, the cycles, the flux, the complexities of nature.

Living on the Edge of Nature

Inevitably, near these summer spots north, south or off to one side, there's a patch of green daubed onto a map otherwise crowded with lines of varying colors. State parks, reserves, national forests form those swaths of green, cutting across otherwise populous states and provinces and offering a view into a more natural world. These parks are the wilds beyond the hedgerows. The Kawarthas sit in the green shade of Algonquin Provincial Park, Squam Lake straddles White Mountain National Forest and Chincoteague huddles up to the wild horses of Assateague Island National Seashore in Virginia. Like the commons before the enclosure, these are lands with universal rights of usage, remnants of nature saved for the communal good. Summer houses cozy up to this expansiveness. The big green patch exists nearby, comforting residents with a sense of wildness, its spaciousness spilling over.

Carved into mountainsides, propped up on beaches and planted by lakes, summer houses obscure the border between civilization and wildness. They offer us a blurred vision of a wilder world, leaving an impression of wildness. The ideal summer landscape seems untouched by human hands, but in reality, it is like the hedgerows of England, a thin, leafy border between cultivated fields. The hedgerow has been logged and mined, pruned and trimmed like a row of shrubbery. The wild things—snakes, animals, uncultivated plants—have been pushed into this no-man's-land of bush and vine, seeking refuge from the hoe and the rake. The hedgerow represents the border between nature and culture, a border that the metal reach of the train has pushed back, and the automobile has pushed farther still. Like the rabbit who digs his burrow at the edge of the field, we seek refuge in the hedge.

In *The Experience of Landscape*, Jay Appleton suggests that humans are attracted to two complementary aspects of landscape that once aided our survival: prospect and refuge. From that hedge, there is prospect into the landscape; in that hedge, there is refuge from being seen. Now the summer house sits precariously between the natural and cultivated world, in an ultimate position of prospect and refuge. As much as we seek connection with nature—to get closer to it—at the same time, we seek protection from it.

Winslow Homer relished being on this tenuous edge, and pushed the boundary farther and farther back. His studio, along with his family's summer compound, sat on an exposed piece of rock at Prout's Neck, Maine, with a view of the ledge and cliffs. In the 1880s, the Homers were the first to site their house on the exposed sea, as most cottagers of the time chose to set their houses farther from the ocean. At Prout's Neck, Winslow Homer painted the ocean. Like many of the mariners he used as subjects in the early years, he worked outside in the harsh elements, in the ocean spray that misted salt on his face, salt on his paint, salt on his cold hands. After several years of standing on the cliffs with easel and palette, as waves crashed up around the rocks, he retreated into a booth.

He had a portable painting box built—a little room eight by ten feet that he moved around the shoreline to suit his compositions. A wood stove kept him warm inside and a plate glass "viewing window" brought him outside. A picture picture window, it framed his compositions. Usually, the box looked onto Eastern Point where the sea's fury roared most ferociously, as Homer stood protected. Fascinated as he was by the power of the sea, the box let him get as close as he could be to the ocean without being carried out to sea. Waves broke practically at his feet, the sea surged, but still Homer stayed warm and secure inside his box, buffered from the effects of nature by the most itinerant of shelters and exposed enough so that he experienced the ravages and redheaded temper of the sea. Although a roof stood over his head, he remained both inside and outside, with refuge from and prospect into the natural world.

Winslow Homer's box mirrors a cottage's relationship with nature. It, too, lies on the verge, as far as an artist's studio can go into the natural world without being overpowered, crushed or swept away. As much as we think we want to live closer to nature, we insist on bringing our box, and all its comforts. Living near nature and civilization at the same time, being in nature with civilized comforts—these contradictions are just the beginning.

Like Homer, we want to hear the roar of the breakers, without being sprayed with saline mist. We want to live at the mercy of the sea, while keeping two feet on the solidness of the ground. We want the wildness of nature, and the roof of civilization. Although living in the brush is a tantalizing fantasy, few of us are outfitted with the skills and knowledge needed in real wilderness. Even the pioneers of Adirondack camping vacations brought guides with them into the woods; these woodsmen knew the territory, they knew how to build bark shelters, where to find meat and fish. Summer visitors to Murray Bay depended on the *habitants* to help them explore the back country and wilder rivers and lakes. If let loose in the wild, most would end up like the circus bear of Adirondack legend who escaped into the woods and was found performing his act in a clearing, hoping a fish would get thrown his way. We just wouldn't know what to do. So instead, we build a house, in nature, near nature, on its periphery.

Shelter-making seems part of human nature, as Thoreau observed: "Man didn't live long without discovering the convenience there is in a house." Once a cabin gets planted into the ground, the spot has arguably become denatured, but it has more nature than a city park, more wildness than a suburban lawn. More birds passing through, more native plants. Still, culture triumphs over nature. Even a crude log cabin represents civilization in the wilderness—a clearing, a claiming of property. Architect Roland Terry, who built himself a sod-roofed house in the wild island landscape in the San Juans, admitted to *Architectural Digest* that his house was at odds with nature. "Actually, this was such a magnificent piece of property that it shouldn't have had anything built on it at all; it really should have been left in a completely natural state." That enlightened acknowledgment did not curb the normal human urge to shelter. The architect built anyway. He wanted both the natural state and the civilized state and compromised by not cutting down any trees to make room for his building, and by roofing it in sod—earth itself.

Nevertheless, getting closer to nature comes with a price. That position of prospect into the landscape exposes us to the vagaries and dangers of nature. So, looking out onto the natural world, we seek refuge in the house. Besides comfort and convenience, we also seek its protection. It's a place of safety we can escape to, warm and secure. Outside the box, there is only the power of nature with its storms and strength and creatures. Outside the box is the natural world, which remains somewhat beyond human control.

There's a roller-coaster attraction to those uncontrollable landscapes. "Below the mountains, the mighty Saint Lawrence River stretched beautiful but treacherous, full of roaring tide rips and too cold for bathing," wrote Reginald Townsend of his summer territory. The power of nature attracts like a child to matches. Nantucket possesses the beauties of heaven, a summer visitor once wrote in his diary. "But nevertheless one can't forget Hell surrounds your shores. Your reefs and rocks are dangerous. I suppose dear old island that this was the price you paid to become on earth a heaven." Beautiful but treacherous, heavenly but hellish—these are landscapes of contradictions where we build summer houses. Poet James Russell Lowell's "Pictures from Appledore" describes the same contradictions of the Isle of Shoals off New Hampshire's coast, where he

flourished in Celia Thaxter's artistic salon as her flowers flourished
in her island garden:

> A heap of bare and splintery crags
> Tumbled about by lightning and frost
> With rifts and chasms and storm-bleached jags
> That wait and growl for a ship to be lost . . .

That "nightmared ocean," said Lowell, was hard to comprehend
on a sunny day. The atmosphere of peril intensifies its beauty somehow, and intensifies the thrill of being there. Along Atlantic coasts,
ferocious tides and storms and waves threaten boaters and sailors,
daring to throw them up against rocks as sharp as broken glass. Dramatic landscapes such as rocky shores, mountains, cliffs, waterfalls,
these are places of danger, inhospitable but beautiful to look at.

The more a house tries to approach nature—its views, beach,
breezes—the more violently nature repels it. As nature becomes powerful, uncontrollable, it becomes female—Mother Nature—and the
reverence is gone. When you get close to Mother Nature, she talks
back, shrieking like a fishwife, swearing like a shrew at those who
trespass—in those woman-hating words. The defense begins with
pesky creatures and ends with tempests. Houses on promontories may
display picturesque panoramas, but they also expose themselves to the
ravages of the sea. At the ocean, every cloud of rain hides the possibility of a hurricane, one of those big, boisterous storms traditionally
named for women but that eat like men, finishing with a mighty
belch. They mark their passage by tearing up docks, taking back
dunes, ripping through screen porches and crumbling beach houses—
leaving piles of woody debris destined for driftwood. Just a few years
ago, Hurricane Hugo appropriated thousands of pleasure houses in
the Virgin Islands and along South Carolina's shore, ripping off roofs
and sweeping them into the sea. A tidal wave once actually flooded
Tybee Island, Savannah's hot-weather playground. Along the coast of
New Jersey, because of a severely receding shoreline, several significant shingle-style houses at Monmouth Beach now sit underwater.

Fire is another way that nature reestablishes itself. And any cabin in the woods is threatened. Around Georgian Bay, with its vast expanses of open water, lightning writes itself every which way against the sky, striking often, furiously, at the camps and cottages tucked into its archipelago, lighting them like a torch. Many of the early resort hotels and cottages, all built from wood, have become humus for the forest as summertime fires raged through shingled walls and gingerbread verandas—some seventy such hotels disappeared from Muskoka that way. Much of the legacy of summer architecture has in fact been reduced to ash. In 1947, a great fire destroyed almost one-third of the houses at Bar Harbor on Mt. Desert Island. Many were never replaced, but reclaimed for the Maine woods, as much of the surrounding land became Mt. Desert National Park. All this is nature's real estate tax.

Outside the city, there are other things from which to seek refuge. Natural Predators, long since eliminated from towns and cities, still inhabit these abandoned pockets of discarded nature. Sharks prowl the waters; even the slightest hint of their possibility sends shivers down swimmers' spines. In the northern woods, bears more factual than fairy tales rifle garbage and leave behind legends of attacks. Even on his country property, which had been cultivated for well over two hundred years, my father met disastrously with a copperhead snake, who was disturbed in the usually quiet hedgerows by an encroaching mower. The snake punished the trespassing of those borders with a two-point bite, which crescendoed into a heart attack, shock and, eventually, an avoidance of the unmowable pockets of land.

Declawing Nature

Snakes, deep water, dangerous currents, alligators, sharks, bears, tropical storms traveling north—all these things so frightening to children on vacation are manifestations of nature, the wild place, just over the line, which is beyond our control. Clearly, nature exceeds the limits of a picture window. More than simply scenery, or a place to play, nature has its own ways, its own agenda, and the uncontrollable reminds us that we are guests, that our house is just resting on a piece of land temporarily, until a hurricane, flood or fire should take it away.

In response to this seeming powerlessness, we seek not just refuge, but control, with concrete pilons, fire towers, live traps, life jackets and—in the case of my father—snake boots and the execution of his attacker with a hoe. As the power of nature challenges the power of civilization, the summer house takes the defensive, trying to keep that power at bay. We build breakwaters to tame the sea for swimming and to protect yachts. We jack up houses on stilts beyond the sea's reach. If those measures fail, we try again. Even after tsunamis and mudslides pull Malibu beach houses back to sea, determined Malibuites rebuild on the same spot with more sophisticated engineering and deeper-set pilons. And so, second-home owners submit to extortionary insurance premiums, paying dearly for such closeness to nature, unwilling to admit that the house may have come too close to the edge.

As much as we want to approach nature, we want nature declawed, stripped of threats and bother. Writer Julia Ward Howe—who created "The Battle Hymn of the Republic," among other songs—once described a little clearing at her Newport farm where the brambles had been cut back and stumps made for sitting as a "charming out of door salon." It seems that's the kind of place we are trying to create, a clearing as safe as a salon, as comfortable as a parlor—without inconveniences, discomforts and dangers. So, mosquito swamps are flooded with pesticides. House pests are trapped and poisoned. Shark nets circle popular beaches. Lifeguards prevent undertows from taking swimmers away. And in Georgian Bay, where Massasauga rattlesnakes once lived on the granite islands, summer people used to weed them from their rocky gardens with a quick blow. Some even carried a snake stick, a walking stick notched with the number of kills. Now so few of these snakes remain that the species' survival is endangered. Yet, once rid of the serpent, the garden is safe.

Applying lessons he learned in his garden, nineteenth-century essayist Charles Dudley Warner saw these territorial disputes between humans and nature thus: "But the minute he begins to clear a spot larger than he needs to sleep in for a night, and try to have his own way in the least, Nature is at once up, and vigilant, and contests him at every step with all her ingenuity and unweaned vigor." In his mind, the outcome is the same: "This talk of subduing nature is pretty much nonsense." That well-engineered beach houses on pilons can crumble in the vortex of Atlantic gales proves his point. And the tenuousness of this edge appears, wherever houses cling to it.

Up in the Blue Ridge Mountains, there's a small weekend cabin near the town of Bluemont, which used to be Snickersville. Surrounded by woods, the cabin sits back a quarter mile from the road, down a rough track whose dried-mud ridge rises like a dinosaur, cutting into the chassis of a city car. That rough entry makes the place seem far from the paved world, yet when one looks from the deck, the white city of Washington appears in a little break on the horizon—a prospect of civilization.

As soon as the cabin is closed for the week, the denizens of nature take over. They set about attacking the house that seems to invade their territory. A piliated woodpecker has drilled hole after hole into the posts supporting the house and raising it some eight feet off the ground. After serving as hundreds of meals to the hungry bird, the posts resemble sticks of Swiss cheese, their structural properties slowly weakened. The woodpecker was attracted by the first invaders, unseen insects who insinuated themselves into the lumber. Other animals peel phyllo-pastry layers of wood fiber from the board-and-batten siding, eat more holes in the walls, oddly preferring plywood to the real stuff growing wild just a few feet away.

"There are all these animals eating my house," says the cabin's owner, waving her hand over the destruction—nature taking nourishment from her house. Any attempt at landscaping with imported plants is foiled by squirrels who eat each flower down to the nub. The trees, too, seem to come in closer and closer, pushing back the clearing.

As the cabin's owner tries to protect her property against animal encroachment, the creatures continue to attack her board-and-batten encroachment. She defends her territory with chicken wire, wrapped like mesh scarves around the perforated posts and peeled plywood. For the present, they are stalemated, until the creatures somehow get through the wire. If that happens, the posts might just break and the cabin could end up like another house on the property, ruins buried in the brambles—like the stone remains of another house, long since disappeared in a new growth of trees.

A Sense of Place

In eighteenth-century England, when the mania for landscape spread with the intensity of a dance craze, aesthetes peered into the loveliness of the landscape through a Claude glass. A peculiarly passive form of outdoor recreation, this tinted piece of convex glass framed the view picturesquely, creating a panoramic landscape in the style of painter Claude Lorrain. It gave an instant, yet ephemeral, snapshot of the countryside, at once formalizing and abstracting nature.

So, too, a summer house, a cabin, a dune shack all frame a smaller part of the landscape. There, we experience a small piece of nature, rather than dealing with the abstract whole, Nature capitalized and revered. Instead of picturing burning rain forests, desertified African fields or north country flooded by hydro projects, we can picture a particular crust of Lake Superior shoreline, a half acre of north Florida dunes covered in sea oats, or the birch and pine woods surrounding an Ontario cabin. We all need a patch of land to connect with, and summer houses make that possible. It's like making friends with one man rather than getting to know all mankind. It puts the land into fatherland, and the country back into mother country; no longer earthless orphans but adopted by a place, we develop a sense of it—*a sense of place*.

The Claude glass gave a purely aesthetic experience of nature, unsullied by concerns for crops, practicality or a livelihood. And city people living partially in the country also seek an aesthetic relationship, although ours is less formal and more direct than that sought by aficionados of picturesque landscapes. When visiting over the summer, or on holidays, we develop a bond with the land that bears no resemblance to that of people who work on and with the land. Henry James noticed this particular bond in a rocky corner of New Hampshire abandoned by farmers to summer people: "The touching appeal of nature . . . is not so much a 'live upon me and thrive by me', as a 'Live *with* me, somehow, and let us make out together what we may do for each other—something that is not merely estimable in more or less greasy greenbacks.'" A living no longer stands between the land and its part-time inhabitants. The land seems to say, "I lend myself to poetry and sociability—positively to aesthetic use." Rather than extract or exploit, summer people merely want to enjoy the land. Nature has become our playground and scenic lookout, where we take pictures, have picnics and just stroll. Certainly, if we had to *live* from the rocky shore and pine trees, we'd feel less romantic about it all, more married.

Although Aldo Leopold lamented motorized tourists reaching farther and farther into wilderness and the crowding of cottages onto coasts, he recognized that "Recreational development is a job not of building roads into lovely country, but of building receptivity into the still unlovely mind." The roads leading to the cottage lead us to that receptivity, to an understanding, knowledge and love of place. Knowing nature requires living *in* the landscape rather than merely looking at it through convex glass. Naturalists have realized this ever since Richard White wrote *A Natural History of Selborne* in the eighteenth century. This English vicar studied the birds, insects, geology, plants, trees and deer of his habitat—what we'd now call an ecosystem—and recorded everything in meticulous detail. Similarly, Thoreau inhabited and studied Walden and its woods, and Leopold tramped over every piece of his farm. Thoreau's direct literary descendant, nature writer John Burroughs, built a retreat, Slabsides, a mile and half down the road from his farm on the Hudson when that area became too cultivated. In his essay "Wildlife About My Cabin," he wrote, "Well, I do not call it a retreat; I call it a withdrawal, a retirement, the taking up a new position to renew the attack." What he intended to attack was the study of nature itself; from his secluded cabin, he could watch the wildlife undisturbed. Most of all, he wanted to be a citizen of the place, not its conquerer, so he sited his house accordingly: "It is never wise to build your house on the most ambitious spot on the landscape. Rather seek out a more humble and secluded nook or corner which you can fill and warm with domestic and home instincts and affection." By placing his cabin humbly rather than arrogantly in the woods, he declared his citizenship in the place.

Better than being a visitor who pulls tent stakes from the ground each dawn, at getaway houses you get to know the nature of nature on a day-to-day basis, as Burroughs got to know the birds who visited at Slabsides. We become like those naturalists who make a science of living in a place. Living and observing tells more than any field guide or natural history museum. At country places and beach houses, nature becomes your address, your place of residence, not some botanical theme park where you ogle the view for a few short minutes but won't see the litter you unwittingly dropped the day before. You inhabit that place and confront your impact on it. It becomes like your house; you do not rush through your house as if were like a train terminal; you rest, you roost, you put your name on the door. You belong. Part of belonging is familiarity.

Every summer place I've ever visited displayed a map on the wall: nautical charts, survey maps, ordnance maps, orienteering maps, contour maps and aerial photographs detail every creek and bump and contour of the surrounding landscape. These maps signal a desire to explore deep country, like Champlain or Lewis and Clark. These explorations go beyond normal cartography into the smallest natural details. The Iron City Fishing Camp drew up its own map without roads, hospitals, railroad tracks: the legend lists crawdaddy pools, frog territory, natural rock fort, red cedar bush, turtle territory and the site of the 1976 bear incident. The land is shared by the families that spend each summer on this Georgian Bay island, who know every inch of the place and navigate by these natural landmarks, as easily as looking at the back of a hand. This is the geography of naturalists. Probably each and every person who has summered at the camp could walk eyes closed, blindly navigating every stump of the terrain, committed to memory like conjugations.

A woman who has gone to the same cove all her life, as her mother had before her, tells me, "I could walk over there with my eyes closed; I know every root and stump and tree." It's a rare but deep pleasure to know a place so well. Farmers who plow and seed and reap the same fields season after season develop that intimacy. Some gardeners do as well. Hunters who frequent the woods each fall in search of game soon learn which trees hide their approach, which valley resonates footsteps that fall on dried leaves. Successful farming, hunting, gardening or even wartime combat all depend on some level of connoisseurship of the land. In the languor and space of summer, there is time to explore the environment—to develop connoisseurship.

There is something immensely satisfying about knowing a piece of ground so intimately that you can watch it change and see the processes of nature at work. Knowing nature doesn't necessarily require great travels. The larger principles surface on a smaller scale, just as they did at Leopold's farm. And the part reveals the truth of the whole. Although just a five-minute drive from suburbia, the

47

scrawny woods and stream of my studio show the cycles of life and the processes of death so essential to the natural world, which I noticed once I started paying attention. There is the bark-stripping hunger of wintering deer, the nights of brush wolves howling after their prey and the scattered bones and antlers marking the violent death of a weakened stag. There is the marvel of wild phlox, which strengthens its bloodline every summer, regenerating itself miraculously and copiously into the shady spots—a bottle of eau de toilette overturned in the woods.

Returning year after year, weekend after weekend, we get to know the landscape, which yields more, the more it's explored. That intimacy lets us see beyond the superficiality of scenery. We see details and qualities the visitor could not. The details come up to the surface, like bubbles of air revealing a presence below the water. It's a matter of seeing the specific beyond the species. A tree is not just a larch, but the larch that fell down in the storm and became the drum for the grouse. It's not a de-constructed vision of nature in various parts, but a reconstructed view of the whole. We can see the connectedness among all things—the web of relationships that weave together in our territory. However, unlike the outlines of Everest or the curve of Niagara, that maze of root, stump and tree is known to us only. It's virgin territory, a private bit of ground, a sacred spot.

Sacred spots joined together by the songlines color and cross the landscape of Australia. Aborigines see the creation of the world and the mark of the first godlike animals in the buttes and rocks and streams of the countryside. Their tribal and family history wraps around each tree like Virginia creeper. What's now prosaically called the outback is a landscape of associations, myths and dreams. In familiar territory, our past gets embedded in the terrain, fossilized and permanent. Life weaving into the landscape creates a personal sense of place. There's the tree planted during the first summer. The edge of the woods, rife with wild raspberries, recalls an experiment in jam. Or there's the big dune children used to jump off, landing on sandy banks some twelve feet below. The rocky point holds the left-over memory of annual picnics laid out by the shore. Children watch their names scratched into bark grow thicker with each passing year.

These memories, drawn like tattoos over the landscape, are equally indelible. Even after the land's been bulldozed and built on, those ghostly moments still appear to those who see what happened there rather than what is there now. When I walk along the hundreds of paths woven around the studio, past moments jump out at me like ghosts—déjà-vus that already were. While shaded by a summer canopy of maples, I'll suddenly see that path covered in snow the night we skiied through thin blue paths. As I turn a corner, an image of the dog appears, her eyes shining big and black, as, clearly thrilled by her instinct, she holds a bloodied rabbit. My life, with its walks and discoveries, is permanently but quietly embedded into the landscape, like the Indian sign tree whose lowest branch was stretched with rocks into a right angle hundreds of years ago. So our own personal history is tied to that of the land.

It creates a sense of belonging that few of us in this peripatetic world have experienced. In Newfoundland, where so many families have persisted for generations, living off the sea's capricious abundance and the shore's miserliness, natives say they "belong" to Newfoundland. Most of us envy that belonging. We move too often to develop a real sense of place; long-time family roots have been transplanted so often that they're mangled beyond recognition. It's difficult to develop a deep sense of belonging in the cement of the cities: the walls are too smooth to encourage the growth of any vine of belonging. Before being jammed into cities, people identified with, and were identified with a place. Think of Leonardo da Vinci, whose name reveals what place he belonged to. Retreats offer a glimmer of that belonging. Writer Wendell Berry found this sense of belonging at his river camp, earned it: "The wild creatures belong to the place by nature, but as a man, I can belong to it only by understanding and by virtue." After spending many years there, Berry understood that it didn't belong to him, it was the other way around.

Greater than the urge to own land is the need for land to own us. We seem to need a patch of earth with which to connect. And it's not a new urge, it comes from living in cities. Lack of rootedness is actually landlessness. Discussing how city people had created summer homes in the country in the 1860s, architect George Woodward noticed, "They have bought and built, and planted, until they have identified themselves with the chosen spot, and as their trees have taken root in the fertile soil, so have their affections taken root in the beautiful country." The bankers, prosperous merchants, professional and wealthy men he described developed this attachment in a courtship that lasted a few idyllic summers, and today we do the same. So that people who actually live in Montreal, Washington, D.C., or Boston feel they belong to the Murray Bay, the Outer Banks of North Carolina or Martha's Vineyard. This taking root seems as natural as any plant extending itself into the earth, grabbing hold of each gritty little particle with a determination to stay put, even when it's soon to be transplanted.

The feeling summer people develop for a place develops past the hot-weather romance, until they begin to see the beauty of a winter landscape, braving the cold and snow to have Christmas there. People without that bond and sense of belonging to the land might not see the beauty. When people said to Frances Hutchinson that there was nothing to do in the country in winter, she wrote in *Our Country Life*, in 1912, "Shall I try to explain the daily changing beauty of the winter landscape, from the hoar frost which transforms my world into fairy-land . . . that first snow which, clinging to every crevice, gives a new contour to my familiar scenes?" Sort of like a marriage after the bloom of romance, a deep tie binds. When people get to know a place, a spot, a bit of earth, they develop a protectiveness for it. As Horace wrote: "The land now known as Umbrenus' was recently called / Ofellus'; It will never belong to anyone, really: / It is loaned to us for our use, now mine, now others'."

Feelings go beyond ownership, as we become custodians and protectors of the place. Any developer who has tried to build—

either big or small—in summer territory learns the ferocious protectiveness of summer residents who band together as legal guardians. Even with all the land Alexander Graham Bell had acquired surrounding his Nova Scotia fiefdom, he bought two square miles in the mountain lakes north of Baddeck in order to protect the land from timber speculation. That land did not border his summer house, nor did keeping the trees on those mountains preserve his view. Rather those protected, treed hills must have given him a different kind of comfort, the comfort of seeing blank spaces on the map—a feeling of spaciousness that he could stretch out into wild nature. Mt. Desert Island in Maine was saved for the future by its summer people—one person in particular. A man called George Dorr from Boston had hiked the mountains for most summers of his life, wearing a pith helmet and carrying a biscuit for sustenance. Eventually, he decided that those mountains must be preserved and shared by all. Dorr lobbied Congress and recruited the Rockefellers. He devoted years of his life, and much of his fortune, to establish what is now Acadia National Park.

Being deeply connected to a landscape, as Dorr was with Mt. Desert, develops a protectiveness that goes beyond mere bestial territoriality. No longer merely exploiters, we often become protectors, custodians, stewards who work toward that relationship freed from those "greasy greenbacks" that Henry James talked about. Rather than keeping the land for personal gain, people like Dorr want to preserve, maintain it, become partners in its future. The not-in-my-backyard syndrome grows over the fence into a larger world. It grows as users of the land become its stewards.

But that protection of the landscape extends to a deeper understanding of nature beyond the view—that includes its inhabitants. After spending many summers at Prout's Neck, Winslow Homer's family established a bird sanctuary in the 1880s. This idea of giving sanctuary to birds was a relatively new one. It's still there, and it's still called the Sanctuary. In the Thousand Islands, a businessman who once tooled those waters in powerboats bought an island that he gave to the blue herons—or rather to the nature conservancy who established it as a heron sanctuary, as the increasing building of cottages and peopling of the islands cut into the birds' usual nesting space. That kind of preservation would not be necessary if summer houses did not encroach on the green, blank spaces in the first place. But at least these acts of nature philanthropy preserve what initially attracted us—rocky islands where herons nested and then sprang to wide-winged flight over passing boats.

Beyond knowing and belonging to a place, we seek an even more direct connection—a tangible communion with place. This urge to connect with nature reveals itself in the dozens of souvenirs of the natural world brought inside and displayed in the summer house. A rock, a feather, a nest, a shell, a bleached bit of bone, a scroll of bark. Look around a cottage and you'll see these artifacts of nature. Dozens of stones, smoothed by the tides, are exhibited on a side table, or a flycatcher's nest without flycatchers. Other times, a piece of driftwood is taken in, made functional, as it holds back a thick door to encourage an incoming breeze. A cockleshell holds cigarette ash. They are natural bric-a-brac that we pick up with the collecting urge. Nature's cemeteries surround us, and like grave robbers we sort through the remains, scavenging things of value from skeletons of life forms. A simple awe pushes us to pick up that red leaf or dried starfish whose appendages point away from its center in perfect symmetry. And so we bring it back into the house, where the smell of the sea dries out eventually. These sticks and stones are the souvenirs of walks. They are like the torn ticket stubs stuffed inside a drawer, proof of admission. It's as though possessing its pieces will bring us closer to an understanding of the whole.

Aldo Leopold said, "We can be ethical only in relation to something we can see, feel, understand, love or otherwise have faith in." In a society of landlessless, where concrete carpets roll under our feet, places like the shack let us see, feel, understand, love and have faith in a tiny piece of the earth.

Elk Horn Ranch

3. SOJOURNS IN A SIMPLER LIFE

"Nothing can be more foolish than for an easterner to think he can become a cowboy in a few months' time," according to Teddy Roosevelt, who worked at it himself for years. After his wife's and mother's deaths, which occurred just a few hours apart in 1884, Roosevelt went west to his ranch in the North Dakota Badlands. On endless plains where he saw melancholy and loneliness, Roosevelt silently lived out his grief. He exchanged a life of politics in New York for what he called a more elemental life, a seat in the New York legislature for a western saddle. Taking what amounted to a cowboy sabbatical, he stayed there, off and on, for the next three years, living in a rough world of men, far from the New York, Oyster Bay and Cambridge of his past.

In the early 1880s, cattle ranching was all the rage. As a pastoral dream, it was shepherding on an industrial scale, and had captivated the cultural imagination. Like many of his eastern friends and colleagues, Roosevelt had made some cattle investments, and bought his own ranch in 1883. And he wasn't by any means the only part-time rancher from the East; even in the town of Medora, a marquis had built summer homes for himself and his wife's parents.

Roosevelt's Elkhorn Ranch was a long, low log structure hidden in a clump of cooling cottonwoods. It had what Roosevelt called a veranda, like any porch overlooking Long Island Sound, yet here the Little Missouri River gave only a trickle of water during most seasons. Reminiscent of Thoreau's sparsely furnished cabin, Roosevelt's ranch, with rocking chair, two or three shelves of books and a rubber bathtub, satisfied all his wants: "And then I do not see how any one could have lived more comfortably," said the Rough Rider. Roosevelt, too, sought simplicity and self-sufficiency.

The ranch was self-sufficient. They made their own butter, grew potatoes if the grasshoppers let them, as well as other vegetables, and kept hens for eggs, in case their guns brought them no meat. They got their own firewood, and quarried their own coal. Civilization seemed remote, and Roosevelt said he felt he was living in an age long past. In addition to raising meat to sell, Roosevelt lived off a bounty of game then still roaming in the West. He shot prairie chicken, elk, bighorn sheep, keeping the ranch supplied with fresh meat by the prowess of his guns, of which he had several different kinds. It was a healthy life, he said, that ". . . taught a man self-reliance, hardihood and the value of instant decision." He reported that he had become one of them—a cattle rancher. In some ways he had. The future president went on roundups that lasted several

weeks, as he camped out and ate canned beans like the rest of his
men. He did all the work of a cowboy, in addition to writing at night.

Still, ranching wasn't quite a full-time occupation. "In the days
when I lived on the ranch I usually spent most of the winter in the
East . . ." Caretakers he had brought with him from Maine looked
after the ranch when Roosevelt stayed in New York, just as any
summer house is entrusted to the care of winter residents who check
the pipes during cold weather. Roosevelt led the life of a rancher for
several months a year from 1883 to 1886; and, of course, like many
other sophisticates who experienced the simple life, he wrote about
it. In 1885 he published *Hunting Trips of a Ranchman*, which he followed three years later by *Ranch Life and the Hunting Trail*, both of
which were illustrated by Frederic Remington, who later became
known for his sculptures of cowboys on horseback. He and Remington painted a picture of the wildest western fantasies, telling stories
of trappers, horse thieves, towns with several Bill Joneses, posses,
and Indians who are quoted by the future president as saying, "Me
good injun." These two easterners added to the mythology of the
Wild West.

Although Roosevelt described ranch life as one of hardship and
anxiety, full of dirt and rough fare, he posed for publicity pictures
wearing a buckskin suit of great expense, and his knife and scabbard
bore the mark of Tiffany. In the tradition of the gentleman farmer,
Roosevelt was a gentleman rancher.

"Really I enjoy this life; with books, guns and horses, and this
free open air existence," he wrote a friend. "It would be singular if I
did not." He said he had lost his usual restless caged-wolf feeling.
After a few years, the wolf became domesticated, returned to civilization back East, became civil service commissioner and more
involved in politics, so his visits were less frequent. At one point, he
brought his second wife out to see the ranch. But after losing substantial amounts of money, just as in his books he'd warned inexpe-
rienced easterners they would if they tried western life, he sold
Elkhorn. Soon after, his ranch became a cultural relic; the house

was exhibited at the St. Louis World's Fair, and later moved back to the Badlands, where it's now a museum.

Roosevelt's ranch prefigured the dude ranch—in its original form—where ranchers took in paying guests from the East who sought a western vacation, except he acted as both host and guest. Roosevelt certainly never thought of Elkhorn Ranch as his summer house—he would have given Sagamore Hill in Oyster Bay that distinction. Nevertheless, living part-time at Elkhorn Ranch provided escape and a momentary stay in a more primitive life that was quickly disappearing. Even while immersed in that life, Roosevelt described it elegiacally, realizing its transience: "In its present form, stock-raising on the plains is doomed . . . The great free ranches, with their barbarous, picturesque and curiously fascinating surroundings mark a primitive stage of existence as surely as do the great tracts of primeval forests, and like the latter must pass away before the onward march of our people . . ."

Despite his Tiffany knife and hired hands, Teddy Roosevelt did experience the simple life. Looking back in his autobiography, Roosevelt realized that living and working in cattle country allowed him "to get into the mind and soul of the average American of the right type," people who might be called simple folk. The Badlands—those empty plains where social position counted for nothing—represented a huge leap for a man of his class. He gave up material comforts, intellectual companionship, the right society, and politics to experience the wide-open life of a frontier, which in turned opened him to a lifelong love of the land. Like people today who escape to a rustic fishing cabin or an old farm, Roosevelt reached toward a simplicity that he knew was being lost.

Teddy Roosevelt was by no means the first sophisticate to forsake the city and all its meretricious pleasures to take up the simpler life of a working man—for a time. Thousands of years ago, the poet Horace delved into agriculture at his cherished Sabine Farm. Contact with the soil and a long day in the saddle are things that purify the soul, though sooner or later the simple clothes of the working man are replaced by the togas of town. "I need plain bread much more than honeyed cakes," said Horace, who adored the plainness of farm fare after the oyster-laden feasts of Rome. His poetry praised repeatedly the simple life of the country. In his "Ode to Maecenas" he wrote, "Leave worrisome luxury and your house that stretches to the very clouds. Cease to admire the smoke, wealth and noise of Rome, so blest." Horace left all that for his farm, given to him by his patron. Unlike the showy villas then being built by the very rich, his farm was a working estate—a *villa rustica*—that referred to Rome's noble and recent past. "No ivory nor ceiling of gold glitters in my house, no slabs of marble lie heavy on columns quarried in utmost Africa, I do not ask the Gods for anything more . . . blest abundantly in my single Sabine Farm." Despite his descriptions of simplicity, slaves worked the estate. Still, Horace played the farmer, and wrote about it as any poet would.

Ever since the pastoral poetry of Virgil, sophisticates have harbored a fanciful love affair with the rustic and primitive. So they tryst in the country, seeking amusement and respite from complicated lives. Marie-Antoinette adored the rustic, if it were confined to an afternoon spent playing at the Hameau. Chinese officials of ancient dynasties sometimes lived in luxurious cottages outside the city, unpretentiously called grass huts. According to Yi-Fu Tuan, they retired there when the political situation became dangerous. Some eighteenth-century English gardens, with grottos and follies, where cows and sheep grazed in the distance kept out by ditches called ha-has, perfected this pastoral scene with real live bedraggled hermits. These hermits were paid to populate the property with their poetry and poverty (or poetic poverty). Like professional hermits or houses called huts, simplicity is often nothing more than artifice, a luxurious idea embraced by those with time and means to enjoy it.

The Simple Ideal: a cottage, a cabin, a shack

With traditions of Puritanism, Jeffersonian agrarianism and Thoreauvian austerity, the desire for simplicity is coarse thread running through our cultural homespun. But material progress, and the realities of modern industrialized life, made that simple agrarian life impossible for most people. The summer house has allowed urban people to reconnect with that idea of simplicity. It represents the garden without the machine—to paraphrase Leo Marx's book of that name—a temporary Arcadia where signs of technology and machinery are banished. It represents a return to the essential things of life. In the evolution of the summer house in North American culture, a desire for simplicity has, for the most part, reigned, rising in reaction to the growing clank and whir of the national machine. The simple ideal still attracts us, although it's become more elusive and we now interpret that ideal more loosely than before.

Even our use of the word *cottage* illustrates just how essential the idea of simplicity is to the summer house today. The cottage is, by definition, a simpler house. Widely used to denote our inessential houses, the cottage has its root in simpler soil—actually the mud and muck of English villages. Originally, a cottage was a laborer's dwelling of few rooms and even less pretension, what might be called a hovel, if one were speaking plainly. According to Mary Gilliatt's *A House in the Country*, in the sixteenth and seventeenth centuries these one-room structures were likely to be constructed of mud, with reeds laid on branches making a roof, or they were timber structures also filled by mud. Certainly a far cry from the so-called cottages of Newport, Bar Harbor and the Muskoka lakes. Nonetheless, that we choose to call them cottages expresses our longing for simplicity—in spirit, if not in fact.

So how did rustic estates come to be called cottages? Did they start out with mud walls, and get renovated later with plaster, billiard rooms and all the Victorian comforts of home once a family's ships came in laden with bounty? According to Cleveland Amory in *The*

Last Resorts, our current usage of the word *cottage* descends from the large resort hotels, where, to contain the overflow of guests, plain little buildings surrounded the main lodge like nestlings around their mother. Eventually, resort guests realized that those separate cottages had advantages of privacy over regular rooms, and the simple out-buildings gained in prestige. Today, a bungalow at the Beverly Hills Hotel costs much more than rooms in the main building, and carries big prestige in a culture founded on fleeting privileges. When the hotel guests decided to make summer life more permananent by building their own houses in the area, they kept the word *cottage*, and returned to the hotel for dances and dinners.

Nowadays, if people talk about their cottage, they could be referring to anything from a twenty-room shingle-style manse over-looking the water to a one-room cabin with matching outhouse. Second homes dress down by adopting plain Jane names. Calling a vacation house a cabin also points to a rough, pioneer existence supplied only with necessities. These retreats are often called shacks in Newfoundland. In Quebec, northern Ontario and New York, a summer house is a camp, even if the last vestige of tent is long gone. A Quaker woman in Saunderstown, Rhode Island, called her little guesthouses "shanties."

We still call it simple, even if it isn't. We like to return to humbler beginnings on our vacations—or at least imagine that we're doing so. To refer to the Newport extravaganzas patterned on the White House or, in the case of the Vanderbilt Marble House, on the Petit Trianon, as cottages seems like fashionable artifice. As indeed it was.

This simple ideal reached its height in the cabin—the North American equivalent of a yeoman's mud-and-timber cottage. Hewn out of the very woods the pioneers cleared, the log cabin represents the beginning stage of our civilization. The cabin is an icon of culture—a fantasy in which urban refugees have often sought temporary refuge. John Burroughs retreated to his Slabsides. Poet Robert Frost spent time at his Spartan cabin during the many summers he

attended the Bread Loaf Writers Conference. At his Homer Noble
Farm, he disdained the farmhouse for the slabsided cabin where he
wrote on a plywood tray, surrounded by dense woods that he logged
for his imagination.

A cabin in the woods is still the ultimate address of the simple
life. It speaks of self-reliance and a life in nature. As Conrad Meinecke discussed in *Your Cabin in the Woods*, the cabin comes with a
"philosophy." These cabins were built by lovers of the "Great Out
Doors" (which makes a significant acronym). It must have the
owner's handicraft and rustic furniture and, Meinecke says, old-fashioned kerosene lamps become a luxury once more, throwing inter-
mittent light like the moon through clouds. Clearly, a cabin is more
than just simple shelter. Novelist Stewart Edward White, who built
his own summer cabin in the Sierra Mountains during the 1920s,
compared cabin life with that of the pioneers. If he wanted something, he had to make it. "So in our summer home we find ourselves
very much in the position of those early backwoodsmen." Hunting
cabins and fishing shacks rise from the same impulse for the great
outdoors; they shelter a longing for a rough, outdoors existence—
plain bread with the crust still on.

Ever since cottages and cabins have replaced the more sophisticated
European notion of a villa, the summer house has been built around
simplicity. It's part of the experience itself, as integral to a vacation
as swimming. Not accidental, that simplicity is chosen, self-con-
scious and purposeful. According to Cleveland Amory, millionaires
on Fishers Island off the Connecticut coast lived in small cottages
reached by dirt roads, even when they could clearly have afforded
much more. The conceit goes so far that a log house of baronial proportions recently built in Telluride, Colorado, was roofed in tin, to
pay homage to the miner's shack. Simplicity, in theory, if not in
fact, remains essential to our idea of an escape. And it has, ever
since people loaded their trunks on trains traveling from the city to
great lakes set deep in dark woods.

A History of Roughing It

Roughing it has a long tradition in North American summering. Early visitors to Maine in the 1870s and early 1880s were often called *rusticators*. Rusticity itself was their destination. Life was indeed rustic in mid-nineteenth-century Maine, where the fisheries had been heavily taxed, the hills shaved of trees. Summer travelers stayed in boardinghouses or with farmers. In those days, beds were often stuffed with corn husks, and chowders and potatoes completed the fare. The visitors' lifestyle differed little from that of their hosts. If summer visitors weren't charmed by the potato-and-chowder conditions, they were certainly willing to endure them to experience the delights, scenery and cool weather of Mt. Desert Island.

Even after they built their own cottages and settled in for the summer, the atmosphere remained simple, and the nickname stuck. Living among the lobstermen and lumbermen, these rusticators sought simple pleasures, hiking, fishing, boating in wood canoes and sailing vessels. The carriage processions of Newport were unknown here. In the 1870s, *Harper's Magazine* reported that walking expeditions were the rage, and the correspondent noted that the rusticators had a "vigorous, sensible, healthy feeling in all they do, and not a bit of that overdressed, pretentious, nonsensical, unhealthy sentimentality which may be found at other places." Simplicity was a resort virtue as valued as the view or the right people.

At about the same time as the rusticators explored Maine, the Adirondacks were colonized for holiday pleasures. The idea of summer simplicity thrived in the mountains and lakes of the region. Even today, the tradition continues, blending rusticity and comfort into a mixture palatable to city people. Not simplicity for its own sake, plain living and high thinking met in these dense woods of upstate New York. It all began with the Philosophers Camp, when Emerson joined other thinkers and scientists for a camping expedition in 1858. They hunted, fished, explored and wrote about it, as Emerson did in his poem "The Adirondacks." The simple life was a conduit to nature and nature was a conduit to God, following the transcendental thinking of the day. And so the intelligentsia of the day—writers and thinkers such as Robert Louis Stevenson, Richard Dana, Mark Twain—ventured into this near wilderness.

Indeed, the ideas of the simple life, and of experiencing a closer connection to nature, were pressed from the same vintage. People first came to the Adirondacks to experience the woods and the wilderness. But it follows that those who wanted to travel deep into nature had to leave comforts behind. To live in the woods, one lives like a woodsman, taking down trees for heat and then crafting them into shelter for the night.

When Reverend William Murray published *Adventures in the Wilderness; or Camp Life in the Adirondacks* in 1869, the craze for camping really took off. This best-seller caused a stampede, called "Murray's rush," into the woods. In his practical guidebook explaining what to bring, what kind of guide to hire and where to go, Murray described miraculous cures for consumptives as well as religious communion in the woods. He praised the simplicity of camp life: "O luxury of luxuries, to have a lake of crystal water for your wash bowl, the morning zephyr for a towel, the whitest sand for soap. . ." Parties of men traveled to the Adirondacks to hunt and camp like noble savages let loose among the pines of red and white color. (Although Murray included a packing list for ladies, women were not generally included in these camping trips.) Campers hired guides to act as go-betweens between them and the wilderness, helping city people hunt for food and build their shelter.

One of the men who followed into the wilderness was Charles Dudley Warner, editor of the *Hartford Courant*, who described the camping experience in his essay "My Summer." In the heart of the woods, near the foot of Mt. Marcy, his party had built a camp for the night. "Out of this basin we had just taken enough for our supper which had been killed and roasted over the fire on sharp sticks and eaten." So simple were their wants that they did not even keep any to mount on the wall.

Their huts were actually three-sided shelters, probably built by the guide who served as a general factotum and valet of the woods. Campers either built their own lean-tos, as they were called, or, like the hermit crab crawling into an empty shell, occupied shanties left by previous campers. The lean-to represented the Adirondack experience—to sleep with one invisible wall open to stars and pine-scented air, amid a mattress of balsam, sheltered by its limbs and cossetted by its hair.

The campers lay in their spruce bark lean-tos, they reclined on fragrant balsam boughs while birch logs burned, they talked to the guide Old Phelps (probably one of the most written about mountain men ever). At night, men gathered around a fire in the wilderness seeking to reconnect with more primitive elemental life—just as some men do today.

But the human instinct to civilize soon invaded this wilderness, as visitors imported comforts into the woods and stayed all summer. The camps became more permanent, and the few permanent camps described in the early guidebooks grew in number. By the early 1880s people from New York and Boston started buying land, putting up tent platforms and log cabins. They pastured cows and pigs on islands, lived off canned goods and local venison and fish. Roughing it became more civilized, as evidenced in Warner's next sojourn in the forest. Some years later, he rented a cottage near Keene Valley, where he picked blackberries, fished and went camping in the woods. A cook replaced the guide, the stove replaced the campfire, and Warner brought along his family. Philosopher William James had such a camp; along with a few other doctors and intellectuals, he owned a share in what was called Putnams' Camp. From there, he ventured out on long hikes up Mt. Gothic or Mt. Marcy.

On his 1909 visit to America, Sigmund Freud visited Putnams' Camp and was quite perplexed by the studied rusticity of the Adirondacks. "Of everything I have experienced in America, this is probably the strangest," he wrote to his family, "a camp you must imagine in a wilderness in the woods . . . there is a group of roughly made cabins with a name to each, as one discovered everything is rough and natural in character, seems artificial but it comes off somehow." The benches along the wall reminded him of a peasant dining room, and Dr. Freud noted that mixing bowls served as wash bowls, china mugs for glasses, and so on, "but naturally nothing is missing and is supplied in one form or another." This stage of Adirondack life was neither hair shirt nor silk shirt. At one of the earlier camps built in the mid 1880s on Birch Island, three cabins and fifteen tents composed the compound, which was well staffed with servants brought from town. (One chef had even worked at the White House.) Life in the Adirondacks still maintained a simple exterior, however; women made calls in flannel suits and gentlemen wore knickerbockers and coarse stockings.

The simple woods life became yet more civilized, and reached ironic heights in the camp's next stage of evolution. Tented villages were soon surpassed by so-called great camps, built for millionaires on hundreds of pristine acres, grander and more complex as wilderness life became even more fashionable. These great camps, or bark-covered estates, looked a hybrid of Swiss chalet, log cabin and Long Island estate, and were often decorated with the Japanese fans and lanterns so popular before the turn of the century.

In the 1922 edition of *Etiquette*, Emily Post described a fictional yet "fashionable" Adirondack camp, composed of a collection of shacks dumped "like a group of packing cases" in a clearing of pine trees. Inside the guest crates, the bedrooms recall "box stalls," with nothing more than curtain-covered shelves, bed, dresser, chair, washstand and rag rug. But, says Post, "Let no one, however, think that this is a 'simple,' by that meaning either easy or inexpensive form of entertainment!" Despite the bark-covered walls and rough stone fireplaces, such camps were well staffed; a ring of the bell summoned every comfort of home. At Post's fictional camp, twelve guides bring water, other locals do the washing, two people serve the food to twenty-odd guests and food travels by express hundreds of miles. Post did note the hardships: ironing posed a problem, and guests used their napkins *twice* before getting a clean one.

Instead of fishing for their dinner and picking their own berries, guests at the camps depended on their own farms, greenhouses and icehouses for food, operating as self-sufficient enterprises. One of the most famous, Marjorie Merriwether Post's Top Ridge, even supplied a funicular for bringing guests up and down the slope to the lake. In addition to the woodsy pleasures of hunting, fishing and canoeing, at the Vanderbilts' camp, Sagamore, guests bowled in a covered alley of rustic design where young boys reset the pins after each strike. Actually, great camps were city living with the bark left on.

Yet even the great camps retained the lean-to. The bark-covered symbol of Adirondack life was recreated as a permanent outdoor room, paying homage to the idea of woods life. But it was no longer for sleeping with the eyes to the stars. According to Post, an evening's entertainment at a camp centered on an outdoor fire where guests huddled in the lean-tos—which she described to the uninitiated as a "sort of penthouse or windbreak." At Sagamore, even that simple shelter was crossed with urban luxury, and offered room service. Lying on pillows of balsam boughs, as guests watched the flames of the fire, they could pick up a telephone attached to a post and order some snacks sent up. But after the evening's entertainments in the bark-covered parlor, the guests left the couches of balsam boughs to sleep indoors between sheets.

Today, this twinned tradition of rusticity and comfort still exists in the Adirondacks. Automobiles course through asphalt veins into the heart of the park. Settlements consisting of a diner, outfitters and outboard motor dealer gather tightly along the line of the road. Recycling, grocery stores, even movie theaters have arrived in the villages dotting the park. On the 2,300 lakes, and along the 1,200 miles of river, city people have transplanted prefabricated cedar homes and insulated log homes where they spend their vacations.

Yet the old Adirondack tradition endures at a place called the Ausable Club, located in a mountainous region south of the famous Ausable Chasm, up mountain of the Ausable River and between the two Ausable lakes. Suddenly, an incongruous spread of pastures looms, where golfers graze the sea of green grass. A grand old hotel, wrapped in a long veranda, surveys both the course and mountains beyond. No normal hotel, the Ausable is a club where members and their guests are welcome to stay and enjoy the thousands of pristine acres.

Yet Ausable members leave the comfort and golf of the club for a collection of rustic camps in the upper reaches of this very private preserve. To get there, they take a yellow school bus up a one-track road for several miles through the woods to the tip of the Lower Lake. Dense woods finally part to reveal Lower Ausable Lake, sitting among peaks like milk poured into a deep blue bowl of mountains. There's nothing on the Lower Lake save a boathouse filled with Adirondack guide boats—perfectly crafted wooden vessels resembling canoes slightly flattened at the bottom. Packed with supplies, these guide boats and a small portage get members to the Upper Lake.

At the Upper Lake, there are eighteen camps with names like Inlet, Panorama, Moonrise. In other places in the country, they would be called log cabins, but in the Adirondacks, where a tradition of camping in the woods under makeshift lean-tos has long thrived, any human habitation in these mountains, be it a chalet-like mansion or a shack, pays tribute to this tradition by calling itself a camp. Families own some of the camps, and the club owns the rest, letting them out to club members for a time. These camps are much like Adirondack summer life a century ago. A wood stove warms cool nights. Outhouses are at the back, and liquid propane refigerates food and does other sundry jobs. Even the Adirondack guide still exists at the Ausable, taking care of each camp and helping their "sports" with fishing. Until the 1960s all cabin owners were required to keep a guide; now only four camps have guides. Like their predecessor Old Phelps, they cut wood for the winter, cook and weave the balsam boughs for a woodsy night's sleep, although most families do everything themselves. Little else has changed.

Refusing the four walls of the cabins, Ausable habitués still sleep cradled in layers of balsam boughs in the lean-to. Few would have it any other way. A balsam bed is part of the Adirondack mystique—a sort of sleeping porch in the wilderness. Making a bed of balsam takes a better part of the day, as one must layer and weave the boughs into each other like braiding. Closed tents and air mattresses pale in comparison to the lean-to and boughs. To sleep under a bark roof, open on one side to the accompaniment of the stars, nestled in a sweet bed of green needles, is to sleep in the trees.

Between Plain Bread and Honey Cakes

Simplicity is a luxury, and a craving for it only affects a select few, as Charles Dudley Warner perceived. "The instinct of barbarism that leads people periodically to throw aside the habits of civilization and seek the freedom and discomfort of the woods, is explicable enough; but it is not so easy to understand why this passion should be strongest in those who are most refined, and trained in intellectual and social fastidiousness." (Philistines, noted Warner, dislike the woods until they become fashionable, and once they discover the woods, trash them with sardine tins and paper collars—or nowadays, septic tanks and satellite dishes.)

Even for rarefied palates that have acquired the raw taste, the simple life remains elusive. While trying to escape civilization as we know it, nonetheless, we pack bits and pieces, gimracks and gewgaws that find space in suitcase and squeeze into valises. There seems to be an inevitable movement toward civilization that is hard to resist, just as the simple woods life in the Adirondacks first found shelter in lean-tos, then cabins and finally the great camps. While living in a purposefully simple cabin in the Sierras, "ten days away from a starched collar," novelist Stewart Edward White noted this inevitability in *The Cabin*. "If he possessed in his soul the yeast of civilization, then most surely, little by little, as sure as he may, he will construct and accumulate the customary appurtenances of that state." Within a few summers he had made two bedsteads, a bureau, eight chairs, three tables, shelves, cupboards, meat safe, bath house, a two-stall barn, a dog kennel, as well as splitting nine hundred cedar rails—making his cabin into a compound. Wherever people go, it seems that a bread-crumb trail of civilization and comforts follows them through the forest, as do more and more people. Time and time again, summer Edens are spoiled by a surfeit of civilization. And honey cakes replace the plain bread on the baker's shelves, as they did in the rusticators' territory.

When first praised as a healthy, sensible place in the 1870s, the town on Mt. Desert Isle was indeed named Eden. This town, where men and women rusticated in the summer garden, soon changed its name to Bar Harbor, and life in the garden got complicated. Sophistication elbowed out rustication. In 1882, the Bar Harbor paper noted that women attending a ball wore both mountain or walking costumes *and* ball gowns—a state of dress indicating a transition period. But the ball gowns triumphed, and Bar Harbor soon boasted several Italianate villas with enough bedchambers to accommodate a harem. It became a social scene, a watering hole where the wealthy hosed themselves down with money, for all to see.

Simplicity seems a delicate balancing act, like a teeter-totter between extravagance and austerity, walking costumes and ball gowns, hair shirts and silk shirts, honey cakes and plain bread. In his essay "Confessions of a Summer Colonist," W. D. Howells said that his town was "in that happy hour when the rudeness of the first summer conditions has been left far behind, and vulgar luxury has not yet cumbrously succeeded." That happy hour he described as one of "sylvan distinction," which probably means a long day in the woods followed by a hot bath drawn by a maid. Yet, that moment between rudeness and luxury lasts only briefly.

Over and over, the civilizing mechanism sends simplicity tee-
tering back the other way. Quebec's Murray Bay had once attracted
"athletic fellows, fond of camping and fishing and golf, all bristling
with an abhorrence of bringing citified ways into Murray Bay Life,"
according to Henry Dwight Sedgwick. In his *Memoirs of an Epicurean*, he lamented the later influx of Americans who built new
and bigger houses with luxurious furnishings. He goes on to say that
influx was bearable only because "a number of superior men came,
and some lived very simply." Although he names President Taft in
that company, Sedgwick doesn't elaborate on how simply they really
lived. Simplicity, after all, is relative.

Yet often an influx of new people into a simple summer town
could quickly turn sylvan distinction into what Howells called
vulgar luxury, as it did at Bar Harbor, which became a grand summer
city to rival Newport or Long Branch, New Jersey, about which
turn-of-the-century newspapers printed social columns of who was
and wasn't in residence. When visiting the American scene in
1907, Henry James scathingly described that town, as well as his
own childhood haunt of Newport, where summers as simple as
meadows had since been cultivated into elegant parterres. At Long
Branch, James compared the string of seaside villas to monstrous
pearls "where the huge new houses, up and down, looked over their
smart short lawns . . . and confessed, oh yes, we were awfully dear,
for what we are and what we do." Ostentation ruled here: city
people built summer houses for status as much as pleasure; James
said these houses had a "candid look of having cost as much as they
knew how." At places such as Long Branch and Newport, simplicity
and simple pleasures were unknown. James writes that "They
danced and they drove . . . and flirted and yachted and polo'd." A
far cry from the days of his childhood, when summer visitors merely
walked the beaches for amusement.

Fortunately, the theme of simplicity did not drown in the current of post–Civil War prosperity, but arose in other vacation
haunts around North America: in fishing camps in Huronia, farm-

houses in Murray Bay, Quebec, woodsy camps in the Adirondacks. For the excesses and extravagances of every Newport, Long Branch or Bar Harbor, there were dozens of small, simple summer communities spawning and spreading on lakes whose names are not commonly known, and purposefully kept that way.

Toward a Lost Simplicity

Not merely roughness and rude conditions, simplicity often seems to be defined as society's earlier incarnation. Back in 1912, a writer for the American magazine the *Independent* described the appeal of vacation houses in the woods. "To those of us who live and work amid the artificiality of the city, there is something attractive in the idea of being close to the heart of nature, wearing old clothes and living for a time the free and easy life which we like to imagine we lived before the call of the city became insistent." It's a groping toward the preindustrial past—away from the city and all the progress and industrial efficiency it represents. So for these summer fantasies, we rediscover rural life, immerse ourselves in an old-fashioned atmosphere of what seems to be a less complicated time. Still, that simplicity seems to lie just beyond reach, traveling fast toward the horizon with the last quick hurrah of sunset.

Since Horace's time, people living in cities have sought a return to the rural life at country houses and weekend farms. Just as Teddy Roosevelt became a modern-day shepherd in the Badlands, people seek to recreate the simple life. In an article from 1940 on weekend farming in *The American Home*, the author describes commuting thirty miles every weekend to a farm where he maintained a perennial border, an annual garden, a garden of grapes, berries and asparagus and a sixty-by-eighty-foot vegetable garden. Curiously, the automobile and the highway made his part-time farming possible; typically, a complicated existence supports the simple life.

At these farms, labor is grafted on to leisure, and the result resembles the gentleman farmer. "I play the yeoman . . ." wrote William James about life at his New Hampshire farm, "the mother earth is in my finger-nails and my back is aching and my skin sweating with the ache and sweat of Father Adam and all his *normal* descendants." Farming counts as exercise, and purifies the soul by contact with the soil, no longer seen as dirt but the magical maker of food and fruit, oil and wine. I know a chef who goes to Italy every year, where he works the olive harvest on what was his great-grandfather's farm. Shaking olives into nets, gathering them and pushing them through the press becomes a holiday activity, as enjoyable as a bicycle tour through Burgundy. Suddenly, what are chores and work for farmers become recreation.

In the late nineteenth century, New Yorkers of not-too-great means spent their holidays at Catskills farms as boarders. Many found themselves helping out with haying and other farm chores, since few sports besides porch-sitting were available to visitors. Such activities provided exercise and exposure to the natural world, even if it was plowed and planted. At the time, many city people would board at farms for their holidays. In their original form, dude ranches also provided exposure to cowboy life at a working cattle operation. Today, this fascination with rural life continues; a Minnesota company rents farmhouses to vacationers. Not just abandoned houses, these cottages are located next to working farms or in the heart of an Amish community. To immerse themselves fully in agricultural life, vacationers can board in a farmhouse with home-cooked meals; interestingly, the price for that experience is nearly double the cottage price. It's called a farm vacation, a phrase that must sound strange to a professional farmer, who knows the only thing resembling a vacation on a farm is winter. And even then, there's always preparation for next spring.

Pastoralism mixed with a vacation imbues us with greater moral purpose, a significance that goes beyond mere pleasure. In the former Soviet Union, the dacha was reinvented in the farm's image.

The dacha's socialist variant, the summer garden cottage, had its own plot in a cooperative garden, and the entire community was often maintained by a factory that offered this bucolic escape to its workers. A bourgeois institution was made to refer to the country's peasant past, and thus redeemed itself morally.

In the same way we savor nostalgia for the good old days, we crave the poetry of simpler lives. Just as Marie-Antoinette indulged her fantasy to be a milkmaid without cares or courtiers, without necessarily doing all the chores. In the summer, we go back to our roots—or the roots of our more complex society. With the same impulse behind Elkhorn Ranch, or the Hameau, summer settlements gather around fisherman's villages, farming hamlets, logging camps, as though the honesty and healthiness of those simpler lives courses through the air like resinous pine vapors. So bankers live like farmers and lawyers live like fishermen during their vacations. They renovate abandoned farmhouses and pay high prices for fishing shacks. City people even dress like the farmers and fishermen of the area, donning work clothes and yellow slickers. Back in the 1890s, a savvy developer profited by this fascination with the lives of simpler folk by building "replicas" of fisherman's houses at 'Sconset, Nantucket. The rooms measured ten feet square, and the eaves practically sloped down to the floor; nevertheless, vacationers were willing to rent the cottages for a summer. Urbanites will gladly pay the price of admission, even if it means stooping.

Even if they don't live the simple life themselves, summer people have prized its atmosphere, tending old potato farms like hothouse roses. At Murray Bay on the St. Lawrence, cottagers have been careful to build their houses in the least productive corner of a farm according to Philippe Dubé, author of *Charlevoix: Two Centuries at Murray Bay*. Indeed, the Seigneury of Mount Murray, one of the area's first properties granted in the 1700s, is still kept as a working farm although it passed into the hands of a summer family at the turn of the century. So great was the desire of the *résidents d'été*, or *rés d'été*, to coexist with the working farms that the first golf course in the area shared its grass with cows and sheep, adapting the rules to agrarian life: if the golfer hit one of the animals, he or she was allowed another shot.

Besides treating the rural landscape as a pastoral park, visitors romanticize the inhabitants as well as the landscape. Describing the "simple peasant" of the area, angling writer William Hume Blake wrote, "On the long roads, in the hours of waiting for game, when pipes are lit and the camp-fire blazes, you may have a profitable discourse with him about religion and politics, life and death and the heart of man, as you are like to encounter across the walnut and the wine." Ironically, city people often displace those very people they so admire by driving up farmland prices with the pressures of a vacation home market. Consequently, second homes in quaint agricultural areas soon grow in the unfertile soil of farms that were probably hard-pressed to begin with. And once again, the simple life is bulldozed over by encroaching civilizers.

A Simpler Past

This return to a simple life is equally a return to the past, particularly a rural or small-town past. In his book *The Shingle Style Today*, architectural historian Vincent Scully discusses the impetus behind the summer cottages of the 1870s and 1880s, covered in cedar shingles and spread about on the Atlantic Coast. About those old Atlantic towns such as Marblehead, Massachusetts, Scully writes, "There one could build vacation houses and hope to achieve, or play at achieving, the ancient virtues once more." Vacations to such places become a form of ancestor worship, and the past itself becomes a vacation destination. What's more, this holiday nostalgia is nothing new; tourists visiting Mackinac Island, Michigan, in the 1840s, reveled in walking the then old streets resonant with memories of missionaries, Indians and the fur trade.

Almost since the beginning, resorts have seduced visitors with an atmosphere of what seems to be a less complicated time—after all, what people were fleeing was the modern city, with its noise, crime and other evils. When Cape May's chic was starting to wane in the 1890s, the Cape May *Ocean Wave* reported that "Someone has made the discovery that this is a quaint old town and that this feature is one of its principal charms." Rather than keeping up with the times, Cape May and many places like it capitalized on being left behind. They kept their main streets alive and eschewed modernities such as malls, preserving their appearance of quaintness and antiquity as a resource to be mined—seasonally, of course.

Towns without malls and islands without cars appeal to people who live by digital time. This explains why so many mainlanders escape to the Maritimes, where the clocks tick to several decades gone by. So, too, the whaling towns of Maine are stopped in time, preserved by the sudden halt of that trade. It seems that economic disaster is the pickling vinegar of architecture; and that disaster makes that architecture affordable for the city people. Nevertheless, the appeal of old-fashioned towns goes beyond the aesthetic. Clapboard or cedar-shingled architecture represents a more virtuous democratic age, when honesty, trust and good deeds traded like baseball cards.

Big-city people and suburbanites jaded by the automobile existence fill abandoned small towns and villages of America forgotten by prosperity, seeking these small remnants of an old-fashioned society. Towns with a one-person post office, a ten-page newspaper, a barber pole and where there's no such thing as a stranger. We escape to small towns for the small-town atmosphere, where people chat with the grocer and trust one another with keys to their houses, if they ever bother to lock them. Those small towns refer to a time when people could walk freely. After considering dozens of lakes, a woman bought a house on Squam Lake in New Hampshire so her son could walk to the store and buy a Popsicle.

During their vacation, summer residents recapture that feeling of the village long since disappeared from modern, movable life.

Along Penobscot Bay in Maine, where so many urbanites have bought abandoned farms, roadside produce stands dispense blueberries on an honor system. Despite satisfying their nostalgic cravings, though, these perfect little towns have a sadness to them, as W. D. Howells noticed eighty years ago: "One of the most American of all American things is the least fitted among them to survive from the present to the future." He saw his Maine town, too, disappearing into what he calls "our extremely forgetful past."

Besides being museums of well-preserved architecture, these places evoke the past by shunning the present. Aware of their archival atmosphere, many seasonal towns try to banish signs of the modern world—exiling the tree of technology from an otherwise green garden. Cars are often the first to go: Nantucket Island refused the automobile for several years. At one Adirondack camp, the staff quickly whisked away automobiles to a remote garage, as though an engine had no place in the woods; using a car to get there was acceptable, but after that, one wanted to forget all about it. To this day, Mackinac Island prohibits cars, even though the island is just hours from the Motor Capital, and frequented by motor moguls. Instead, islanders travel in buggies, or on horseback, bicycle and foot. In this nostalgic summer landscape, there are no factories or superhighways, no reminders of complex, mechanistic modern life.

We want to escape to a preindustrialized life without technology, or at least see less of it. The few rustic cabins that still exist, unwired to the overhead poles of watts and volts, express that urge in the strongest language—of wood and fire. Such cabin-dwellers seek a direct relationship with the ancestors, preferring to light kerosene lamps and stoke fires at cottages, just as their forebears did. It is a form of time travel, a candle-lit, incense-burning shrine. A woman who inherited such a cabin from her grandfather vows to change nothing. She holds on to the patterns of a previous era, like a religious ritual. As she pumps water, chops wood and lights the fire to boil morning coffee, she fantasizes about when people lived like that. It's a museum of a forgotten daily life—simpler in some respects, and more complicated in others.

The town of Seaside is another response to this craving for the past. This planned community on the Florida Gulf Coast, with front porches and gazebos in the park, takes people back. It's an old-time town resembling museum villages such as Savannah, Nantucket, Cape May, Charleston or Edgartown. The resemblance is not coincidence, since those towns inspired Seaside, but here no longtime residents were displaced. A sales brochure explains that Seaside is "a village which recaptures the spirit of an earlier era when the pace of life was slower." Slowing down counts as the town's unofficial motto. Summer visitors slow down enough to just sit on the porch—an American institution that Seaside is credited with reviving. Those porches predate air conditioning and television, and replace them equally well. After dinner, families sit on the porch and watch their neighbors do the evening promenade, a custom similar to the Italian *passiagiata* when townspeople walk through the main square or sit in cafés watching others walk by. Neighbors stop and talk to each other, commenting on the day's dosage of sun, the evening's outfit or the tides of the sea.

Seaside is an old-fashioned small town, made from scratch. This voyage into another time is not accomplished simply by ersatz architectural detail. Liberated from the automobile, Seaside residents actually walk around the town. The pedestrian scale and town center bring people together, creating a sense of community. The grocery stores and restaurants are intentionally run as mom-and-pop operations. At the Tupelo Street gazebo, children race in circles around the little park, while their parents watch and visit among themselves. Seaside's creator, Robert Davis, thinks living there reminds Seasiders of a time when they visited their grandparents—when they walked to the grocery store and gossiped with neighbors in a quiet old town.

In fact, Seaside recreates the old-fashioned summers of a chautauqua, or camp meeting, nineteenth-century resorts after which the town was patterned. (This homage to the camp meeting is quite literal; one residential section of Seaside imitates Oak Bluffs architecturally.) In addition to the atmosphere and beach, life at Seaside is fun and enlightening. The Seaside Institute sponsors poetry readings, art shows, theater, dance and symposia on urban design or planning. Just as at Wesleyan Grove, this community of verandas surrounds a central tabernacle, although this one is thoroughly secular. Seaside has won countless design awards, attracted much press and attention, but most significantly, it has captured twentieth-century imaginations with its nod to nineteenth-century summers.

Of Simplicity

Today, the rusticating of Maine and the lean-to of the woods have all but disappeared. What began as rustic cabins have been insulated for the most part. Most of us are content to put only a little distance between ourselves and the city, so that the electric wires, appliances, noise and telephones of current civilization can follow us. Of all the millions of summer houses scattered around the beaches and lakeshores, most suck current from electrical wires. Water is pumped out of the ground (or received from the city) in vast quantities, so that dishes, hair and clothes squeak with hot-water cleanliness. Heat comes at the flick of a switch, and a magical combination of Freon and ice keeps foodstuffs perpetually cool. We no longer have to forgo any usual comforts, no longer have to rough it.

Still, even with all the distracting detritus of modern life, we like to think of summer life as simple. It is, at least, simpler. Although there are pockets of hardy rusticism here and there, most of us have redefined simplicity to mean that we simplify what we can. We scale down during the summer, just as Jefferson moved from Monticello to the four-room Poplar Forest. Big households move into little farmhouses. Small suburban houses move into cabins. Apartments squeeze into trailers. (This downscaling even spread to permanent residents of summer colonies: in Martha's Vineyard and Murray Bay, natives would often rent their houses to tourists and move into small cabins or shacks for the summer.) Scaling down acually represents a grand voyage, even if the odometer clicks only a few miles or kilometers.

Like the self-denials of a temporary Lent, something must be sacrificed in exchange for the redemptive escape from the city, be it the comfort of home, privacy or specialities of the delicatessen. The cottage isn't the city, and can't necessarily have all its conveniences. In Bluehill, Maine, a sign posted in the bathroom of one of the older wood cottages reads:

The water tank is very tall
the boy who pumps is very small
so please be careful of the water
and use no more than you had oughter.

Using water sparingly, living without ice cream on an island— this atmosphere of doing without, or making do, underlines our definition of simplicity.

A simpler life—when loosely translated—means a life of informality. Away from society, the tight belt of rules loosens. Thousands of years ago, Pliny reveled in not having to wear a toga at his country villa. For him, that draped garment equaled the strictures of a business suit and Windsor knot noosed at the neck for us. We don't have to wear town clothes, we don't have to offer sophisticated hospitality, we don't have to keep a spotless house. There's less to do, and less expected of us, and that is certainly a vacation.

The simple life still has a distinctly moral tone. Interestingly, this tradition of rusticism and Calvinism seem linked; in countries with undecorated churches such as Finland, Norway and sometimes Sweden, primitive cabins are the standard idyll. Traveling toward the Mediterranean, this hardiness of summer soon dissolves in the hot sun. Spartan living is character-building somehow. The large family depicted in *Cheaper by the Dozen* moved to

Nantucket for the summer, doing without hot water, shower or bath because their father believed living primitively in the summer was "healthful." They bathed daily in the sea, no matter what the temperature.

More than connecting us with the past and its pastoralism, a taste of the simple life enhances summer itself. At the cottage, we edit the ephemera from life and simplify, simplify—in the words of Henry David Thoreau. Simplifying pares life down to the essentials: food when you're hungry, sleep when you're tired, and various pleasures in between. When it comes to experiencing life, less is more. The details of life are swept under the rug and easily forgotten. Life maintenance streamlines. Once we remove work, commuting, extra people, formal socializing, we are free to experience ourselves, our families and nature in a deeper way. The direct, ephemeral and sensory pleasures of life take over when nothing stands in their way—like removing curtains from the window to see the view beyond.

When writing about his retreat, Slabsides, John Burroughs praised "simple things and simple folk, a small house, a hut in the woods, a tent on the shore." To him, show and splendor only "set up a false standard of beauty, they stand between me and the real feelings and characters of thought." Living simply is like a fast for the soul. Think of the asceticism of a monk's cell where sparse furnishings and walls bare but for a cross help the communicant to concentrate on important matters at hand. That principle applies to summer quarters as well.

In the early years of the Rockywold camp in New Hampshire, the founder insisted on simplicity of dress and everyday life. No ladies who wanted to be invited back wore summer silks at this community in the woods. Interestingly, Mrs. Bacon, Rockywold's founder, had traveled to Japan, the land of minimalism. She felt an atmosphere of simplicity enhanced her guests' appreciation of nature, which was, after all, the main event. As Thoreau said, "many of the so-called comforts of life are not only not indispensable, but positive hindrances to the elevation of mankind."

Despite the popularity of looser translations, the ideal of a simple life perseveres in pockets of naturalism, hidden Edens in North America. One such place is Algonquin Park, a provincial park where cedar-strip canoes and portages transport visitors through capillaries leading to the heart of the mythic Canadian North, a colony of some three hundred primitive cabins scattered around several lakes. Many cabin owners can get to their place only by water or footpaths, and most have denied the telephone and hydro-electric company entry to their cabins. Here, the canoe is the preferred mode of travel, and summer residents paddle to where they're going. Says one resident, "Short of a canoe trip, it's as close as you can get to a wilderness experience."

Clear across the continent, there's another bastion of the simple life, whose practicants are struggling to preserve it. High in the Sierras, Echo Lake is set into granite like a diamond into gold. And it is one of a dwindling few in the country where the water is clean, and needs no boiling before drinking. There are no roads around this lake surrounded by junipers and lodge pole pines (ironically named for their future incarnation), so cars and most other modern encumbrances are left at the bottom of the lake. What can be said about a place that operates an H. D. Thoreau canoe race, besides that people at Echo are committed to the Simple Life. They have been since the beginning. The landlord dictates it. Just about all of the land surrounding the lake is owned by the Forest Service, which leases it to cabin owners. Sierra Club founder David Brower says in his memoirs, *For Earth's Sake*, that the Forest Service and cabin owners provided "mutual oversight"—neither letting the other do any wrong. This twinned guardianship means that little has changed in over sixty years.

Now one hundred or so families spend their summers on the

edge of this glacially created cold-water gash in the mountains. Drawn mainly from the Berkeley and Palo Alto areas, they come to this pristine lake because of its remoteness and stunning natural beauty, which they have respected and preserved by early efforts at fighting pollution, recycling and ridding the lake of septic tanks. Echo's commitment to the simple life actually preserves the lake environment.

In a way, Echo is stuck in the 1920s, like a sepia-toned snapshot of what a forest cabin used to be. Materials had to be rafted and poled up the lake, as they are still. But since those were the days before portable generators, no power tools helped build the earlier cabins, shelters built of wood or local stone. In 1925, a minister moonlighting as a summer contractor built a cabin for a family at a cost of only $250. Like most others there, it was small and Spartan.

At one end of the lake, there's one such cabin skirted with porches on three sides. Built of wood and shingle, the place is remarkable not for what it has, but for what it doesn't have. There is no insulation, no wall-to-wall carpets, no bathtub, no bedroom, no real walls, no closets, no telephone. Because there is no electricity, there is no television, no kitchen appliances, and best of all, no vacuum cleaner. Not having electricity shapes the life there, according to the house's summer inhabitants. "You slow down; you don't have to vacuum, you don't have to make fancy meals." There's a relaxed lowering of expectations. Instead of munificent volts of electricity that make a household whir, light and heat come from propane whose heavy cannisters are hauled up the lake with the very straightforward energy stored in human muscle. Doing without TVs or telephones reveals their true intrusiveness, and the family coddled inside this shell closes in on itself, indulging in "lots of family storytelling at night that you don't have the time for at home."

Inside this structure the size of a suburban living room, there is a kitchen area, a tiny bathroom carved from part of a porch and a bunkroom, divided off the main space. The rest is called the living room. Sleeping bags on the sleeping porches serve as bedrooms. Over fifty years old, the cabin has survived decades of rough winters and a recent fire that ignited the nearest house like a torch dipped in oil.

In such simple surroundings, life itself simplifies. So there's no need to fix things or replace things when they break. The stove has lost the functioning of two of its burners from old age, like someone who has lost hearing in one ear, but this household just makes do. People learn to make do when living far from roads and electric current; they salvage treasures and do things themselves, no matter how scruffily. The cabin's shower came from a boy-scout camp on the lake that closed down; and the water flowing out of the shower-head comes from a cooperative water company serving thirty-nine families. The system collects springwater in redwood tubs and delivers it via a system the families built themselves. Life in the cabin, according to its owner, is "reduced to the essentials: sleeping, eating, reading, and enjoying life." Despite the apparent discomfort, going there is as comfortable as putting on an old shoe stretched and shaped to the foot.

About living at a mountain cabin without any so-called modern conveniences, a man says, "Perhaps we're playing at being primitive, but it does help you understand our human roots"—roots that normally lie deeply buried and undisturbed. Saying that our skeletons differed little from our ancestors', Thoreau noted over a hundred years ago that "the improvements of ages have had but little influence on the essential laws of man's existence." Living by those essential laws, even by just a few laws, if only for a few weeks, reveals our impact on the world. It's like tearing off the clock's face to behold the machinery behind, with little cogs and springs working in concert. Aldo Leopold said that living on a farm was a good thing because it educated people in those important lessons: where heat and groceries come from. Even if you don't chop that wood, or plant and pick your produce, the miracle behind the grocery store and furnace is hinted at. Living a wee bit more simply shows how we affect the greater scheme of things. Certainly, the cottagers on Echo Lake who export their effluent realize their weight in the world. They actually carry their own waste—surely a sobering thing to confront. They bring along the garbage that can't be burned, lugging it from the cabin to the boat and then from the boat to the dustbin.

When water comes out of a well in miserly amounts, or when you have to hand pump the required dishwater, you learn to appreciate the resource a little more. Back in town, where water runs furiously out of a tap, without effort, that bridled Niagara seems a miracle worthy of consideration, no longer taken for granted. In this way, the return trip from the cabin represents a very great voyage.

Poplar Forest.

4. RETREATING FROM THE WORLD

Thomas Jefferson spent years building and rebuilding his monument, his masterpiece, his Monticello. It's hard to imagine he wanted ever to leave this beloved place, but he did. While still ironing out the details of its gardens, and well into his second presidential term, Jefferson began thinking about his *second* house. As he explained in a letter to a friend, "I am preparing an occasional retreat in Bedford, where I expect to settle some of my grandchildren." Before that bequest, however, he availed himself of the place.

He didn't leave Monticello for his health, or to escape the heat. Nor was he fleeing the ills of a city, since he already lived in deep countryside. What Jefferson craved was not so much a change of scenery as distance from the rest of the world. He found it at his second house.

By the later years of his career as a statesman, architect and inventor, Jefferson had himself become a national monument. Fame, as it always has and will, drew people like nectar, and Jefferson was besieged by visitors. At one count, fifty people sat down to dinner at Monticello. Relatives stayed—one actually gave birth while visiting—and admirers dropped by constantly, expecting hospitality. His biographer noted that the curious would wait outside his study doors, certain to catch a glimpse of him as he kept to his schedule of cloistered work periods in his private wing, and meals taken in Monticello's public quarters. Others gawked at him while he strolled his own gardens. Thomas Jefferson became an exhibit of curiosity caged in his own house.

Poplar Forest, as this second house was called, sat in the shadow of the Blue Ridge Mountains, as did Monticello. At almost the frontier of wildness, though, Poplar Forest and its nearby town of Bedford were far from the more settled and traveled part of Virginia, where Monticello stood. Poplar Forest was out of the reach of admirers, and friends of friends supplied with letters of introduction. To get there from Monticello, Jefferson endured a three-day ride over ninety miles of rough roads; that distance made the house into an unlisted phone number.

Although smaller and simpler in its furnishings than Monticello, Poplar Forest was no ascetic hideaway. The house sat in the center of a vast estate left to Jefferson by his wife, and which he farmed—to varying degrees of success. As at Monticello, he carried out large plantings, adding such exotic trees as Lombardy poplars, calycanthus, European mulberry and tulip poplars as well as orchards and berry plantations; he even planted thirteen poplars to represent the Colonies. As for the house, Jefferson shaped his small Palladian retreat into an octagon. The gardens and two matching privies echoed the octagonal shape of the house, as did the small rooms. (Indeed, the house was so small that he designed beds that hung from the ceiling during the day to make more room.) Yet Jefferson said that Poplar Forest might be preferable to Monticello as it was more proportional to the "faculties of a private citizen." At Poplar Forest, Jefferson was just that, a private citizen who enjoyed his privacy.

Just like the Roman poets he so admired, he sought a pastoral idyll, and savored the "retirement and tranquility" he found at Poplar Forest. He needed a place to muse and think—where his ideas could come and go freely. He wanted to be alone, and indeed Jefferson described living there "in the solitude of a hermit." Only his daughter, granddaughters and his friends Tacitus, Virgil, Ovid and Sophocles kept him company. His granddaughter wrote that he "found in a pleasant home, rest, leisure, power to carry on his favorite pursuits—to think, to study, to read . . ."

Apparently, he craved those pursuits quite often, as during the rest of his life he managed to visit Poplar Forest about three times a year. Just as people today shuffle between two places with a carful of belongings, Jefferson would shuffle certain belongings back and forth in wagons along the dirt roads, asking his daughters or servants to send along his leather chaise or whatever else he had forgotten. If Camp David had existed at the time he was president, he probably would have traveled to the Catoctin Mountains to find peace and quiet. Jefferson did not always want that hermit's solitude: after a few regenerative weeks at his second house, Jefferson returned to Monticello.

Once Jefferson no longer lived there, Poplar Forest reverted to an ordinary house, losing the protective aura of a retreat. Its land was chopped into smaller and smaller parcels, the house itself degenerating into disrepair. A few years ago, a foundation acquired the property, along with a few patched-together acres; and the house is open to the public like Monticello. And like Monticello, Poplar Forest has become a monument to Thomas Jefferson—but to his private self. The octagon is a monument to solace, to solitude and to the kind of silence that makes a person reborn.

Simpler than a main residence, isolated from the world, an intimate enclave of family, Poplar Forest represents an early version of the cottage as we now know it. When Jefferson was building Poplar Forest, octagonal houses were considered chic, yet Jefferson's design transcends fashion. As a circle and square coming together, the octagon symbolizes rebirth; traditionally, fonts and baptistries— such as Alberti's marble marvel in Florence—take that shape. Indeed, during his periods of study and quiet at Poplar Forest, Jefferson certainly experienced a kind of rebirth. Now we call it regeneration, or, more mundanely, recharging the batteries. Poplar Forest represents a retreat in the very current sense of the word: a respite from a life overflowing with people, so there is little time for oneself.

Today, we respond to exactly that same need to get away—at least for a short time anyway. Two thousand years earlier, the poet Martial expressed the selfsame desire. "That farm of mine up country—what / does it get me, Linus? You want to know? / Linus, it gets me away from you."

Getting away from Linus, getting away from it all, just getting away. To go away is to *get away*. And so second houses are called getaways, hideaways and escapes. When armies retreat, they regroup and regather their strength until ready to do battle again. After advancing, we, too, retire, just as Jefferson did, to be reborn—an inchoate feeling people describe on their return as rejuvenated, relaxed, revitalized, regenerated.

The Search for Seclusion

This notion of getting away from the world was relatively uncommon in Jefferson's day when the aristocracy gathered at springs to take the waters. Yet it flourished along with the vacation. The verb *to vacation* didn't come into being until the end of the last century, and a vacation itself was not a universal privilege until the 1920s when holidays were extended to labor and federal workers. Unlike trips to the springs or stays at a seaside without hay fever, a vacation wasn't simply a health cure or preventative, but a time of rest for its own sake, the vital pause between heartbeats, the moment between breaths. In *Lotus Eating*, a "summer book" from 1854, George Curtis describes various American watering spots—often comparing them to European equivalents. Saratoga's United States Hotel, for instance, is "an oasis of repose in the desert of our American hurry. Life is leisurely there, and business is amusement."

The idea that life is a desert that people need to leave from time to time took off, until eventually it was an accepted notion that everyone deserved to leave the desert, and drink freely and thirstily at the oasis. In other words, they *needed* to get away. In 1904, a travel article about Nantucket, called "The Isle of Rest," asked, "Are you weary and worn and distracted with the multitudinous cares of this work-a-day world, and are you dreaming of some quiet, restful, out-of-the-way spot where you can forget it all . . . ?" That doesn't mean forgetting your name, or which fork to use—forgetting it all meant forgetting all the *unpleasant* things in life for the duration of the vacation.

Soon, getting away came to mean getting *far* away. In the late nineteenth century, when the train tracks' reach spread farther and more and more people crowded the old resorts, vacationing city people went farther and farther afield, putting more distance between themselves and the city. By the 1880s, Montrealers were venturing to St. Andrews, New Brunswick, Pittsburghers to Georgian Bay in Ontario, New Yorkers to the inner reaches of the Adirondacks. These longer migrations meant leaving the world so far behind that it couldn't possibly follow. Seclusion became part of the appeal. In fact, one of the earlier summer visitors to Raquette Lake in the Adirondacks, a doctor named Arpad Gerster, moved his camp to the less populated Long Lake, as soon as the railroad line reached Raquette. That seclusion was the primary medicine in what was called a "rest cure." A 1927 article in *Good Housekeeping* magnanimously stated that housewives, too, needed a vacation, noting that "a quiet spot on the seashore" rather than a celebrated resort resulted in superior physiological rest—meaning that the farther away from "normal" life, the better.

The search for seclusion went even farther, as the same wealthy crowd who had colonized the Adirondacks continued upstate, into the St. Lawrence River and to the Thousand Islands—a collection of 1,700 rocky islets floating in international waters between Canada and the U.S. This unique conglomeration of geography allowed a society of people to escape, each to his or her own island and beyond reach of the world. Indeed, some of the islands sat on Canadian territory, and so were actually out of the country for the Americans who first settled there. During the postwar boom of the late nineteenth century, millionaires who made fortunes from Pullman cars, Singer sewing machines, the Waldorf-Astoria and Bellevue Stratford hotels and McNally atlases built themselves island retreats. As if the isolation of an island weren't enough, local legend has it that the cabal of millionaires made certain the railroad didn't travel all the way into Alexandria Bay, making it difficult for the crowds to follow.

More important, this was perhaps the first time that people thought to have their *own* island. Not content to share Mt. Desert, Nantucket or New Hampshire's Isle of Shoals with hundreds of other people, hotels and various boardinghouses, the industrialists who colonized the Thousand Islands in the St. Lawrence River lived privately on their own granite outcrops. They didn't just build cottages, but erected huge castles with dozens of rooms that accommodated bowling, billiards, a library and dancing, not to mention guest and servant chambers. One even came with its own deluxe houseboat, named *La Duchesse*. Unashamed of their baronial pretensions, the industrialists named these summer houses castles: Boldt Castle, Singer Castle, Jorstadt Castle, Castle Rest. Just like the castles of feudal Europe, these places were fortresses, secure from invasion. The interminable St. Lawrence acted as a communally shared moat, dissuading intruders of the thieving or the merely curious kind. To get to an island castle, a boat was required, which, in robber-baron days, before the advent of Chris Craft and outboard motors, few commoners owned. The Thousand Islands offered their residents refuge, in the company of peers.

Although this kind of island refuge was accessible only to millionaires, today the Thousand Islands offer a safe harbor to many. Refuge has become more democratic; now just about every little island has a cottage peering out from a thin screen of trees. Riverine topography is no longer an impediment to unwanted visitors; anyone with a credit card can rent a fishing craft with outboard motor for $60 per day, and lake freighters, waterskiers and tour boats cruise the waters. The castle is now metaphorical, its battlements conceptual yet secured from invasion by No Trespassing signs. Secure and secluded it must be, because even Yale's secret Skull and Bones Society quietly maintains a place on Deer Island, where intrusive phones and televisions are forbidden.

A century after the barons built their castles, middle-class Americans and Canadians spend their summers on these rocky islands, just as the gilded millionaires once did. Although a fraction of the castles' size, the modern cottages rising from the pink-tinged, lichen-covered rocks offer similar retreat from society. Some islands don't exceed the footprint of a typical suburban house, yet to its residents, such a grouping of rocks is a continent unto itself.

An island, being separated from the world by a daunting body of water, represents the ultimate retreat. These errors of geography, either rock or sand, good for little other human use, have been expropriated for recreation. So summer houses move off the mainland for an added sense of remove from the world and multiply—the Gulf Islands, their twinned San Juan Islands, the Sea Islands, the Elizabeth Islands, Nantucket Island, Block Island and the secretive Fishers

Island. Archipelagos such as the Thousand Islands, the 30,000 islands of Georgian Bay, and the scattering of islands near Stockholm have become communities of getaways—a rocky massing of hermitages. Although it was rare a century ago to have one's own island, and difficult even to reach one, island retreats have become more accessible with better, faster boats and the roomy convenience of ferries. And they've become more desirable: before the turn of century, Muskoka and Thousand Islands properties were sold for little—fifty dollars even—whereas that sense of isolation now costs dearly.

Living on an island represents a sincere desire to get away from the world. The border of water, which makes getting things there and getting things done more difficult, furthers the sense of distance. Divorced from society, islanders must bring what they need with them. Supplies must be planned down to the last potato and brought in one by each, as if preparing for an expedition up a forbidding mountain. In that remove, there's a sense of danger, an aching anxiety that civilization may not be close enough. The mainland looks terrible at first, but after a while, that mass on the horizon seems more inviting, friendly, comfortable and safe—unlikely to disappear like Atlantis.

An independent civilization, an island has its own rules and laws; on the island where I spent summers, any child tall enough to see over the steering wheel was allowed to drive. The more inacessible the island, the greater the amputation from society. Ferry service erodes that seclusion, and an island with a bridge becomes nothing more than a peninsula. Chappaquiddick, just off the island of Martha's Vineyard, relies on a ferry to bring people back and forth. The barge makes the two-minute trip without rest throughout the day. Still, the residents of that island staunchly refuse the construction of a bridge over the five-hundred-yard gap. Their sense of isolation has been ruined already by scandal, headlines and curiosity-seekers looking for the infamous bridge—and who have taken away so much rubble that it has had to be rebuilt.

Having your own island bespeaks utter misanthropy; there you can remake the world in your own image, ruling without any impediments of democracy, living without any neighbors. To live on an island is indeed to rule your own queen- or kingdom. It matters little whether your island is half an acre or half a mile long: you rule.

Yet, metaphorically speaking, all summer houses are islands, secluded, cut off from the world, if not by water, then by intent. They are islands of fantasy, islands of paradise, where all dreams come true. There, one *can* be an island unto oneself. Bridgeless, the other world melts away. Arriving at his Sierra cabin after several days on horseback, Stewart Edward White felt this island remove: "California has been whisked away. We are back again in our magical country and other places are not."

Often, the remove of these houses is itself metaphorical. An inlet can seem like an ocean, and being near water can make one feel transported a great distance. Being away from daily life is more often a feeling than a fact. After visiting a camp in the Adirondacks in the 1890s, socialite Adele Sloane wrote: "Lake Lila is very pretty and Uncle Seward's camp is the only one at the lake, so there is a delightful feeling of loneliness and being way off from everyone about it." In fact, other camps were close by.

That feeling of "loneliness" matters more than the fact. And the illusion of it takes many forms. At the lakeshore, trees rim the edge of water, a green veil cast between the lake and the house. An accepted convention, that screen of trees at water's edge hides each house, so that when looking out onto the lake, one has the illusion of it being unpopulated, pristine, remote. When there are no voices floating in the air, no human habitations exposing themselves, that particular moment and place makes it seem that one is in the garden the very first day, like Adam and Eve.

This metaphorical remove serves just as well as the real thing. A real hermitage might be overwhelming. A 1914 booklet about Victoria Point on Lake Simcoe perfectly explains the contradiction: ". . . the going and coming of craft of all kinds—which are so desirable to avoid the feeling of ennui where the seclusion is complete. And yet on the other hand the residents are ensured all possible privacy and protection from the interference of strangers . . ." Victoria Point offered civilization's comforts and conveniences, without its drawbacks. Writer Paul Theroux explained that when buying an island house in Florida, he wanted something both remote and accessible. The desire to be both far out of reach of certain things, yet close enough for safety, for sustenance, pulls us in two directions. We do not really want to be hermits—after all, we bring our family—but just crave a dose of what we call peace and quiet: an imaginary destination where there is no man-made noise, no reminder of civilization.

That illusion of remove is becoming harder and harder to sustain, or even to find. The screen of trees may still fence off the lake, but too many houses are crowding in behind. One hundred years ago, the *New York Times* speculated that the Adirondacks would become the Central Park of that populous state. The prediction comes close. Although hikers don't risk getting hit by Frisbee crossfire, the park is getting crowded: the winter population of 120,000 almost doubles in the summer to 210,000 people living among those three million acres of mountains, woods and lakes.

While wandering those woods last summer, I met a couple who had vacationed there twenty years, spending their holidays canoeing down the quiet rivers and placid lakes of the Adirondacks. They rented the same cottage year after year, but weren't sure about next year. Suddenly, Long Lake was no longer a haven for them. Motorboats raced by during the day, throwing tall wakes in the path of their canoe. More and more cabins squeezed around the lakeshore, peering from behind the screen of trees. More and more human voices, murmurs and shrieks pierced what once had been still afternoons. Peace and quiet hibernated during the summer, coming out only after Labor Day. They had decided to look for a less discovered lake, and embarked on a four-day odyssey in search of calm waters.

They drove for hundreds of miles, looking at some of the 2,300 lakes of the great Central Park, but found no untouched place—not even an *illusion* of an untouched place offering a two-week rented retreat. Waterslides, movie theaters and themed cabin villages perched on the side of the road. Maine, they decided, would have more room for them. Maybe it would be better inland, on the countless rivers making their path to the more crowded seashore.

In the Adirondacks, as well in many other previously remote places, it's getting more and more difficult to find a place of retreat from the world. Roads go just about anywhere, and are strung with the gaudy lights of commerce, complete with waterslides and minia-ture golf. Waterfronts have been chopped into bite-sized pieces as small as fifty paces across. Vacation homes have sprouted up in once-vacant fields, undiscovered idylls have been written up in glossy mag-azines, then discovered by thousands of loyal readers in search of the last idyll. Ironically, the places that originally attracted people for their remove and quiet often become as bustling as cities. The more people seek that remove, the harder it is to get away. As Aldo Leopold observed some fifty years ago, "It began to be noticed that the greater the exodus, the smaller the per capita ration of peace, solitude, wildlife, and scenery, and the longer the migration to reach them."

Escape

Jefferson may have left Monticello to get away from people, but everyone has a different reason to escape. In Renaissance France, the bishops of Orléans escaped that city and its cathedrals at their own *château de plaisance* at Meung-sur-Loire—which was outfitted with dungeons in addition to gardens. English aristocrats often went to country houses to conduct trysts away from prying eyes. Prime ministers, presidents and princes—people of power—escape to remove the ermine robes of responsibility, and wear jeans like every-body else. Even the dog collar begs to be taken off. According to

Reverend Murray, who wrote the best-selling guidebook to the Adirondacks, ministers need a break from the burdens of spriritual responsibility, and should leave the "unnatural, and often fatal tension" to recuperate in the woods.

There's even a native of Nantucket who leaves his house on that island's tip for a nearby, sparser island in order to escape the summer population explosion. Ironically, the throngs of mainlanders retreating to what they consider a quiet haven have ruined his. Havens are of course relative, as are one's reasons for needing one. But, whatever the reason, we all want to slip away briefly from our lives at some time or another.

Back in Roman days, Juvenal wanted to leave the city, and put it plainly in one of his satires. "Myself, I would value a barren offshore island more than Rome's urban heart / Squalor and isolation are minor evils compared to this endless nightmare of fires and collapsing houses." And that's just the beginning. Later he complains of inflationary rentals, fashion's wincing grip, crockery falling onto the street and burglars roaming outside while Romans stay behind bolted and chained doors. Juvenal wanted out so badly that he cadged invitations by promising to listen to his host's satires: "Whenever you go back home for a break from the city, invite / Me over too, to share your fields and coverts."

Back in 1881, an anonymous poet (who didn't even live in a nasty city) published this lament in a small-town Maine paper, explaining his vacation:

> We grew so weary of each other, Toil and I,
> That when we sat within our little room,
> We shrank apart; a sullen, settled gloom
> Was on our faces, neither saying why
> And so one day, when I was sick and worn,
> I ran away where morning sunbeams fell—

Yet, after a few stanzas of morning sunbeams, wild white waves and woodlands of his coastal retreat, this wearied laborer resigns himself: "Then I'll go back with lightened heart and song, / And fill with joy the old, deserted room."

In this era of faxes and phones, it's much harder to escape toil. I did, however, hear of a computer science professor who built a cottage an hour from his home, just so he wouldn't have a phone. That way, his weekends were not disturbed by panicked phone calls; as soon as he retired, a telephone was installed.

Winston Churchill escaped to what he called his "country basket," to recover from sadness. During World War I, he was stripped of his post as First Lord of the Admiralty following the disastrous Dardanelles campaign. The very same month of his misfortune, Churchill and his wife rented Hoe Farm in Surrey, where they retired every weekend that summer to "lick their wounds," as their daughter describes. In that beautiful garden, Churchill first picked up his sister-in-law's watercolor brush and began to paint. He explained later how the Muse of painting came to his rescue when he was bursting with pressure, overflowing with anxiety, burdened with too much time to think about the horrible happenings of the war. The Churchills left London as often as they could for the salve and solace of the country.

The distractions of a retreat absorb us. Suddenly, learning how to paint—or to sail, or to spot tracks—seems to be the most important thing of the day. With a different horizon to scan, with dozens of birds calling out, suddenly there are entirely new things to think about. This is the magic of retreats, substituting one thought for another, replacing worries with wonder.

The Retreating Mechanism

Why build another house just for escape? Couldn't Jefferson have sent everyone away? Couldn't Churchill have painted in London's flowery parks? Can't work just stay at the office? Can't we just sit in a chair and escape through some involving literature? Isn't that what dens are for? Why can't people simply escape into their imaginations? Powerful tool that it is, the mind should be able to erase itself without having to pack the car and cross county lines. After all, hobbies—whether building model airplanes or gardening—are absorbing activities. Even a cocktail has the same forgetting effect as a cabin in the woods—or does it?

What underlies this feeling of being away? How do we build whole islands, whole worlds out of mere cottages?

Somehow, a cabin in the woods promises unassailable defense, like a burrow hidden in the briars. Symbolic barriers—fences, moats, islands or even a wall of balsam boughs—separate one place from another. While summering at Murray Bay at the turn of the century, Reginald Townsend recalled building "cubbies"—two-room houses built of spruce and balsam with a casino for playing cards. In his memoirs, *God Packed My Picnic Basket*, Townsend says, "the cubbies were our retreat from grownups." Even though those same grown-ups were not far away, those walls of balsam boughs declared it a separate and secret place, possessed of vaguely misanthropic intentions.

Children who build tree houses high in the boughs or forts deep in scratchy brush have retreated from the parental sphere of influence; they have traveled beyond the dinner bell, which can clank furiously out of their hearing. Dinner, Dinner, *Dinner*. At this other place, children are creating a world where they're in control; it is safe, nothing can get you. Actually, the tree house is a model retreat, far from the constraints of cleanliness and scheduled meals. Make all the noise you want, eat what you want, say what you want. Brothers and sisters can be banned from the premises; parents can't climb up the precarious ladder, which can be withdrawn back inside. The same motive and mechanism is at work at summer houses. They are a declaration of independence, of momentary separation.

Like a snake rubbing against a stone to shed the old skin, the separateness, the traveling, the very intention to go scrapes off the old sheath—which is as light as paper—making it seem that the world is being left behind.

As soon as the trip begins, life's details fall away. Crossing borders, going over provincial or state lines, marks the beginning of transformation and transcendence. Although some people manage to escape without going very far, most of us need to mark more mileage than a quick trip down the lane. Usually, getaway houses are about 150 miles from the main residence, a good three-hour trip. But it seems that the more arduous the trip to the cottage, the more desirable. Vancouverites who summer on Savary Island must drive for hours and take two separate ferries to reach their getaways—at least a six-hour trip. A quick seaplane voyage also gets them there, but I suppose that many prefer the more attenuated voyage, since those ferry rides only emphasize the separation, underline the sense of remove. That arduous drive and ferry ride finish in a point of beautiful scenery where all else vanishes in an ingenious system of perspective. These complicated trajectories resemble the paths of criminals on the run, crossing in and out of water to wash off their scent, to throw the law and bloodhounds off their tracks.

To get to the island idyll of my childhood, we used to take a seventeen-hour train ride followed by an hour's drive. After an overnight stay, we would pack up the car, drive for three more hours, take an hour's ferry or motorboat trip and then bump down a sand road packed into hard washboard for a very long half hour. No wonder islanders never seemed to think about life beyond the island—it was a day and a half away.

Still, retreating is as much psychological as it is physical. Just as Marie-Antoinette's Hameau was but a few steps from the palace, I know of a couple who had a house in a country town and a country house just one mile down the road in the countryside surrounding the country town. Driving down the lane in their Land Rover stocked with picnic food was like crossing the river Styx into a different world, although their return trip was no harder than driving uphill. Likewise, in a hidden corner of Mark Twain's estate in

Elmira, New York, you'll find a little gazebo, a sort of den in the open, where the writer in residence at the big house went to find some peace, some quiet, some escape. It's the trip from *château* to *hameau*, from the top of the lane to the bottom, from the big house to the playhouse that marks the separation, even if it's a trip of just a few hundred yards. Ultimately, the real destination is an interior one.

Weekend Waldens

Like monks who give up common clothes for clerical robes, so, too, we take off the garments of social pressure, position and work while at the cottage, getting down to the skin. After all, the word *vacation* comes from the Latin *vacare* meaning "to empty." A vacation empties out a person, body and soul. A vacation house does like-wise. Once you're relieved of all duties and responsibilities, no other needs matter but your own. Getting away from the world is really about leaving the outer world for an *inner* world, going from without to within.

Weekend Waldens, these houses are places of self-culture where we can make that trip within. Unlike Henry David Thoreau, few people can spend two years at cultivation of the self, but instead plow those fallow fields in snatched spurts of spare time, weekends and vacations. Thoreau wrote about our being the Lewis and Clark of our own streams and oceans, and a getaway house allows for that kind of exploration in its time and quiet. Certainly artists and writers have long retreated to country places to reconnect with the self, to search for the sleeping chrysalis. Not quite as wholehearted an escape as the hut at Walden, today's occasional retreats more resemble its contemporary—Daniel Ricketson's shanty, which was a sort of Walden with compromise.

Around the time Thoreau lived on the shore of Walden Pond, Daniel Ricketson found a similar escape at his shanty outside New

Bedford, Massachusetts. He never lived there full-time, but went occasionally, as a respite. After reading *Walden*, Ricketson wrote to the author, saying he recognized many of his own experiences. "I have often felt an inclination when tired of the noise and strife of society, to retire to the shores of this noble old pond . . . but I have a wife and four children, and besides, I have got a *little* too far along, being in my forty-second year, to undertake a new mode of life." So instead, Ricketson traveled three miles from New Bedford to his "shanty," a twelve-by-fourteen-foot board-and-batten shack outfitted with two desks, a wood stove and a long bench. And Thoreau visited him there, later noting in his journal that the walls facing west and northwest were papered with various quotations and paragraphs celebrating simplicity, retirement and the country that Ricketson savored over and over: "How charming is divine philosophy!" (Milton), or (roughly translated from the unattributed Latin), "I come here for solace, hope and happiness."

Ricketson's shanty, like Thoreau's hut, was a place of reflection and study, a place from which he ventured into the natural world. Ricketson observed the birds, took long tramps through the woods and read the poetry of Virgil and Cowper, who sang the pleasures of the countryside. "Still I am not entirely given up to these matters—they are my pastimes." He did not—or perhaps could not—devote himself entirely to his pond, having a farm to attend to and a little business in town. Yet Ricketson managed to uphold his responsibilities as well as maintain this private place for himself. He kept one foot in the outside world, and the other in his own private world. At places like the shanty, we can retire from the world, to be alone, and to think. There, town business and farm matters—other needs and obligations—are left at the door; only the self and its needs enter.

Summer houses are among the few places that accommodate, even encourage, solitude. Indeed its very symbol, the hammock, is an unsociable piece of furniture designed to cradle but one person in its cocoon. Think of all the altars to the self, benches in the garden, swings under trees, rocking chairs, gazebos on a point. Those are places for reverie, for just relaxing and having a muse about nothing in particular. Despite the large numbers of family and guests usually gathered, sociability is optional—at certain times of the day. Strangely, there's nothing antisocial about leaving the group to find a moment of aloneness outside. Solitude grows in profusion in the out-of-doors, in quiet spots in the woods, among the dunes, on an outcropping of rocks where the only company is silence.

> You wonder why I retreat
> so often to my barren acres
> and shabby farmhouse at Nomentum?
> It's because there's no place in the city
> for a poor man to get a little peace
> and a chance to think, Sparsus.

As Martial wrote, we have to leave the city to think. Places like Walden Pond reflect life with the clarity of a clear pool. Poet Edna St. Vincent Millay wrote about Ragged Island in Maine, where she lived with her husband: "There thought unbraids itself, and the mind becomes single." While visiting his brother's home in New Hampshire, Henry James wrote about "the insistent hush of a September Sunday morning; nowhere greater than the tended woods enclosing the admirable country home that I was able to enjoy as a centre for contemplation." He compared the place to a sacred grove, a place prepared for high uses, "even if for none rarer than high talk." The atmosphere is meditative, there are no distractions—no voices, no buildings, no people. Explaining why people should travel to the Adirondacks, Reverend Murray said that a person "must leave the haunts of man—where every sight and sound distracts his attention, and check the free exercises of his soul . . ." In the woods, the mind runs as freely as untapped mineral springs, and the soul follows.

Retreats and Religion

Leaving the world has always had a spiritual dimension. Moses ascended the mount to hear the word of God. Jesus stayed in the desert for forty days and nights, seeking his faith. Buddha left his home, traveling in search of enlightenment, and eventually found it under the bodhi tree. Monks and nuns sequester themselves from the secular in monasteries and convents. Getting away from the world—or the world of civilization—is supposed to bring people closer to God, as the worldly yields to the otherworldly.

Surprisingly, this abandoning of the world has much to do with the development of the summer house. After all, the word *retreat* referred to a religious withdrawal from the world well before it meant a vacation house.

It all began with camp meetings—religious festivals held in the woods. During the religious revival of the early nineteenth century, dubbed the Great Awakening, pioneers traveled to sacred groves hacked out of the forests where they sat on log benches and slept in tents or wagons. At these meetings, which lasted several days, worshipers experienced conversions and a renewal of faith. The drunk and dissolute also came, but lived wildly—foreshadowing the hedonistic atmosphere at future resorts.

Eventually, the Methodist Church embraced this notion of religious meetings. One of the earliest proponents, Reverend Gorham, wrote the first meeting manual in 1854. Comparing the meeting to the Feast of the Tabernacles, he asked, "What better thing can she [the church] do than to retire from the cares of the world for a week and renew their vows . . . just at that period of the year when the faith of the faithful is likeliest to wane." Finally, abandoning all religious argument, Gorham explained that Methodists needed to be "disburdened of worldy cares": "The truth is, human life needs to be dotted over with occasions of stirring interest. The journey asks its milestones, or rather, if you please, its watering places along the way. Our nature requires the recurrence now and then, of some event of special interest; something that shall peer up from the dead level of existence—an object for hope to rest upon in the future—an oasis in the desert of the remembered past . . ."

Many of these oases soon grew up green in the desert. (Oasis seems to have been a popular metaphor for these resorts, as if they contained life-giving substances as essential to the soul as water to the body.) In 1835, the Methodist Church began Wesleyan Grove on Martha's Vineyard, which was followed over the next few decades by dozens of similar summer communities, such as Ocean Grove in New Jersey, Pacific Grove in California, Bismark Grove in Kansas, Thousand Island Park on Wellesley Island in the St. Lawrence. A town named Grove often hints at holier beginnings, as does a lingering practice of temperance. Since their peak around the turn of the century, many Groves have since been swallowed by summer colonies or even suburbs, losing their religious feeling.

Wesleyan Grove, one of the largest, has endured to this day, its spirituality alive, if slightly muted. Set above the bluffs at Edgartown on Martha's Vineyard, Wesleyan Grove was sheltered by a bower of scrub oaks—a true sacred grove. In the beginning, families rented or built tents where they stayed during the revival, but tents gave way to cottages in the 1860s. The campground grew into a village of over three hundred cottages that radiated from the community's nucleus—the tabernacle. As well as praying under that roof, visitors prayed in front of a "consecrated juniper," an ancient bonsai of a tree. Even the landscape took on biblical tones: entering the campgrounds was referred to as "crossing over Jordan."

Wesleyan Grove was often called the celestial city. The cottages, with their gothic windows and pointed gables, resembled little churches all to themselves. Harmonious in design and decorated in gay gingerbread trim, these dollhouses made the resort look like fairyland. Clearly this was a place removed from the day-to-day world. It was always so quiet that the Sabbath barely stood out. Children roamed about freely, labeled with their cottage name like delegates circulating at a convention. Even personal privacy was sacrificed: the double front doors of each cottage were flung wide open, as though the behavior inside were above reproach.

In her study of Wesleyan Grove, *The City in the Woods*, Ellen Weiss observes, "The dynamism of American life demanded solace as well as celebration, both of which residents of Wesleyan Grove managed to achieve." Solace took the form of two daily services, in addition to Sunday worship. Fun and faith mingled cheerfully; after the skating rink appeared in the 1890s, young people could be seen roller-skating, arms at one another's waists, to a waltz version of "Nearer My God to Thee." A band played throughout the noon-hour swim. By blending pleasure and prayer, the camp meeting at Wesleyan Grove and its cousins elsewhere provided an alternative to harmful influences at the resorts that were multiplying madly in the prosperous period of the Gilded Age. Late-nineteenth-century observers commonly contrasted Wesleyan Grove's healthy atmosphere to the decadence and vulgarity of Newport and Saratoga. In the 1870s, Harriet Beecher Stowe took heart that people were traveling "not to places of dissipation but of worship."

Today, Wesleyan Grove—now called the Martha's Vineyard Camp Meeting Association—thrives quietly amid the town of Oak Bluff, a tourist town bursting with Tex-Mex takeout, bike-rental shops, bars and summertime movie theaters where sex and violence alternate at seven and nine o'clock showings. Going to the grove is retreating to an oasis of quiet, small-town America. This mecca draws its pilgrims from points as distant as Georgia, Texas and Colorado. Although the association is now nondenominational Protestant, residents lease the land under their cottages and must submit to an interview by the Camp Meeting Association, which shuns real estate speculators or fast-living people, who would not fit into this wholesome family community.

Despite the invasion of tourists who stroll around the village, gawking at the historically quaint cottages, many things are just as they were. Band concerts have gone on forever at the pavilion overlooking the bluffs. The residents sit on front porches, lined up in rockers and rocking to and fro, nodding at the passersby in the morning, during the hot afternoons and in early evenings. A very old-fashioned community sing draws the campground residents on Wednesday nights. More important, the celestial city has preserved its spirituality. Sunday brings people of all faiths under the tin roof of the tabernacle built more than one hundred years ago. There, a banner still hangs saying Surely God Is in This Place— perhaps less so than before, but the presence remains. "There's a common sense of values which bonds people here," says a young father from Colorado who recently became part of the community. "There's a oneness with people. As people walk by there's no race or no creed—you just talk with people; you see God in each human here." Unlike similar groves that have been overpowered by the modern vacation agenda of unadulterated pleasure, the campgrounds at Martha's Vineyard have retained hints of their holier beginnings.

The Methodist groves eventually evolved into another morally tinged resort—the chautauqua. In 1874, on the shores of Chautauqua Lake in upstate New York, a Methodist minister founded a camp for the instruction of Sunday-school teachers. Beyond that mandate, however, the interdenominational Chautauqua offered learning and culture in its program. Hebrew classes, concerts and noted lecturers were the entertainments. Just as at the campgrounds, families inhabited tents, and later built gingerbread cottages where they spent the summer season year after year. The chautauqua idea spread to DeFuniak Springs in Florida, and as far away as North Dakota, where campgrounds existed at the inappropriately named Devil's Lake. At one count two hundred of these summer communities were spread across North America, offering personal improvement, intellectual stimulation and a wholesome atmosphere. Usually located by a lovely natural setting such as the original Chautauqua Lake, they were popular places to spend vacations. As at the original, visitors to the various chautauquas expanded their minds with lectures, stereopticon slide shows, philosophy and theology, in addition to Sunday school.

With their emphasis on learning, the chautauquas moved toward the secular. However, like the revivalist-tinged campgrounds, they, too, remained apart from the world: Grimsby Park on Lake Ontario had both gate *and* moat, to keep profane influences safely away. Yet inside those boundaries, the wall between temple and nature began to crumble. The tabernacle was done away with, as the vacationers worshiped outdoors. At the Grimsby chautauqua, the auditorium was nothing but benches among the tall trees. A few hours farther north, the 1920s Universalist Muskoka Assembly substituted a walk in the woods for more formal worship conducted in enclosed space. The temple came outdoors and the outdoors eventually became the temple.

Besides spreading the word of God, the camp meetings and chautauquas scattered over the continent spread the notion of retreat, just when cities were growing taller and denser than August cornstalks. Unlike the great resorts of the Gilded Age, devoted only to pleasure, comfort and ostentation, the camp meeting pursued a deeper purpose. Its residents revived their faith and renewed their relationship to God in an Edenic garden.

Unlike the great summer estates built in St. Andrews, New Brunswick, the Laurentians or in the Berkshires, summer quarters at camp meetings were affordable. In 1866, a Wesleyan Grove cottage cost a mere $500. Clearly, these campgrounds and chautauquas were within the reach of the urban middle class, so more people could afford a healthy, religiously tinged vacation.

In fact, these religious summer cities helped democratize the summer house. Having a family tent or cottage was not only *fiscally* possible, but camp meetings and chautauquas made that cottage *morally* defensible—erasing all resemblance to the frivolous and conspicuous villas of the wealthy. It was pleasure diluted with purpose.

Although the religious retreat still exists here and there in the form of church camps, it is for the most part a thing of the past. We still embark on retreats, although nowadays most of us have taken the religion out of the retreat. Yet this heritage of greater meaning has been passed on to vacation houses; hints of higher purpose still linger, heavy as incense. Many parallels exist between religious retreats and the vacation house. Both are about rebirth and communion. Both encourage an atmosphere of contemplation and meditation. Both return the communicant to the world enriched in an uncountable, unsayable way.

Summer houses are secularized retreats—places where we can put the soul back in the body during a weekend's Sabbath. They are miniature monasteries, where matins masquerade as early morning fishing trips and vespers are disguised as the cocktail hour on a deck overlooking a red sunset boisterously blazing a path down the sky.

There's a universal ritual of arriving at the cottage. The car door is left wide open, the luggage and groceries left inside. The passengers run down to the water's edge—even if that water is the chlorine-tinted liquid of a pool—and dive, in a ritual of baptism, rinsing off the sin of city and emerging anew, refreshed, a cleaner version of self. There is something entirely transforming about that first swim. We return to the same waters to spawn, to start life anew. That immersion is the beginning of a vacation-length rebirth—into a warm-weather state of grace.

Beinn Bhreagh

5. COMING HOME TO THE FAMILY

During the golden age of cottages in the 1880s, Alexander Graham Bell and his family were looking for a summer place. They tried Newport, but its grandeur wasn't to their taste. Bell wanted to escape the scrutiny of the press, the assaults of favor-seekers and the pressures of lawsuits constantly challenging his rightful patent of the telephone. His wife, Mabel Hubbard Bell, wanted to find a place where her daughters could dress in boys' clothes and play freely. So they went to Canada, where Bell had once lived, in search of emptier places. While on a steamer tour of the Nova Scotia coast, they landed at Baddeck, a little outpost of Gaelic culture on Cape Breton Island. The Bells got off the boat right there, and stayed three weeks at an inn. The landscape recalled his native Scotland, and the vestiges of Gaelic culture cemented his affections. By the end of that summer the Bells had rented a farmhouse, which they later bought. They built an additional story *under* the existing one and a half floors, and returned the following summer.

Eventually, the Bells bought land and more land until they gradually acquired all the farms on the neck of land called Red Head. It sat squarely between Baddeck Bay and the Bras d'Or, a collection of saltwater lakes filled with water from the sea, with the Wycogomaugh Mountains in the distance. They renamed the place Beinn Bhreagh, Gaelic for "beautiful mountain." To find the ideal spot for a summer house, they drove around sitting on chairs mounted atop a wagon, trying the different views of water and mountains as a lady would try hats in a shop, until they found the perfect vista.

Originally, Bell had envisioned a little cabin beside a brook, but after building a rustic lodge, he added a second house on the property: a manse of several dozen rooms in the great Victorian style, named Beinn Bhreagh Hall. The imagined cabin eventually grew into a vast working estate with dozens of buildings. Bell separated the place into four divisions called the Nursery, Farm, Building Roads and Wharves, and Lab Division, where he conducted countless experiments. Known primarily for the telephone, Bell was a versatile inventor who worked on education for the deaf, invented a precursor to the iron lung and developed solar stills for the desalination of water. He even bred sheep until he could prove that it was possible to create a twin-producing breed. Clearly, this summer home was dedicated to industry, not idleness; at one point thirtynine people worked in the various labs. At the kite house, he conducted experiments in flight that culminated in the first airplane flight in the British Commonwealth. His hydrofoil, HD-4, sped across Baddeck Bay at 70 mph in 1919. Here, away from strictures and structures, Bell's imagination roamed as freely as girls dressed in boys' trousers.

Despite all the speed records and science, Beinn Bhreagh was a family place. Bell loved his children and grandchildren, and did the usual grandfatherly things like flying kites with his daughters' children. One of his first grandchildren was born at Beinn Bhreagh Hall in 1909. From that year until 1922, they published the *Beinn Bhreagh Recorder* off and on. In addition to that newspaper, Bell dictated Home Notes about the family's goings-on to keep everyone informed. (Children weren't always to be seen and heard; Bell often retired to his houseboat, which was deemed off-limits.)

The clan gathered at Baddeck every summer; a photograph from 1918 shows fifteen relatives surrounding the patriarch; his notion of clan was an expansive one. Bell cousins and cousins from his wife's family built their own cottages across the bay, and their descendants still summer in Cape Breton. In just a few decades, Bell had created an ancestral home like those of Britain's landed gentry, the difference being that second sons and daughters shared in this summer patrimony. Beinn Bhreagh was his legacy to his family. Alexander Graham Bell wished for that property to remain in the family, and it has stayed thus and prospered.

Just as Bell generated a generous legacy of descendants, his summer house hatched generations of houses. Within the past one hundred years, those first two houses, the Lodge and Beinn Bhreagh Hall, now called the Point for its position on a point overlooking the bay, spawned another twelve. Burns Cottage, the Nucleus, the Red Barn, Kiaroa House and others are spread generously around the five-hundred-odd acres so that one house's laughter goes unheard by the others. As the family grew, various outbuildings were pressed into service to shelter a growing number of Bell descendants. A boathouse over a canal houses one family. The kite house was converted into a cottage, as was an old laboratory. Another branch of the family bought the schoolhouse, and others have built their own places. The gardener's cottage now serves as guesthouse. Despite all these additons, the succeeding generations have scrupulously kept the Point just as it was in Bell's day; any move to change things in the mother-of-all-cottages is fiercely opposed. It's said that if Bell returned, he'd be able to find his way easily through the house. To this day, he's called Grampie Bell by generations who know him only by family folklore.

Bell's dream of a family seat has survived the invasions of the twentieth century, as his great-great-grandchildren spend their summers in much the same way his daughters had. Scattered around the country like seed pods floated on the wind, they come from Florida, Pennsylvania, Massachusetts, Washington, but of course some do not come at all. Yet unlike Bell with his restless mind, the relatives who come to Baddeck today indulge in normal holiday pleasures such as resting, reading and sailing. Children can run about the place freely. If they're nowhere to be found, they're probably with some newfound cousins.

Still, Beinn Bhreagh represents more than a safe playground for all ages. According to one great-grandson of Bell's, "For most people in the family, it's like their soul. It's the place where they return because it's so much a part of their identity—and a way to commune with parents and grandparents." Some things are just as they were: Sunday dinner at the big house is still a formal affair presided over by the beloved family matriarch. Aside from an annual family meeting, held in Washington, there's no other event or circumstance to bring them all together. In 1990, the clan celebrated the centennial of the Lodge, the patriarch of all cottages. The memorial T-shirt read, 100 Years of Free Thinking, the Rest You Pay For, alluding to the expense of maintaining a family legacy, even when divided into dozens of shares. Despite their varying family names and preferences for sailing or hiking, this mountain in Nova Scotia binds dozens and dozens of distant cousins to a common source. "The family identity is very strong, and returning there reinforces that," says a Bell great-grandson. Visiting descendants also reinforce that identity by study-ing the pictures and exhibitions at the nearby Alexander Graham Bell Museum. Beinn Breagh must be one of few family cottages that has its own national museum.

Few summer places claim such a long and scientifically signifi-cant history as Beinn Bhreagh. Nevertheless, those fourteen houses serve the same purpose as most cottages: reuniting and reinforcing a family. That piece of land in Nova Scotia calls back Bell descen-dants to the summers of their childhood, in a pilgrimage to their source. For them, Beinn Bhreagh is a constant. Grandparents and parents pass on, spouses are embraced into the family, children make their first visit. But over the past century, Beinn Breagh Hall—down to its furnishings—has stayed put, unswayed by chang-ing fashions, and immutable as a mother's love. It's been that way for one hundred years, which is longer than most family memory. Beinn Bhreagh, and places like it, are family enclaves.

Whether it's passed down through generations, shared by siblings or newly built to create happy childhood memories, the cottage repre-sents a family seat, a place of belonging and identity. A family marker as strong as any inherited dimple, it connects people tied to one another by blood. That summer life, with its scraped paddles, island picnics, sailboats and bushwhacked pathways, is one of the few experiences members of a family share. And so the house becomes a symbol for that family—a powerful symbol at that. Like the Bells' nearby museum, summer places store a family's history with found objects and the cottage name, Tall Pines or Shorewinds, whispered like a password among the family, magically conjuring up happy, warm days that ended in a corn roast or a late-night swim, as they have for summers on end.

The family itself was once a much more powerful unit of mea-sure than it is today. There were family farms, family crests, family businesses, family capital, family recipes, family traditions. Now there remain only family packs, family plots and family reunions—a strangely artificial gathering of a clan, many of whom have never met.

As the family recedes from daily life, it asserts its power over summer. The family summer place has taken on more meaning in recent years. It has become a touchstone against which we can measure ourselves—where we are in touch with childhood, coming of age and the passage of time. The damage of one year's winter is compared to previous winters, and the summer's weather is measured by summers past. Sometimes the measuring is literal. At the luxurious Sagamore camp in the Adirondacks, a doorjamb off the grand living room becomes a yardstick of progress: notches on the wood showed the growing height of a Vanderbilt son, just like at any family home.

On the migratory routes of the modern family, vacation houses represent the summer nesting grounds. Like the seals who spend summers on rocky shores, birthing and nursing their young at the spot where they were conceived the summer before, we, too, leave for summer quarters, often crossing the country to return to the same place. (Winter homes change as people seek better and better hunting, but summer places stay the same.) Families are dispersed, thrown all over the country with a roll of the die, moving every seven years or so. Despite moves and divorces, the cottage stays put, the permanent territory to which the clan returns every year to reproduce its identity—to gather and renew ties. It promises the same summer that it has for years. Even if the shell of the building changes, or is moved to another place, the experience within remains the same. It's ironic that in a transient world, the fleeting summer stakes such a powerful claim of permanence in so many lives. Summer places are a constant in a complex equation—something that can be counted on as much as family itself.

The Adolescence of the Family Cottage

This gathering of the clan is a recent function of inessential houses. Indeed, children are absent from early accounts of retreats. Roman writings about villas and farms make no mention of the wife and kids, the closest perhaps being Pliny's famous epistles from his villas where he writes, ". . . I do not interfere with the pleasure of the members of my household and they do not disturb my studies." The two worlds don't seem to meet. The Trianon and Hameau formed a playground for courtiers, as Marie-Antoinette played parlor games with grown-ups rather than peek-a-boo with her dauphin. Thomas Jefferson built Poplar Forest for his grandson to live in, but not while Jefferson was still in residence. Although he sometimes brought his granddaughters for fireside company, the four small rooms could have scarcely accommodated a family reunion.

Early North American resorts centered on adult amusements. Down at the Virginia Springs in the first half of the nineteenth century, the diversions seem quite adult: quoits, hunting, billiards and fencing. With its gambling and horse racing, the later incarnation of Saratoga Springs was hardly the destination for a family outing. Nor could the social posturing at places like Newport be in honor of family solidarity. Travel brochures lured people with promises of good health, descriptions of sublime nature and rejuvenation of the soul, not family entertainments.

During the nineteenth century, families did leave the city for country summers, yet this move was made in the interest of the children's health, not so their parents would see more of them. Oliver Wendell Holmes explained the reasoning thus: "Money buys fresh air and sunshine, in which children grow up more kindly, of course, than in close back streets; it buys country places to give them happy and healthy summers."

Children, then as now, probably enjoyed the change of residence the most. Escaping the city mists of cholera and typhus and as yet undiscovered germs, children played freely and happily. In her memoirs, Edith Wharton recalls girlhood summers at Pencraig, her family's Newport house: ". . . to a little girl long pent up in hotels and flats, there was inexhaustible delight in the freedom of a staircase to run up and down, of lawns and trees, a meadow full of clover and daisies, a pony to ride, terriers to romp with, a sheltered cove to bathe in, flower-beds spicy with carnation, lily, rose and a kitchen garden crimson with strawberries and sweet as honey with Seckel pears." She also mentions the thrilling privilege of being "allowed to be present, and to circulate among the grown-ups" while the archery club met. At the time, the children's summer garden was fenced off from that of the grown-ups with an ornate ironwork grille. The Victorian attitude toward children was a segregationist one, dictating that they belonged upstairs or downstairs—wherever the nursery might be.

That segregation often applied to holidays themselves. In the early days of camping in the 1870s, men often went away together on wilderness adventures, leaving their families in town. Male enclaves, fishing and hunting camps were rugged places not suitable for women and children. When Pennsylvanians camped in Muskoka at Solid Comfort or the Sharon Social Fishing Clubs, the women and children often boarded with nearby farmers. Teddy Roosevelt spent time alone at Elkhorn Ranch during his first marriage, although he did bring his second wife four years after their marriage. Philosopher and psychologist William James maintained two summer places: an Adirondack camp he shared with fellow professors and scientists near Keene Valley, and a farm in New Hampshire where he stayed with his wife and children. The farm, which they called Chocorua, with its spring and soft lawns, was a perfect place for children. James thought the place justified its cost by the education it gave his sons—presumably an informal education in the forests and fields. Although he and his wife honeymooned at his Keene Valley camp, the professor retreated there alone several times a year. There he hiked, wrote and caught up on his reading. (How many parents today would travel to a second house without their children?)

Conversely, another established Victorian tradition left the husband in town. Fathers stayed in the city to work, while wives and children stayed at the cottage for the summer. After all, the holiday had to be paid for. Getting the children out of the city in the interest of their health and happiness apparently counted more than family unity. They had to wait for weekend visits or vacations to see their father. The fathers joined the truncated family at the end of the work week or for a few weeks later in the summer. This institution was so entrenched that it engendered special train fares, as advertised in this 1880s circular: "THESE TICKETS WILL BE SOLD ONLY TO HEADS OF FAMILIES. For businessmen having families in the country, and who desire to visit them a certain number of times during their sojourn." In the Catskills they called the Friday train "the husband train," which a brass band met at the station. Reunion was certainly cause for celebration.

Besides the children, the entire household including furniture, chickens and a cow (for fresh milk) moved to the summer nesting grounds for three months. Nannies and governesses, if there were any, also came along. A Nova Scotia woman whose family moved some eight miles up the coastline for the summer recalls taking the refrigerator. What's interesting about this arrangement is that the mothers were in charge. Several people who remember the prevalence of this manless family arrangement insist that summer households were matriarchies where the women ruled and cherished their short independence. The tradition continued until recently, but now that so many women work, few can leave for the entire summer. Besides, in contemporary non-hierarchical families, it seems unfair to leave the husband slaving and sweating in the city while the rest of the family plays, even if a brass band were to meet him at the station.

Victorian families did travel to summer places together—the notion of togetherness was just taken for granted in those days, not talked about the way we do now. Judd Northrup, in 'Sconset Cottage Life, described his holiday at a Nantucket cottage in the 1880s. "The family now consisted of our own household of seven and my niece and two sisters who had lodgings elsewhere." Their Nantucket visit wasn't just a vacation, but a gathering of the clan. About moving his tribe into this one-story house he wrote, "It was a marvel how we all got into it and turned around when once in it, and why it didn't burst with its plethora of humanity." Families still probably squeeze into these selfsame 'Sconset cottages, happy to be together for the duration of a summer rental, and they probably still marvel at getting the entire dispersed group to Nantucket at the same time.

Still, during Northrup's time the activities of children and adults seem to diverge; the adults picnic, go on expeditions and gather wildlife souvenirs, while the boys go camping. Today, that kind of segregation would be seen as endangering the family unit. The family that plays together supposedly stays together.

A Family of Families

In the New World's democratic and moral interpretation of the summer house, camp meetings and chautauquas, the family was embraced. Old photographs of cottages show some dozen people, ranging in age from babes in arms to grandparents, all perched on the balconies or porches of the tiny houses. Emphasizing religion and temperance, these resorts provided a G-rated version of a vacation. Not only were children taken on these spiritually tinged holidays, but there were also amusements to please and instruct them.

New York's original Chautauqua had a sort of walk-in diorama called Palestine Park, which duplicated the topography and geography of the Holy Land. At Ocean Grove, a Methodist campground in New Jersey, a miniature church complete with bell tower and rose window enticed children with its perfect-pitch scale—it was the house of God made into a dollhouse. Of course, families attended religious services together, squeezed under the roof of some great tabernacle in the grove. The Victorian wholesomeness of these summer communities still attracts people today. Like their predecessors one hundred years ago, families sit out on the porches of the Martha's Vineyard campground, watching children ride their bikes on roadways forbidden to cars.

With their clean living and community parks, these moral resorts inspired another very North American form of the summer house with a distinctly family atmosphere. About the 1880s and 1890s, groups of families—a family of families—banded together in association around the bends of lakes or sandy peninsula; they built their own cottages, but a dining hall and surrounding land were held in common. There are dozens of these places: Iron City in Georgian Bay still attracts descendants of the original Pittsburghers; the Belvedere Club in northern Michigan; the Outing Club on Clear Lake, Iowa, where one long, veering veranda joins each cottage; the Ausable Club in the Adirondacks, and more that have remained so private that nobody has heard of them. Summer at these places is just as it was, minus the large staffs and a few layers of clothing; what's more, the same families still inhabit the cottages and cabins. A low-rent version of this tradition flourished in the Catskills where summering Russian and Eastern Europeans created a kind of group living called *kochelein*—or "cook alones." Families brought their own linen and food and shared the kitchen with others; it kept costs down and allowed immigrant children the country summers seen as so essential to their health.

Like any nuclear family, these communities came—and still come—together at meals, breaking bread in one large refectory. Families belonging to the three associations on Higgins Lake in Michigan leave their cottages and take their meals in the dining rooms, each of which seats some twenty-five families. A history of Iron City put it this way: "From the beginning, members of the club have taken their meals together and fished and played together almost like the members of one large family. This sense of family reaches deeper than the simple physical manifestations of common activities. Iron City is a place where children come to think of their elders as 'aunts and uncles.'"

Indeed, at the Pinewoods Camp on Higgins Lake, children do actually call their elders aunt and uncle, even once those children wear the stripes of grown-ups. It's a tribal notion of family, and so important to summer communities that Point O'Woods on Fire Island, once a short-lived chautauqua, allows rentals only to families with children. If accepted by the committee, a familiy may buy into the summer village with its yacht squadron, nondenominational church, private ferry and blue laws—religiously inspired temperance policies.

What inspired these communal communities? Perhaps at the time there was a sense of security in numbers when people ventured into what was then perceived as wild country. It was certainly easier, and less expensive, to manage a camp collectively. But more important, private camps assured a certain level of society that couldn't be guaranteed at resort hotels. Unlike the campgrounds, where Methodism was the common glue, other values held the community together. People wanted to be with like people during their holidays, rather than be thrown into a larger social pool. Within those closed gates, children play with friends of friends of the family. At these enclaves, even friendships are passed down like tea sets from one generation to the next, as children say to each other, "Oh yes, my grandfather used to sail with your grandfather." Even relationships have continuity, as these family camps continue on much as they always have. One such place, tucked in below New Hampshire's White Mountains, on the shores of the lake called Golden Pond, will soon celebrate its one-hundredth summer of family holidays.

In 1897, Alice Mabel Bacon, a professor at Virginia's Hampton Institute, was inspired to establish a place where people could spend a summer vacation in simple and natural surroundings, living in tents and taking meals in common. She called the place Deephaven, and it was later joined by a sister camp, Rockywold, founded by Mary Alice Armstrong, whose descendants still run the camp.

A family community, Rockywold-Deephaven is also a community of families that have known one another for generations. In the early days, Mrs. Bacon had encouraged mingling in the evening in the Longhouse living room. Today, guests invite one another over for cocktails at their cabins before dinner. Activities are geared to the entire family: picnics at Loon Island or square dancing, talent shows or movies at the Playhouse—sort of a living room in common. There are also games of capture the flag, and the softball game—guests play employees, who are either college students or locals. In addition to all those entertainments, there's the ritual educational presentation on the icehouses, which, cool and soggy under mounds of sawdust, the camp resolutely maintains. Despite some bending to the times, Rockywold-Deephaven holds on to camp traditions such as vespers on Flagstaff Point or services at the lake's own Church Island. Temperance is another steadfastly held tradition; no drinks are allowed in the dining rooms, although alcohol is now permitted and consumed quietly in the family cottages.

A collection of some sixty wooden cottages surrounds the rocky shore of the lake, each set at its own angle of comfort in the landscape, connected to its neighbors by well-worn dirt paths. Gnarled roots reach onto the paths, but habitués who know each root, rut and turn can navigate the woodsy arterials even by moonlight. Eventually, all the arteries lead to the dining room. Rockywold's wooden refectory overlooks the lake and its loons, dispatching meals by the hundreds, cafeteria-style. A card in each table's center indicates which clan occupies which table (being seated near the wall of windows marks a long and distinguished lineage at the camp). The camp becomes the Great Mother, feeding everyone and taking care of all chores: each cottage receives daily housekeeping, wood for the fireplace and ice from the icehouse, which is carted around in wooden wheelbarrows. Inside the cabins, the style here is Adirondack lodge mixed with a bit of old Waspy frump; the furniture is worn down a bit at the heels, having its own history.

Many families have been coming here for generations, and continue to come even from places such as Maryland, Connecticut, New York, California or even London. In the beginning, families built their own cabins over the wooden platforms where tents originally stood. In those days, guests stayed for the leaves' green season, instead of popping in for a week or two, as they do now. Each family takes its own cabin, the same one they have rented for years, so there's a sense of attachment and permanance. After several years, a family gets a "lock" on that cabin for a particular period, coming for the same week or weeks each year. That way, they reunite with the same family friends who also lock the same couple of weeks. And they develop the same feeling for the family cottage, investing it with feelings of home.

Besides spending their vacations here, Rockywold families come for reunions or to hold weddings at Church Island. The camp functions as a gathering place and annual tradition. Some extended families meet there for a shared holiday, and a second-generation Rockywolder says, "That's the one time when we see each other, besides funerals and weddings." The assorted cousins and aunts live too far away. A recent history of the camps, *Our Spirit's Home, Rockywold-Deephaven Camps*, says, "The outstanding characteristic of the camps is they are a place for simple and wholesome family life with freedom from domestic cares. This has made it possible for families to do things together."

Perhaps this recognition—that a summer vacation should include freedom from domestic routine—is left over from days when servants were the norm, or perhaps it's because women founded the camps. Whatever its origins, with all the food, ice, wood and maintenance taken care of, everyone can get down to the business of a family vacation.

After all, family vacations are now the raison d'être of summer places. Hunting and fishing camps have gradually evolved from manly enclaves to rustic abodes that embrace the entire family. (Although I know of one fishing cabin where the grandchildren were invited to be guides, do chores and hunt for bait.) Aldo Leopold originally purchased his shack in the sand counties as a hunting camp, but soon his family joined him there, making improvements, pursuing wildlife and spending time together.

The Iron City camp was originally founded in 1879, when Episcopal-Methodist ministers and dentists came to fish in the wilds of Georgian Bay, where pines bend like contortionists in Lake Huron's west winds. The men came up from Pittsburgh and camped for several weeks in search of smallmouth bass, pike and other fish stories. Some years later, wives and children, not to be left at home, accompanied the fisherman on their sporting jaunts. Despite its masculine beginnings, today's Iron City campers would call it a family place.

Vacations, and especially vacation houses, have become a family institution. A concern for health of the body has given way to a concern for the health for the family body. So much so that by the 1950s Cleveland Amory was describing the accepted paragon of resort virtues as a "family place perfect for all ages." Eventually, family atmosphere becomes a selling point for a resort, as much as good ozone or a fever-free climate once was. A recent brochure for Florida's Seaside claims this new town's essence is ". . . sharing time and creating memories with the people you love."

Reuniting the Family

Even when living in the same town, today's family is a divided, weakened unit, rent asunder by schools, activities, meetings, errands, business trips, camps, sleep-overs. Besides joining for the evening meal, there are few moments when the family even occupies the same room. Fathers go to one office, mothers to another, children spend their days at school and practices. Even Saturdays get swallowed by errands and playdates. Summer, along with the two other high holidays of family life, Thanksgiving and Christmas, is often the only time to unite. The summer house is where families go to be alone together—like honeymooners. Indeed, going off together seems a natural thing. Even mating chimpanzees leave their group for a few days to concentrate solely on their purpose, creating a family, just as we re-create our families during a vacation.

That kind of single-minded togetherness is what we're after when we go to the cottage, that very unity is the goal. The clan makes a circle of wagons, closing itself off to the howling dangers of the prairie. Going to her primitive cabin in the Sierra Mountains is a way for one mother to shut out outside influences, as she finds the isolation "strengthening for relationships and family, because you're just not diverted by the usual stuff." It's odd that something as concrete as a cabin can affect relationships, can make a family close.

A house makes us close by bringing us together. Sitting on his seaside porch, a young father told me, "Here we have a common commitment, one just to enjoy each other." Spending time with family is the primary entertainment at cottages, as novel as mountain climbing or other adventures that don't fit into the daily patterns of life. Many parents would agree with the founder of Florida's Seaside, who thinks that the primary job of a vacation is to play with your children. Cottages keep families together for the full cycle of a day, from fishing at first light to finding Cassiopeia in the night sky. And so the family walks the beach together, a silhouette of different heights and shapes. The family packs into a sailboat for a day's adventure on the waves, where the younger play crew to an elder captain. Families play the same card game over and over again, giving handicaps to the younger players. Living together, doing things together, having adventures—this thickens the bond like cornstarch in sauce.

Parents, children and grandparents all come together on the playing grounds of summer. Summer itself is a return to childhood, a timeless and tactile sphere of being. In the holiday orbit, the planets of grown-ups and children finally collide. Grown-ups become like children, living a life of play and pleasure, getting down on all fours into their childhood, close enough to smell the grass, all green and sweet grazing. It's a life of no responsibilities and no decisions other than what boat to take or what game to play. Just like a child's life, the day is filled with games. For the most part, childhood vanishes from adult life. Yet during vacations at the same golden pond or rocky beach, a kaleidoscope vision of childhood colors the landscape.

Come September, parents separate from their young again, until next summer. Summer is, after all, nature's season of nesting and breeding. When Inuit children were forced to study in government schools during the winter, parents would take them traveling to a round of summer hunting camps. Summer became a de facto school of indigenous culture where parents or grandparents passed on Inuit knowledge gathered over centuries: how to make stone-circle fish traps and how to build tents. In a similar way, summer places let parents reclaim their children. Once the center of all things, the clan's job has been reduced. Other people educate your children; other people play sports with your children; other people read the books of religion. However, during summer, these jobs are restored to the family. Most important, during the summer, children learn from parents. A child learns skills: how to cast a line to where fish forage; how to take a whiting gently off the hook; how to clean and fry a fisherman's breakfast. Parents impart skills of lifelong usefulness: a back dive, identifying trees, a putt, coming about or steering a motorboat.

These are skills that linger, that get brought out once a year. Who but parents show us how to beachcomb or take a proper siesta. Third-grade penmenship rules may fade into the pea fog of memory, but hot-weather education is imprinted with the permanance of heat-stamping. My grandmother's admonitions about sun, hot-weather digestion and the importance of filling a glass to the rim with ice to make a proper iced tea will be with me always. Not part of any curriculum in particular, these lessons belong to summer places.

Returning to a family cottage as an adult is stepping back into your childhood. You can bring your own sheets and cook all the meals, but you remain a child trapped in older wrappings. Once there, the whole family slips into its past and its patterns. Those patterns are reassuring, in some ways; the family may not be attached, but like ghost pains of amputees, the feeling is remembered. Living among these people is as comfortable as being without clothes, for these are the people who knew you before you wore the propriety of a tie or the messages of meaningful T-shirts. Quirks need no editing. Stories need no preface. Nothing could be more relaxing than that kind of familiarity.

Like any heraldic crest engraved onto pinkie rings, the cottage becomes part of the family identity. With rituals and traditions repeated each summer, the family bonds like members in a secret society. So secret, in fact, that novices must be initiated into the group. Often a summer place serves as a test for suitors. Boyfriends and girlfriends are subjected to the Cuttyhunk or cabin tests; can they endure the outhouse, the ticks and tricky currents, actually *like* the place? A failure to appreciate someone's summer indicates irrevocable incompatability, and almost a refutation of who they are. After all, if a suitor doesn't like a beloved's summer place before things get serious, he would never consent to yearly vacations in the family fold.

Compounded Families

The vacation notion of family extends beyond the nuclear to something more like the Chinese Tsu that joins parents, concubines, sons and daughters-in-law and their children under one tiled roof. The summer house is one of the few places where the larger family meets—a family consisting of cousins and uncles and other undiagnosed relatives. Often, the cottage is built to lure an extended family by giving them a place to spend vacations—a place where grandchildren can explore the barefoot terrain of summer. Whether it's just in a wooden cottage with a few bedrooms and folding sofas to handle the overflow, or a compound of grand houses, a family assembles for a reunion lasting longer than a five-course catered banquet. The object is to gather as many generations and relatives as possible in one house, on one property or one island. Barbara Bush manages to fit twenty-three members of her outstretched family into the rambling cottage on Walker's Point in Kennebunkport. Yet this yearning for unity is not exclusive to families whose sons are called scions. Along the shores of Keuka Lake in the Finger Lakes, where lots stretch to only fifty feet, edge to edge, where the houses are even thinner, deck after deck crowds with grandparents, parents and children eating dinner outdoors to the accompaniment of a sunset.

This seasonal assembly of relatives created the compound, another institution unique to summer. One house may not fit everyone, and so the one sprouts others from its stalk. The Bell summer house has sprawled thusly into a tribal village where third cousins can meet over their vacations—probably just what Alexander Graham Bell had in mind. Over the generations, these places grow along with the family. Kykuit, the grand country house built by John D. Rockefeller, Jr., later enticed his sons, three of whom built houses on or near the Hudson Valley estate. Fanny Kemble Wister, in her memoir of the Owen Wister family, describes how their cottage in Saunderston, Rhode Island, was built on land bought jointly with cousins back in 1906. Her summer playmates were in fact related. These compounds go one step further than the exclusive family camps with common dining rooms; genetically speaking, everyone is alike. It's the ultimate closed club.

What is it like to live in a big family tribe? Its related ingredients yield a richer taste of family—not to mention a quorum for team sports and kick-the-can games. Children see their parents parented. Cousins search for commonalities among themselves. Ties are everywhere, and there's an inescapable sense of connection. The idea of clan conquers individual identity. Surrounded by so much flesh and blood feels as secure as your own body. (Those close connections also mean there's no dating in summer compounds.)

Assembling a family in one place is not always so purposeful. Relatives often flock together, choosing to return to the nesting grounds of youth, be it Chester, Algonquin or Stony Lake. Relatives of the MacKenzies have summered at Ontario's Stony Lake for five generations. In the early years of this century, two brothers, a headmaster and a professor, each built himself a house, related by brotherly names: Loch End and Gairloch. The two MacKenzies even built a church, St. Peter's on the Rock, in the tradition of family chapels at great estates. They eventually handed the wooden chapel over to the Anglican diocese after running it themselves for several years, and their descendants still wed and pray there. Gairloch was sold and torn down, but its brother, Loch End, remains in the family, along with a baker's dozen of related cottages scattered around islands and coves of the lake. Over the past eighty years, various descendants divided their land and constructed their own houses; some bought their own lots and put up cabins, or even bought another family's summer history and moved into the house. They have been there so long that the MacKenzies are written onto the landscape; the water by their original island is called MacKenzie Bay.

Nowadays, the great-grandchildren of the original MacKenzies spend their vacations at the lake, competing against one another in regattas and canoe races. Should they point their compass at the lake, the needle would point to second cousins to the northeast, third cousins to the south. Some cousins return from as far away as Vancouver to summer here, rather than on the Gulf Islands or lakes in the western mountains. They return to canoe the same coves, tramp in the same woods, and gather at the Juniper Island community center as they always have. The homing instinct rules; choosing where to vacation clearly involves more than considerations of the best sailing winds and fewest mosquitoes.

Like a magnet, the home territory draws us to the past. In the Thousand Islands, I visited a house that has stayed in the same family over a hundred years, transferring to distantly related but closely connected cousins. Some things about the place have changed: the kitchen moved into the main house; electricity, indoor plumbing and a telephone have made life easier, cleaner, faster. Yet the Victorian-era furniture has remained just so. The same paintings and sepia-toned photographs, as well as snapshots of more recent good old days, decorate the whitewashed wood walls. The lady of the house, who had been coming to that island since her marriage, now supervises a houseful of grandchildren. They swim and sail all day long, as her children had done some forty years ago—and as her husband had spent his days some sixty years earlier.

She retrieved the house's album from its place on the shelf, and pointed at a photograph of a summer picnic taken well over one hundred years before. It had been a lunch excursion to another island. A group of young men and women lounged on plaid blankets at the water's edge, dressed in the starched and high-collared clothes of the time. "They did exactly the same things that we do now," she said. Summer clothes have since shed their starch, collars and underlayers; but a hundred years later, the household embarks on similar expeditions. Grandparents, their children and their children's children pack into a boat and sail to a remote and uninhabited island. There they spread their feast on the shore, buttering bread and sipping tea in the open air. Family names have changed, boats have come and gone, once remote stone islands have been covered in a brownish moss of cottages, but those island picnics join generation to generation.

Families are about continuity, yet that continuity is rarely apparent, except in the curve of a brow. Not too much else is shared by generations. But the young and old can meet on the timeless pleasure grounds of summer, blessed with a sense that things will continue as they always have. Returning to familiar summer places

connects us to memories of childhood, and thus with children; it is
one of the few links maintained with that past, easily reached with a
map and a memory of how things once were.

E. B. White once brought his son to the Maine lake where he
spent his childhood Augusts in a woods cabin. Since then, his tastes
had turned to saltwater, but the sea's temperature and tempests
made White long for the calm of an inland lake. So he returned to
the summer place his family had frequented, which he decribed in
his essay "Once More from the Lake." "But when I got back there,
with my boy, and we settled into a camp near a farmhouse and into
the kind of summertime I had known, I could tell that was going to
be pretty much the same as it had been before—I knew it, lying in
bed the first morning, smelling the bedroom, and hearing the boy
sneak quietly out and go off along the shore in a boat. I began to
sustain the illusion that he was I, and therefore, by simple transposi-
tion, that I was my father. This sensation persisted, kept cropping
up all the time we were there." Oddly, this continuity asserts itself
when we've broken with regular life and traveled to the magical
never-never land of summer.

Never-never land is never changing, and like childhood, the
charms of summer life have changed little, be it the summer of '42
or '92. Outboards and built-in appliances may be new, but the
essence of summer life remains the same: picnics and early morning
paddles. There, we can dive into the future and springboard into the
past, sending only the faintest ripples over the surface. Vacations
have turned into rituals resembling the aboriginal pilgrimage to the
ancestral lands—rituals of connection. And the connection is not
unpremeditated. Like Bell, parents envision an unbroken future of
summers connecting their lives to their children's, and create a
place for that to happen. It's an experience parents want to share
with children: after his camping stay in the Adirondacks, Ralph
Waldo Emerson wrote, "That we should build, hard by, a spacious
lodge / and how we should come hither with our sons." Watching
his children play in their summer garden that had belonged to them

only a few years, a father told me, "We fully expect that our children will come back here." It is a legacy of leisure.

A Legacy of Leisure

The childhood home is sold, family stories are lost in the telling, but the family cottage remains, boarded up and waiting for the summer. Families manage to hold on to cottages despite cyles of recession and richness, rises and falls in social mobility. That tenacity applies to hunting cabins as well as seaside villas. It's not uncommon for a summer house to count its fifth generation. Somehow, these places remain impervious to the hurricanes of economic fortunes. This type of family heritage is inherited rather than sold. British Columbia's Savary Island rarely has any cabins for sale; only acts of God part owners from its prized sandy beaches. The cabins are rather cramped, crowded and compared to shacks by some. In many summer communities, the only way to acquire a cottage is to inherit it. Having an old family cottage means your family had once been clever and well-to-do enough to afford a second house; it also means these clever and well-to-do genes have persevered. After all, what is family prestige besides tenacity? There's an undeniable prestige in having an island compound that's been in the family *forever*.

More amazing than the longevity of summer legacies is that this compulsion for legacy applies to the even humblest summer habitation. So clearly, it's not about greed or status, but something other. Describing the fishing cabin that her grandfather and father considered selling, a writer for *Wisconsin Trails Magazine* says, "But that humble one-room cabin, with its pot bellied stove and patchwork quilts, has become a legacy that neither my brother, nor sister, nor I would trade for anything right now." Summer real estate lies beyond ordinary markets but trades on an exchange of memories, emotions and sentimental attachments—all untaxable commodities. Like an antique, its value lies in its age; the longer a place has been in a family, the more valuable it is.

Even leases possess the same kind of value as real property, freehold and owned. At the Methodist campground Ocean Grove, 250 canvas tents still stand as they have since 1894. Many of them are leased by descendants of the original family, though not for want of a market. Apparently there's a five-year waiting list for these cloth jewels by the sea. When that lease is willed to the next generation, it's a bequest of Atlantic breezes and belonging to a tribe and a place—more than simply the shell of a tent. Cabins on land leased from the Forest or Park Service also pass from one generation to the next, with a pair of signatures sprawled across the bottom of the page. Some leases at Echo Lake in California date from the first decade of this century, and have belonged to three generations of the same family. Despite the Forest Service's attempt to eradicate the lease program, it has found that parting a family and its cottage is no easier than separating a lioness from her cubs. More than property, summer places are artifacts of family history—souvenirs of childhood not easily thrown away.

Why this compulsion to keep and preserve the family cottage? It's not about passing down wealth, for there are no monetary dividends. If it's about prestige, that prestige is hard to see. Perhaps bequeathing a cottage assures descendants rooms full of good times and a roof to shelter the old memories. That kind of bequest wishes on those who follow the perfection of a summer afternoon. It's a heritage of experience. At Higgins Lake in Michigan, where many families have summered since the late nineteenth century, some parents find a pastor liberal enough to baptize new children in lake water—water that they consider the clearest and bluest of so many Midwest lakes. Besides faith in God, they bestow upon their children faith in a place. That different kind of holy water represents a hope that the children will nurture the same feelings of place their parents did. However, inheritance taxes, or death duties, are starting to imperil bequests of holiday property. Dedicated summer people

are finding ways around them, by deeding the property to children
before a gift becomes a bequest or by arranging conservation easements or land trusts in order to tame taxes.

Passing it down often means cutting it up, so that everyone
shares in the leisure legacy. Sometimes inheritances get handed
down in pieces; summer places get divided among the heirs like a
choker of heirloom pearls made into separate strands. The place gets
chopped up into fifths, sevenths or tenths of a house. The revolu-
tionary real estate concept of timesharing dates back to the first cottage held in trust for siblings. The heirs divide the season and the
bills. The negotiations go something like this: you take July, and I'll
have August, since your family had August last year. Some families
incorporate their summer house, giving each sibling shares in the
corporation, so that it becomes a business expressed in red and
black ink rather than the garishness of sibling rivalry. When the
parents are still living, that arrangement works fine, but when their
authority is gone, anarchy often ensues.

Unfortunately, when written as an equation, owning two-sevenths of a cottage equals lawyers' fees and long silences. Getting
seven people to agree—especially when they're related—is no easy
task. A woman who has shares in two family places with two different family groups says that, in her experience, this kind of democratic arrangement only works if a self-appointed dictator is willing to
call the shots and get things done. Usually, that iron-willed leader-
ship is badly received by siblings or cousins operating under delu-
sions of democracy and different ideas. Without a leader, however,
it's cottage by committee, and you can guess what that looks like:
persnickety signs all over the place; summer life divided into charts
of chores and responsibilities; repairs left undone until the committee unanimously agrees to the expense of draining the septic tank.
Sharing skills have hardly improved since the nursery, and the
smaller the place, the harder it is to share. A guesthouse allows
some compromising when it comes to divvying up the first week in
July, but otherwise, there are fights—fights about taking turns, con-

trol and money. These two-sevenths fight about who uses the cottage more. They dispute how the place should be run. Then they fight about bills—some siblings don't pay their share, citing hours of chores they performed at a high billable rate. It may be because they can't afford as much as the other brothers and sisters, a fact that recalls ghosts of parental disapproval and opens up wounds of rivalry. Ugly family politics suddenly trespass on the neatly clipped lawn of summer, leaving divots of divisiveness in the soft grass where babies toddled and children played croquet.

For as much as a summer place can unite a family, it can wrench that same family apart. Fights over family cottages are about as bad and bitter as they get because people are so emotional and possessive about their summer place. Because it's not simply vacation property, childhood memories and a person's very idea of family is at stake. Once the wars have played out on the porch and verandas—the family hearth—the invisible carnage makes the place uninhabitable. I've seen it happen many times. This place so cherished, and so viciously fought for, becomes spoiled and unwanted by the very people who fought over it, as they become disillusioned with the fantasy of a happy family life. Unwinnable, these blood wars are about home, because in a rootless world, the summer house takes on all the meaning and magic of home.

A Loyalty to Home

This attachment to a summer house spreads like ivy to the ground it sits on. While visiting Maine before World War II, Katherine Butler Hathaway noticed a fierce loyalty among the seasonal residents. "The real summer people who owned houses there and had come year after year for many years seemed to feel and understand something more concerning their favorite town than could actually be seen. There was some kind of hidden fascination about it which the real initiates were aware of as nobody else was." Hathaway says the feeling was secret, inexpressible, unexplainable. Yet as she relates in her memoir, *The Little Locksmith*, she acquired that fascination once she bought her own house, and spent summers in the balmy and balsam-tinged air. That understanding and feeling she noticed is shared by summer people all over—rather like a summer romance with a sense of place. The romance is as intense and hot as the weather. Summer people say theirs is the most beautiful place in the world, they call theirs the cleanest lake, they insist their mountain view is matched by no other. That attachment Hathaway perceived actually represents a notion of home—a loyalty and love of place.

Strictly speaking, home means the place where we live, the place of our origin, the place of our family. Second homes often come first in the heart and memory, even though they are not where we're from, even though we only spend a few weeks there. Home, after all, represents an emotional attachment more than a verifiable fact of residence like license plates or postal codes. The attachment we form with summer nesting grounds is one of home-ness; it's a sense of place woven with memories of people. I know of a couple who, even with three houses, count their summer address as home, for only in that small town does the postmistress know them—by name, by face. While imprisoned for political offenses, Czechoslovakian playwright and later president Vaclav Havel often thought of home as his place in the country at Hrádaček, rather than the apartment in Prague. He instructed his wife to paint the fence, he dreamt of his homecoming, he suffered nightmares about the government condemning the place.

Perhaps it *becomes* our place of origin because we recreate and re-create ourselves there, baptizing ourselves with each and every swim. Wendell Berry wrote about having begun to be born in mind and spirit at his river camp in Kentucky. It just *feels* like home. A young woman who spent her summers on a little lake near Petoskey, Michigan, even honeymooned there and continues to vacation there as an adult, traveling back in time when she does to her childhood. While staying at Florida's Captiva Island one winter, she actually became "homesick" for the Michigan lake. It was as though the pleasures of water and idleness belonged among pines rather than palms, and were out of place in other locales. To switch such associations of pleasure would be like substituting another man for her husband just for the vacation—it would be disloyal. That nostalgia would be understood by Eleanor Roosevelt, who once wrote that she felt sorry for people forced to sell country places they enjoyed for years, because "One has so much more sentiment as a rule about one's country life." That sentiment comes from an unequal distribution of good memories which collect in the langour of the countryside.

Yet home goes beyond inchoate feelings of attachment; home is also a ceremonial center. In five short years, the river house my parents built has become the family's place of reunion and ritual. We squeeze around the table for holiday dinners. Churchless for years, we used to borrow one for special occasions, but now the tiny church a few miles away has held a memorial service and a family wedding. Women often choose to get married at their summer homes; at an Adirondack wedding decades ago, the church was decorated with whole birch trees. These days, it's a definite trend to marry at country places. Of course, the natural setting is romantic and there's room for a big marquee in the country, but love of place is the deciding factor. That love of place is indeed so strong that it often becomes the site of another love ritual—the honeymoon, when a new love is introduced to the beloved place.

Often cottages even host the homecomings funeral parlors call final rest. William James was buried at his beloved Chocorua; Alexander Graham and Mabel Hubbard Bell's graves sit on the summit near his house in Baddeck; a man whose family has summered at the same Quebec lake for four generations wishes his ashes to be scattered about that landscape. Why be crowded into a cemetery where one hasn't spent any summer afternoons picnicking or lying in the grass? A guest at the Vanderbilt camp in the Adirondacks, Fifi Wichfield, even sent her dog to be buried at Sagamore, as in his owner's estimation, Inky was happiest while visiting Raquette Lake. It's doubtful the Vanderbilts felt the same way about Inky, as the grave sits on the back path toward the service area of that great camp; Inky's marble headstone reads, "Always the best friend I will ever have."

Some have seen their summer place as the very final resting home—even beyond death. A man who lived at a house called Sevenacres in Blue Hill, Maine, is said to have come back as a ghost. A few years after his death, he returned to his cottage, making his presence known by sweeping bottles off shelves, turning lights on and off in the pantry as he poured himself a drink, and by occasional pinches and bumps. The new residents probably wondered why he didn't bother his house in Baltimore. Somehow, the ease and pleasure of Blue Hill probably seemed more like home.

Camp David

6. COTTAGE CULTURE

In 1978, President Jimmy Carter invited Israel's Prime Minister Menachem Begin, Egypt's President Anwar Sadat and their wives to his place in the country. They accepted his invitation to the presidential retreat buried in the lush woods of Maryland and left, thirteen days later, with the Camp David accord.

Although not far from Washington by helicopter, Camp David was a separate world, where the intracies of diplomatic protocol evolved over centuries at European courts somehow didn't belong. No one wore medals or sashes on their chests. Nor did uniformed guards line each walkway, arms raised, sabers crossed at the tips. Here, deep in the lush woods of the Catoctin Mountains, heads of state became just people. As any cabin or beach house, Camp David had its own culture of informality, communality, with a free atmosphere of play and pleasure. In her memoirs, *First Lady from Plains*, Rosalynn Carter recalls her husband's saying, "It's so beautiful here. I don't believe anybody could stay in this place, close to nature, peaceful and isolated from the world and still carry a grudge." The magic of the place became a kind of lingua franca among three cultures. Indeed, Begin even said that Camp David seemed like heaven on earth.

Camp David is, first and foremost, a retreat. Razor-edged barbed wire, electrified fences and Marine guards helped shut off those one-hundred-odd acres from the rest of the world. Retreating from the world also meant retreating from the curiosity of the world—the bewitching glare of cameras and the treacherous thicket of microphones. Public personae could be left behind; looking back in his memoirs, Carter says, "We had no need, while working in the privacy of Camp David, to convince the public that we were wise, forceful, consistent or superior in our negotiating technique." Carter barred the press from Camp David, and encouraged the participants not to relay any information about the talks' progress, to avoid making any news until there was something substantial to report.

So for thirteen days, men who represented countries that had been at war with each other just years before slept in cabins in sight of each other—mere waving distance from their front porches. Begin and his wife stayed at Birch Lodge, the Carters occupied Aspen Lodge and Sadat stayed at Dogwood alone, as his wife couldn't come at the last minute. Staffers dined communally in Laurel Lodge, which forced interaction among the three countries' delegations. As at a family cottage reunion, privacy was sacrificed in the interest of communality. Even with its thirteen cabins, Camp

David was stretched to its limit. Quarters were crowded and somewhat cramped, and some advisers had to double up; Zbigniew
Brzezinski, Jody Powell, Hamilton Jordan and Bill Quandt shared
Witch Hazel Lodge. Since the camp couldn't accommodate everyone, Begin and Sadat could bring three aides each, but Carter later
wrote that these limitations were actually a blessing, as they kept
out hundreds of bureaucrats, advisers and hangers-on.

So Camp David became a small community, a different kind of
global village, where everyone walked to his or her destination.
Both Begin and Sadat took solitary walks in the woods for exercise;
and one morning, the two crossed paths on the trail, as neighbors
might. They were, after all, practically living next door to each
other. Three cultures—three religions, in fact—coexisted. And
each of the three traditions descended from Abraham maintained
its own Sabbath: Sadat was given a temporary mosque made from a
theater, and Begin held forth over a Sabbath supper, with kosher
food filling the tables.

Despite the seriousness of the negotiations, Camp David managed to retain the atmosphere of a summer camp—of pleasure and
relaxation. The Carters played tennis. The Israeli defense minister
and U.S. secretary of state played pool. Menachem Begin played a
game of chess with U.S. National Security Adviser Brzezinski—the
first he'd played in thirty-eight years. In addition to the tennis
courts, there was a golf tee, badminton, a skeet-shooting range,
Ping-Pong, pool, and bicycles left in racks for anyone who might
like to take them. (Curiously, there seem to have been no team
sports at the camp; perhaps they would have proved too divisive.)
Movies played almost continuously to distract staff members with
time on their hands. Mrs. Carter remembers fifty-eight movies being
shown, including the war epic *Patton*. To lighten the tension, the
three leaders took a sightseeing trip to the nearby fields of Gettys-
burg, Pennsylvania.

The rustic setting even changed the negotiating procedure
itself. Rather than sitting at formal conference tables, the three

leaders and their aides held meetings on porches or on patios, surrounded by the glint of leaves just starting to turn color. They
worked in shirtsleeves in bright sunshine. After an initial group
meeting, Carter shuffled back and forth between Sadat and Begin.
Still the talks stalled several times. Sadat packed once, and as a
helicopter waited for the Egyptian, Carter prevailed upon him to
stay. Eventually, after more than twenty drafts, Israel and Egypt
came to an agreement. After almost a fortnight, Menachem Begin
had also understood American cottage culture. At the signing of the
accord, he said, "Today, I visited President Sadat in his cabin,
because in Camp David, you don't have houses, you only have
cabins. And he came to visit me."

Afterward, dozens of different groups besieged President Carter to
take them to Camp David to resolve conflicts of civil rights, labor, borders, the environment, as though the deciduous woods of the Carolin-
ian forest exuded vapors of compromise and reason. Carter replied that
"in the future my preference would be to go to Camp David with Rosalynn and Amy, and not with George Meany, Ralph Nader or President Anastasio Somoza." To have invited other disputants through the
Camp David gates would have turned Camp David into a Conflict
Resolution Center and its magic would certainly evaporate. No longer
an enchanted enclave hidden to all but the initiated, it would have
become like any other woodsy conference center.

Camp David was designed to be a retreat, not a White House in
the woods. Despite the necessary office facilities and bedside telephones, the motif of the place is pleasure and privacy, relaxation
and recuperation.

Just as the porticoed grandeur of the White House differs from the
woodsy cabins of Camp David, life within that ceremonial mansion
differs wildly from Camp David; they represent two entirely different
cultures. To talk of cottage culture may seem strange, but it's as real
as any anthropology. As the institution of the vacation house has
thrived, so, too, a particular culture has evolved.

Twinned Cultures

Following our usual dualistic thinking—good/evil, country/city, cottage/home—cottage culture acts as counterpoint to normal life, the other side of the looking glass. Cities center on the wonders of art and culture; cottages on the wonders of nature. The fast pace of town slows down at the cottage to a sauntering gait through life. Work and schedules of the city give way to the leisure and idleness of the cottage. Cars yield to boats: we travel by water, checking who's home by counting the boats lined up at docks, like slippers at the foot of the bed. Indeed, the Otherness entices. As First Lady Barbara Bush explained in an article about her summer house, "Our way of life in Kennebunkport is very informal. The difference between Washington and Maine is night and day. I play tennis, garden, and plot and plan everyone's day . . ."

L'Espace et son double (Twinned Spaces) investigated the culture of second homes in France; another house allowed people other ways of being. For example, a woman who cooked dinner every night in town would escape that duty at her *maison de campagne*; conversely, women whose days did not normally include the regular chore of cooking dinner reveled in preparing complicated repasts with all the necessary sauces and pastries. It allowed for a reversal, a switch, a taste of the difference.

Summer-house culture expresses and celebrates those differences with its own traditions and institutions. Like any culture, it has rituals, mythology, codes, traditions, taboos, folklore, totems common to most everyone who holidays at a vacation house. Naming houses, warm-weather mores, special etiquette, antagonism between winter and summer residents, games are just a few ingredients in the cultural soup of summer.

This summer culture, gauzy and light, is indeed vastly different from normal life, and nowhere is this more apparent than in Finland. In Finland, a culture of wood and fire surrounds the summer house, or *mökki*. Finns leave the city for the taste of a life in nature, living like the woodsmen of their country's past. They return to the forests—called the soul of Finland—which carpet the countryside. They live in log cabins by the shores of one of countless lakes, which are dotted with little sauna houses. Like North Americans, they spend their days fishing, boating, lounging around. Yet the *mökki*'s main attractions are the sauna and the fire. Although it may not have hot water, or a water closet, just about every summer cottage in Finland comes with a sauna, a wooden bathhouse that includes another room for bathing or lounging. In fact, the tradition of heat bathing is so integral to summer life that Finns often build the sauna first, and add the main house later.

Families take the sauna together, reveling in this ritual of health and cleanliness so long a part of Finnish life. They prepare by chopping wood and making birch whisks, which stimulate the skin and smell wonderful. They complete the ritual by stepping outside and jumping into the lake. They sizzle and return to the heat bath.

Afterward, they start another fire, this time in the fireplace, where they roast sausages. Watching the flames rise and fall, crackle and turn blue provides an evening of entertainment—something to look at, something to talk about, something to attend.

Still, the summer's big fire is the midsummer's night bonfire. On 21 June, the sun stays up all night with the Finns, as they build a huge bonfire, as if to brighten the night sky even more, and sing around the flames. There's also a midsummer's sauna with its own festive traditions. After the bath, Finns throw homemade whisks like bridal bouquets, with the handle acting like a love compass, pointing in the direction of a future sweetheart.

The vacationing Finn probably spends a fair amount of time chopping wood, splitting birch logs with an ax and creating a woodpile. In a country with more forest than field, wood gives them steam to clean by, heat to cook by, colorful flames to dream by and a bonfire to sing by. Not just a return to nature, summertime brings Finns back to their country's traditional culture.

While perhaps not as romantic as the Finnish return to woods life, summer culture is as well defined in North America. Summer towns are pretty easy to spot. To city people, they seem to be sleeping—they speak of a different age. The emporium on the main street calls itself a general store, and like the other shops displays a wooden sign with gold painting. A fancy food shop does catering, and a boutique or two sells what retailers call resort lines. It has a library and a movie theater, incongruous for the size of the town, which expands in the heat and then shrinks in the cold without the slightest warping.

Strangely, in the ephemeral, informal summer, each little coastal town or woodsy hamlet develops its own particular culture, carefully tended by the part-time residents. As the Eastern European character in Margaret Atwood's story "Wilderness Tips" noted, traditions were "thin on the ground" in Canada, except at his wife's family cottage, where the deck chairs were like "escutcheons elsewhere." Like him, so many of us are hungry for tradition and ritual, and we find it in the summer. Summer culture is accessible, so that in just a few summers anyone can develop, learn, master and feel a part of it. That culture serves to reinforce a sense of community; it glues people to a community.

There may not be museums or libraries to safeguard the culture, but still it gets passed down, passed around, preserved. Some communities on Fire Island carefully guard their atmosphere, and ban barbecuing or eating on the street. Many summer towns produced warm-weather newspapers, which were named *The Wave*, *The Buoy* or such, and reported on cottagers' comings and goings. Newsletters sent to town addresses unite a summer community throughout the year, reinforcing the culture. The tightly knit community Echo Lake produces *Little Echoes*, which reports on canoe races, boat safety, wildflowers to watch for, stars to watch, as well as stories of lake life and cabin history. Lipps Beach, Saskatchewan, Foresta in Yosemite Park, Iron City, the millionaires' Beaumaris in Muskoka— just about every lakeshore or summer town produces a historian, who bestows a small self-published history of the area on all of the guest-room reading tables, telling who was the first summer resident, how that person got the land, what kind of things he or she did in the early days. Such histories also invariably contain stories of fires and hurricanes that took certain houses away. Perpetuating folklore like any storyteller, the history of Yosemite Park's community Foresta includes a cautionary tale concerning a bear electrocuted on the power lines while climbing after a squirrel, and whose body fell onto a cabin and ignited it, in a powered version of a forest fire. This is the stuff of culture.

Each summer culture develops a totem entirely its own, and stays close to the buoy: it tells them where they are, gives the comfort of familiar waters. In the Adirondacks, people maneuver the flat-bottomed guideboats around. Nantucket visitors declare their allegiance all winter long, with a braided rope bracelet, plaited forever onto his or her wrist. Fudge is a theme and a common snack at Michigan and other midwestern summer places. At the Virginia springs, where in the nineteenth century young Southerners courted, there was a tradition of serenading a young lady under her window the night before she returned home. At Murray Bay in Quebec, the *rés d'été*, or summer residents, from both America and Canada adopted the French-Canadian culture as their own, naming their houses in French, singing Québécois songs at bonfires and wearing striped socks particular to the neighborhood. A boat type, a bracelet, a song—these totems mark a culture as much as any beaver or eagle.

United in a common culture, summer folk get together at the village green—a marina, dock or post office porch. We unite at yacht clubs, casinos, beach clubs, regattas, firework displays or even churches built by subscription for the summer residents. We gather wherever to reinforce that sense of community so forgotten in anonymous cities and suburbs. Thousand Islanders worship at Half-Moon Bay, a rocky inlet where vespers services happen each summer Sunday. Members of the congregation sit in their boats as an organ plays and the the offering gets passed around, over water.

At Higgins Lake, Michigan, residents gather in a natural amphitheater for Saturday evening Concerts in the Dell, and listen to recorded orchestral music that seems to come from the trees.

Ultimately, however, culture comes from people. "The summer colony is so discreet and understated that from either road or lake it hardly shows," wrote novelist Wallace Stegner about the fictional Battell Pond. "Of its two thousand or so summer residents you rarely see more than a couple of young people in a canoe, a woman at a mailbox, or a gray scholar disappearing toward his think house." Only village auctions or the *New York Times* delivery bring the cottagers out, like a swarm of bees leaving their hive. The kind of Vermont lake Stegner decribes is a haven of New England Wasps and intelligentsia, a place where canoes outnumber motorboats and where any money is carefully hidden in the rustic cover of bark and log houses. No television antennae stick up like wire trees among the birch and firs. Here, all the children learn to identify the local flora and fauna, assisted by a humid copy of Roger Tory Peterson.

As Stegner observed, the personality, and hence culture, of a summer place is determined by the type of visitors it attracts. There was once a saying that proclaimed Bar Harbor was for those with money but no brains, Northeast Harbor wanted brains but no money and in Southwest Harbor one needed neither brains nor money. People find solidarity and community among people like themselves.

Not written in permanent ink, summer culture mutates as the summer people change. Typically, people hate any change, especially at these places that represent such constancy and changlessness in a fast-seeming, fast-changing world. When different, more or new people come to a summer colony, the earlier residents regret the new cottages, as the original year-round residents probably resented their arrival. It happens over and over again, as it did at the turn of the century in Murray Bay. "But with the coming of the Americans, everything gradually changed; Americans built new better and bigger houses, they furnished them more luxuriously, they brought ways that they had been used to at home, if not really urban and sophisticated, yet more so than those of the Canadian pioneers," Henry Dwight Sedgwick (an American himself) lamented what he called a social change. "The Americans infiltrated, they came in numbers; they brought evening clothes and wore them, they gave afternoon teas and dinner parties, they played bridge; they treated the *habitants* . . . as servants and inferiors." Whether that luxurious lifestyle he described in the early century holds true, I have no idea; the culture could have changed several times since then. Nowadays, French-speaking Montrealers have displaced many of the English-speaking holidayers. Newport endured three different cultural reincarnations as a resort town—four counting today's era of tourist buses disgorging crowds who plow through the preserved "cottages" en masse. In the 1820s and 1830s, planters from Savannah, Charleston and the Caribbean Islands appreciated the cooling sea breezes; interestingly, Newport wasn't visited for its natural beauty, which is hardly legendary, but because it was conveniently situated between New York and Boston. Later, in the 1840s and 1850s, Boston Brahmins and intelligentsia such as Julia Ward Howe, Henry Wadsworth Longfellow and the elder William James frequented the town. Later, of course, Society claimed Newport as their warm-weather capital—a sort of Versailles on the rocks.

These places change with the fashions, as resorts are perpetually upwardly mobile. Staking social positions has long been a function of summer resorts; John Foster Dulles called them a social leveling ground. Yet one kind of social leveling rarely takes place: any truck between summer and permanent residents.

A Clash of Cultures

In truth, there are two cultures inhabiting summer territories: city people who spend time there, and the people who live there. As visitors, we might find it hard to confront the fact, although we get

along with the lady at the post office, the man at the marina, that
our two cultures are very much at odds, even at cross purposes. The
pursuit of pleasure collides with the stark reality of making a living.
Yachters and lobstermen do constant battle in North Atlantic
waters, as potwarp gets tangled in yacht propellers. Some yachters
cut the cables, leaving the fisherman's catch at the ocean bottom,
like money thrown down a well. Nonetheless, the presence of *real*
fishermen makes a seasonal town seem more real, more down to
earth, more desirable for those of us leaving the supposed artificiality of the city.

Economics is the underpinning of any culture, and economics is
the source of this cultural conflict. Money comes between the two
tribes: one has too much, the other not enough. Summer visitors are
like relatives from a long time ago, who left the village or farm to
strike out for the city and make money, leaving their country
cousins behind to fish or farm. Those who stayed struggled with
rock farms, declining fisheries, lumbered forests, while their cousins
struck gold in the city, prospered and returned a generation later, to
purchase a pleasure farm and create a seasonal economy. They are
attracted to economically depressed areas where the real estate is
affordable, a steal, in comparison to the city.

Seen through the eyes of year-round residents, summer people
come into a town, take over nice houses, drive fancy cars, powerful
boats and spend their days at leisure while everyone else works.
Their money sticks to them. They stand out from the year-round
residents—even from the road. The houses that are old and worn
down are owned by the real people who collect rotting and rusting
machinery, be it tractors, cars or old plows in a pile on the front
lawn. For country people used to making do, those piles are a sav-
ings account whose balance is shown to all—and it's a wealth the
summer folk can not understand. A house inhabited only in the
summer looks different: the trim is painted, the yard is neat and
flowering and, of course, the house has a name. Like all colonialists,
they are resented by those they colonize, who come to depend on

the outsiders for money and work. I saw this resentment scrawled on a roadside sign: Slow Down, Maine Has Kids Too!—demanding respect for local *lives*, if not the local way of life.

The summer population explosion is not all bad, however. Summer residents of Castine, Maine, in the 1890s established a village improvement society, which improved the town lamps, street posts, benches, town gates and a cemetery. Besides handing out odd jobs and other cash, city people plump up a declining tax base. Towns and counties have learned to tax waterfront and shoreline property, at double, treble or quadruple the standard rates, in order to target the well-to-do visitors. If you want to play, you have to pay, say the local governments. In that way, summer colonists subsidize poorer places, evening things out with tax.

When it comes to summer people's impression of the native, W. D. Howells, the ever perceptive observer of the summer scene, doubted its accuracy. "He is, perhaps, more complex than he seems; he is certainly much more self-sufficing than might have been expected." Nonetheless, locals think the vacation people are shallow, show-offy dunces who know nothing of the countryside. And town folk think the natives are quaint, endearing, wise and simple peasants. Curiosities like museum pieces, the locals amuse their seasonal and sophisticated neighbors who reward their hosts by mythologizing them: the farmer who acts as the country sage; the fisherman with ribald stories; the handyman who answers in monosyllables. And they call each other names: people who visited Indiana Dunes on Lake Michigan were duneites or duneheads, in New Hampshire summer folk are flatlanders, and Michiganites call tourists fudgies, a name that originated from daytrippers who snacked on fudge from confectionaries sugared like ant-traps.

In the northerly lake country of Quebec, the fervent throes of separatist feelings in the 1970s exacerbated this antipathy between full-time and part-time residents. Not only did the English-speaking people have the upper hand in the summer community, but they also seemed to control the political power and the country itself. It got so bad that village children once stoned a dog belonging to an English-speaking summer resident.

It's easy to tell who belongs to which tribe. In the harbor counties on the eastern shore of Lake Michigan, visiting Chicagoans never reset their watch to local time, so that a flick of the wrist shows who's who. There are other subtle ways to underline the difference between indigenous and imported. In some places locals refer to a house by the family who had previously owned it for decades as the Smith house, although the Joneses from New York have spent the past twenty summers there. Invoking the name Smith reminds the Joneses none too subtly that they trespass in their own house—it takes their property away from them. Almost forced underground, locals form their own secret society. In Nova Scotia, there are two real estate prices: one public, inscribed on ads and signs intended for rich Yankees, the other private, a lower unadvertised price reflecting what local people can pay. Town meetings often convene in the dead of winter, to exlude the summer people who hold resident association meetings of their own in the city; and their agendas often differ.

Labor Day weekend comes like the tolling of the bell, calling us back to a winter at offices and work stations. It's a sad time of resignation for the migrating tribe who pack up, drain the pipes and fantasize about staying. Yet the locals rejoice at being left alone, with no one to take orders from, no one flaunting their money about town. Up in New Hampshire in early September, locals walking into the town post office greet each other by saying, "Well, that's the last of the blackflies and the flatlanders." Both hot-weather plagues abate with the slightest chill. Howells imagined the natives danced a farandole to celebrate the colonists' departure. In the San Juan Islands of Washington State, natives do just that. They throw a "Taking back the Rock Party" after Labor Day, rejoicing that one-third of the island's residents have returned to the mainland, leaving them to the quiet of winter, their place to themselves and their ways. As much as some may dance when we go away, some may also dance when their town fills again with the returning robins, just as glad as we are to have a change.

Summer Mores

At the cottage, rules change. By leaving the city, we discard its complicated and constricting social codes. Summer mores are like a sundress, cut low in front for air, cut low in the back for air, and cut dangerously low under the arms. In the early nineteenth century, at one of the continent's first seaside hotels at Nahant, Massachusetts, women were seen playing billiards. And that kind of wildness continues today at the summer shares on Long Island, notorious for an unrestrained sexual atmosphere. Still, that décolleté mode of behavior seemed especially daring to the buttoned-up Victorians. Perhaps summer resorts thrived in that era because of this laxity. Strict rules about chaperonage and Sabbath observance loosened considerably. Adele Sloane, the young society woman, went on picnics or long hacks through the countryside with beaus, without escort. Of course, not everyone approved of the rules themselves taking a vacation: one mother said that Mt. Desert around the turn of the century was "a wild place where girls from New York and Philadelphia walked up mountains swinging their arms." Whether hiking or arm-swinging constituted wildness, neither would play in Philly. Young men and women of the Adirondacks hunted in pairs for deer; the twosome would sit patiently in the woods and wait for a deer to pass. This practice scandalized a visiting Englishman who described it as a bacchanale. In the woods, the rules bent and twisted, like a pine whipped by the wind, until they were hardly recognizable.

Emily Post discusses summer mores at an Adirondack camp. The "Kindharts" have invited the "Worldlys" to Mountain Summit Camp, but asked them not to bring a maid. Mr. Worldly worries about sacrificing his valet, from whom he has not separated in twenty-four years. Mrs. Worldly wonders how she will do her hair herself. Excepting Mr. Worldly, Post writes, "The other men all look upon a holiday away from formality (which includes valeting) as a relief, like the opening of a window in a stuffy room." Finally, you can open the window, let down your hair or grow your beard. You can pick up chicken with your fingers and spit out watermelon seeds. W. D. Howells wrote that his summer colony was impatient with ceremonies that separate people: "It is part of our splendor to ignore the ceremonies as we do." Informality indicates a lack of rules—a comfortable caftan of behavior in whose roominess we can hide. And like red dye in a white wash, it colors everything. At the church St. Peter's on the Rock on Stony Lake, Ontario, the worshipers who arrive by canoe or motorboat often attend services wearing shorts and sometimes bare feet—a uniform unthinkable at a town church.

Basically, you don't have do anything you don't want to do, even if there are rules. Talking about her family summer place on Walker's Point at Kennebunkport, Barbara Bush says, "Every day is different, although I do have certain rules posted on the doors which no one really keeps: picnics should be planned early for the beach, please pick up wet towels and use them twice; please be down for breakfast between 7 and 9 or no breakfast." Despite the posting of house rules, she admits everyone breaks them constantly.

Indeed, the rules of summer are so slight that almost nothing is taboo. Only formality itself would transgress the code of informality. In her reminiscences about the Adirondacks, Mildred Phelps Stokes Hooker remembers how a couple caught canoeing to a dinner party in a tuxedo looked ridiculous—penguins trespassing on loon territory. What would be as unwelcome today at a summer house as evening clothes at an Adirondack camp? Cellular telephones represent one forbidden object. To bring one to the cottage negates the atmosphere of retreat, and ushers unwelcome technology to the Edenic garden. It signals a perverse intention to keep working, and stay in touch with the world. I've also heard that if someone must work at a vacation house, he or she is expected to do it quietly and out of sight, so the others are not reminded of duty, and rudely woken out of their pleasure.

Guests

Generally, hospitality involves a host's providing a bed and a meal or two. Yet in the country, at the beach or by the lake, the rules of hospitality turn upside down, or at least skew a wee bit—they must, considering the situation. The farther away the house, the more those rules change. It's by no means unusual to be asked to bring your own sheets, the makings for one meal and to help with the building of a dock; there may be no washing machine, nearby stores or available day labor. Summer hospitality resembles a barn-raising where we all help raise the beams for the eventual safety of a roof. In the earlier days of Georgian Bay, people used to bring their own booze when visiting neighboring islands.

It's accepted that things are different there, and expectations change on the part of both guest and host. Rather than do all the work, the hosts let the guests help, which would rarely happen in town. It is everyone's vacation. Furthermore, we invite guests to a summer house to *entertain* us rather than the other way around. So good guests display an avidity for the chosen parlor game; spend time teaching all the children how to dive, fish, or locate frogs; suffer being beaten at chess and staying up late to talk, even if they're tired. Perfect guests, as they've been described to me, do all that, as well as bring fabulous bread and wine, cook a meal and plan an activity to do on their own. And if the wine and meal are really good, they're sure to be invited back. But guests who stay indoors, decline invitations to go sailing, play croquet or pick berries will not be—having failed to appreciate the special gift it is to be invited to share this favorite place.

In her chapter on "The Country House and its Hospitality," Emily Post proclaimed, "In popular houses where visitors like to go again and again, there is always a happy combination of some attention on the part of the hostess and the perfect freedom of the guests to occupy their time as they choose." Post listed certain guidelines for the country host: meet guests at the station or boat landing and, during hot weather, provide them with a hand fan, and a fly-swatter in August. Since her day, summer entertaining has changed immensely: few country houses or camps have staff, most people arrive by car, hand fans have fallen out of use. Yet her advice about fly-swatters and giving guests a long leash still holds. Otherwise, friendships built over years can disintegrate over a period of a few days as friends get too close. This explains why *guesthouses* accompany so many summer places.

At a summer house or beach cottage, guests and hosts live together for several days, cohabiting like husband and wife. This intimacy necessarily changes the guest-host dynamic.

Summer guests are treated more like one of the family, and so must do as they are told and go along with the house rules. None of the regular dispensations for company apply. Often, these rules and ways of doing things seem a bit queer; everyone may have to wash his or her own dish after every meal; each guest may be assigned one quotidian task, either to stack the firewood or light the fire. To conserve every brackish drop of water in our well, my grandmother insisted on hosing the sand off our guests herself, which caused everyone appreciable humiliation; luckily few families visited. Summer informality also seeps into entertaining. There's no pressure to perform, no putting on the dog. Entertaining is as simple as throwing meat and some vegetables on a charcoal fire, and having everyone eat with their hands. Even simpler than the barbecue, the picnic represents the lowest common denominator of entertaining.

Ceremonial Meals of Summer

Summer's main ceremony is a picnic, or a string of picnics laid in meadows, on riverbanks or by the sea. In the city, a picnic, or a *déjeuner sur l'herbe* in a manicured park, counts as a nature outing. At the cottage, though we can dine outdoors on terraces, porches, dining porches and decks, we have and always will pack picnics. In the country surrounded by nature, a picnic becomes an expedition, blending adventure and eating into a delectable pastry. Not simply a meal, it's something to do for the entire day. It's a destination to sail to. It's something to plan for.

Preparing for a picnic unleashes an unchanging sequence of events: you fill up a hamper or basket with treats, leftovers or simply crackers and champagne. With blanket under one arm and hamper on the other, you search for a perfect spot, considering a nook under a tree, then moving on to a hilltop in a sea of tall grass fields. The perfect picnic spot is flat, but on high ground, giving views to devour along with the food, so that you can look east during lunch, and southwest while eating dessert. The picnic spot should also be shaded enough to keep food from spoiling, and far from people and their messy scribbles on the landscape so that you seem totally isolated in nature.

Picnics represent one of the most long-lived and universal traditions of summer living, although they have also changed with the times. In *Lotus Eating*, George Curtis described Saratoga visitors in the 1850s picnicking at the lake, where "a select party is dining upon these choice trouts, black bass, young woodcock." While visiting her family's Berkshire estate in 1893, Adele Sloane recorded in her diary the details of a *fête champêtre*: the food came separately by buckboard, as she and her friends rode horses to the spot and dined in an apple orchard, where they played in trees and felt "wild."

Yet picnics go beyond lunches in orchards; the genre has evolved into a buffet of outdoors meals. Katharine Butler Hathaway listed eating expeditions at familiar watering places during summers in the 1930s: ". . . the motorboat lunch picnics at High Head or at Indian Bar, the swimming tea picnics at Craig's Pond, the painting picnics on the hill in Penobscot . . ." Topping it all off, like a flambéed dessert, as "the best and most characteristic of all the institutions," were suppers at the cliffs. Maids descended a staircase to the bottom of the cliffs, bearing baskets filled with frying pans, a lumberjack coffeepot and biscuits bundled up in napkins. The group supped just a blanket length from the bay, watching the darkening sky until the coast outlined itself in black on black. Dining in the dark, to the roar of the sea, Hathaway said, "The perilous wildness was made more thrilling by the safety and coziness" that her hostess wrapped around them like a "magic shawl"—as if food were a defense against the sea.

Night picnics were once popular in Murray Bay. The *rés d'été* would boat along the St. Lawrence to a choice location, light a bonfire and sing Québécois folk songs accompanied by a chorus of stars, which never perform near the city. It was a bit like singing around the campfire but without the real bother of tenting, mosquitoes, supplies and roughing it. And in New England, the clambake provides an interesting twist on the picnic idea. Reginald Townsend describes this New England institution in *God Packed My Picnic Basket*: a professional bakemaster layered sausages, corn, chicken and of course clams in between layers of damp seaweed into a large pit where a fire cooked the food by steam, simmering for hours and hours under a tarpaulin. The title of his memoir suggests Mr. Townsend's clambakes were blessed. The corn roast is another picnic variant that has been around some hundred years and still carries on today. Corn figures on the menu, of course, during its sweet, short season, but other foods and meat accompany the cob. Nevertheless, it's named for the vegetable, like a harvest festival that pays homage to the goodness of what is grown.

Interestingly, certain spots in summer landscapes attract one picnicking party after another, becoming a lunchtime mecca. Like those generations of Thousand Islanders who leave one island to lunch at another, we love to pack up a basket and take our food to another, more remote place—like a dog who takes a bone to where it can lick the marrow in undisturbed pleasure. We love taking our nourishment in the open air, while lying down in Roman couches of grass and blankets—deliciously informal. Rather than just looking at a view while we eat, we are *in* the view, as the air flows around us, fluttering napkins and cooling the wine bottle wrapped up in a wet sock. The picnics of the season, like wedding suppers, birthday dinners, Thanksgiving meals, bond together the celebrants in a ritual of red-checkered cloth, wicker baskets, deviled eggs and the magic of the thermos flask, when the only worry is the mayonnaise.

The Log: summer's diary

Before photographic film was life's preserver, cottage logbooks kept summer memories as fresh as a mason jar. Keeping a logbook is a Victorian tradition that has persevered in some older houses, and that has been adopted by newer houses. Some people call it a guest book, but in any case, it's the sacred text of summer. And it stays in the cottage—not borrowed and lent like regular books. For some, it replaces the family Bible, the book of records that continues for several generations. Its storehouse of the past is so valuable that many take it back to town for the winter just for safekeeping. The log means little to strangers, saving its signifigance for the confirmed and initiated who have learned to read its text.

The book is filled with journal reports of the day's activities: farmer's almanac recordings of the weather and wildlife; lyrical descriptions of the place; and gushing thank-you notes from grateful guests—bread-and-butter notes preserved forever. In one house I visited, a guest wrote, "Had a lovely afternoon up Red Hill Pond (1 loon, 1 turtle, 1 colored coromorant = three daiquiries)"—a record of a summer day's different accomplishments. A 1928 entry in an Iron County, Wisconsin, cabin journal reads: "Stayed all day Thursday—tramping, fishing and resting. Three perfect June days of rest and recreation. A.C. says, 'dam poor fishing.'" Ten years after the fishing weekend, guests wrote, ". . . a finer time in a finer place in a finer camp in a finer location can never be enjoyed by two people more than we have enjoyed our stay here . . ." Unrestrained hyperbole usually guarantees another invitation.

The logbook stores family mythology and records history. Besides passing on family myths like storytellers, the book records the first back dive, the size of fish, the strength of storms, the outcome of a regatta and when the sea turtles were last discovered on the beach. Putting the summer into words represents another attempt to make it permanent somehow, to reduce the experience to a bound object, something that you can hold on your lap, store on a shelf and read from. Some families make a ceremony out of the tradition, by reading previous entries when they arrive, calling the meeting to order with a reading of the minutes, with storytelling from summers past.

Rituals

Saying hello to the lake is a greeting like any curtsy or handshake; it's a paying of respects to the landscape. Saying hello to the lake, ringing a bell upon arriving or checking feet against footprints, hand against palmprints are just a few of the rituals that come with an inessential house. All represent rituals of arrival, a moment that needs to be marked somehow, as the entry into the fantastical world of summer. Of all the summer rituals, those of arriving proliferate, making the transition from one world to another like a passport stamp. My family was one of many that rang a bell when arriving at the cottage; oddly these objects to mark time and announce schedules are quite common at cottages and used only ritually—to ring when arriving, to welcome guests, to mark Victoria Day.

Rituals are procedures performed in a certain prescribed way and order; they give importance to the matter at hand, elevating an action into ceremony. Rituals of summer underline the fact that this is summer, we are here and the fun is about to begin. Other rituals squeeze themselves in between arriving and departing. Maybe it's a midnight skinny dip, perhaps it's a treasure hunt played with a neighboring family. Each maintains its own. I know a family that has guests sign their names on the door. Another has created a ritual surrounding a doll. When a child requests to see the doll, a grown-up takes it from the shelf, and the child plays with it. When all is done, a piece of paper records that the doll was "taken down on July 14, 1985," for whomever, and is stuffed into the hollow of the doll. This practice evolved for no particular reason and captured the family's imagination.

Rituals like that just happen, as Katharine Butler Hathaway noticed while staying with friends in Maine: ". . . the Goodwins' love of the place had expressed itself in certain spontaneous, happy adventures which later grew into a ritual, which became increasingly important with the passage of time, because, by linking each new summer with all that were gone, it brought the past, happy years back again." This is the comfort of rituals: they link one summer to another, one generation to another, one person to another.

Even vespers services at Half-Moon Bay came about accidentally, as visitors in the late nineteenth century boating in the little inlet broke into hymns and were delighted with the sound. Since then, hymn singing has become organized sermons. Like any family, summer communities also create their own rituals. Lakes come together for the annual regatta, when sailors or canoeists compete against one another, and then celebrate together, after passing on the paddle or cup that serves as the prize. Just like the village *vendange*, harvest festival or midsummer's bonfire, these rites unite a community—yet unlike those events, summer rituals are not inspired by any natural event, but are just pulled out of the air as a reason to get together and celebrate. In Beaumaris in the 1920s, there were evenings of lighted floats. Residents of the Berkshires held a gymkhana, and tub parade.

But one of the most long-lived summer rituals is Illumination Night on Martha's Vineyard, which punctuates the summer in a blaze of light. Since 1869, the cottages of the Methodist campground have strung Japanese lanterns from every porch and tree on an August night. The governors of Massachusetts used to attend the event. A brass band plays in the tabernacle, and a voice cries out, "Let the lanterns be lit." Candles strung around the cottages make the whole grove glow for hours with an ineffable spiritual quality. And thousands of people pile into the campground to behold it. Illumination Night will probably continue as long as the campground is filled with summer people who preserve the gingerbread trim as respectfully as the other traditions.

Naming: the stamp of home

Whether it's called a camp, cabin, country house or beach cottage, it's sure to have a name, like any aristocratic country seat. Driving around summer, looking at the house signs by the road, reveals your whereabouts with compass precision. By the woodsy Kawartha lakes, houses are inspired by the trees that surround them: Silver Birch, Glen Maple, Seven Oaks. So in the Blue Ridge Mountains in Virginia, houses called Woodhaven, Bouldercrest, Misty Mount, the Ridge, White House Rock line the curving roads. Near the sea, the names take on a nautical theme: Seascape and Shorewinds from Martha's Vineyard; Two If By Sea and High Tide in Nantucket. Even the fact that the house is named indicates its poetic use— being a place of fantasy, rather than day-to-day life.

Originally, naming cottages solved a practical problem: giving a reference point in a landscape without street names or numbers. Carved onto a sign, or splashed with house paint onto a rock, that name makes it possible for guests and mail to find their way to Rose Cottage, Shorewinds or Kismet. However, in summer towns where the streets have been named and numbered for postal convenience, vacationing families still baptize their second home, burning their brand onto it. Why? Not only is it tradition, but the new name erases all previous owners as well. It provides an opportunity for self-expression, and adds a bit of fancy.

Titling the house is a creative act, although sometimes it's just a reach for the nearest cliché, as accessible as a book on a shelf. Oftentimes, it's a flaunting of mastery over the pun or interpretative orthography: Pomme de Mer, ITLDU, O-So-E-Z. Appropriating Indian names adds a little cultural romance to a house and indicates a naive desire to live as harmoniously with the land as its native inhabitants. After I spent several months of reading and recording these signs, they began to seem ridiculous yet significant because they signal the freeing nature of summer places, where the imagination is indulged. And that name acts as the thesis statement of summer, expressing how we feel about the place and our expectations for it. Poking fun at the whole tradition, a place off the Conneticut coast was dubbed Hoover Hall, in honor of a ridiculous dinner party conversation regarding merits of household appliances. The house also has a Latin motto that means something to the effect of, I clean, therefore I am. The name inspired a heraldic crest of two vacuums crossed over each other; that clean heraldic crest decorates both stationery and china for the house.

A stream, a rock, a cave, a cove, a beach, a dune, all take on their own names like the house. We become cartographers, geographers, explorers seeing a landscape for the first time, naming it like the Creator. The smallest bump of a rock somehow asks to be ennobled, singled out with its own name—as if that recognizes its being. Often, people animate the outdoors, giving rocks and trees their spirits. The sandy mounds in the Indiana Dunes near Chicago were often named for the people who spent time there. Naturalist John Burroughs named a jutting bit of geology, Julian's Rock, above his cabin, Slabsides, in honor of his son. In the Adirondacks, I even saw a birch tree separated into three trunks, named after three sisters, who all sprang from the same root. Even when long gone, these women peopled the landscape for their kin, their spirits living on in trees. These names link people with place.

In Muskoka there's a Skinny Dip Rock, where the swimming is particularly good. Perhaps the saddest is a rock called Mrs. Under-

hill's Chair on the Isle of Shoals off New Hampshire, named for a
lady who used to sit and read there until a tidal wave took her away.
Some place names can't be agreed upon: Harrington Lake, where
the prime minister has a house, is also called Lac Mousseau. Owning
an island gives the right to name it. So mundane place names are
replaced with more romantic titles; Potato Island became Chingam-
agusi, and the countless, hog, cow, farm and garden islands take on
their owners' fantasies and expectations. And place becomes property.

"The act of naming was part of the transformation of Sandy
Beach into our Iron City," says a history of that camp's hundred
years. When the American visitors first reached the Iron City Fishing Camp in Georgian Bay, the island was called Sandy Beach.
"Gradually, over the years, the campers learned the existing place
names and provided new ones of their own invention that gave the
campsite and its surroundings the stamp of home." Now, an Iron
City habitué can point to Men's Beach, Twosers Bay, the Hole in
the Wall, the Moon, Champagne Point, and other campers know
exactly where to look, but visitors are lost. It's a shared yet secret
geography, beyond maps, that unites a summer community.

Games and Sports

In the late nineteenth century, summer visitors to coastal Maine
practised rocking. Not as strenuous as any Scottish rock-throwing
games, to rock was to lounge on the large rocks of the coast that lay
like meteorites fallen here and there. A guidebook from the time
explained, "A gentleman can take his lady canoeing along the
shore, they can land and indulge in that time-honored pastime of
rocking." Somehow, the name gave lying around a geological and
scientific air, as if lounging with one's sweetheart actually counted
as some sort of nature appreciation. In this culture of leisure, health
and physical activity, games and sports rule.

During the day, we play at golf, tennis, water polo, beach volley-ball, waterskiing, hiking, surfing, kick the can, hares and hounds. At night the play continues inside with parlor games and card games and now board games: charades, Botticelli, coffeepot, cribbage, canasta, hearts, poker, Monopoly, Scrabble and the sterile pursuit of trivia. Alexander Woollcott used to enlist his guests into an evening of anagrams, challenging vacationing brains to solve word problems. For those of us used to retiring to the television or homework, these games bring people together—like a dinner table with a purpose—and encourage a playful sociability. Parlors were made for talking, and so, too, parlor games. Around a game of hearts, Monopoly or charades, talking, teasing and joking become the main activity.

A game's popularity goes in and out like the tides, but *playing* itself never dies—only the balls and costumes change. Edith Wharton described how the new game of lawn tennis surpassed archery at Newport in 1879, and Newport soon became a mecca for the sport as matches took place on the lawn of the casino. Yet, she notes, "The regular afternoon diversion at Newport was a drive." Victorias, barouches or the vis-à-vis ambled up and down Bellevue Avenue. Each summer colony develops certain sports or games that become a particular part of local culture. In Bar Harbor's heyday, walking the hills of Mt. Desert Island represented the summer sport. Apparently, prestige added up with the number of miles walked. Mackinac Island, Michigan, holds an annual stone-skipping competition. The record is twenty-nine skips over the water. In places where the water is too cold for pleasant swimming, sailing takes over as the passion, allowing some contact with the water. Other times, we adapt games to the topography of summer. Boats helped people playing scavenger hunts on Echo Lake in the 1930s, as they went from cabin to cabin looking for a piece of string or recent newspa-per. At the Iron City Fishing Camp in the 1920s and elsewhere, people experimented with water golf, teeing off into the lake.

Basically, two types of games happen on the playing fields of summer: sports that connect us with nature, and those that connect us with other people, such as parlor games. As they all developed along with the summer house, swimming, canoeing and croquet exemplify summer.

Swimming

Swimming, or what was once called sea-bathing, represents the oldest diversion of summer resorts. In fact, the English seaside town of Brighton was built around the theories of a Dr. Russell that sea-bathing aided in the cure of ailments and disease. Previously all the dyspeptics and gout sufferers spent time at Bath, as Britons have done since it was Roman territory. The early sea resorts constructed "bathing machines," a sort of enclosure to hold people. (Few people swam at the time, and if they did, could not fight the currents.) At other beaches, a rope that was anchored to a barrel forty feet away extended into the surf. Bathers could hold it as the waves crashed and broke around them—like a towrope that didn't go anywhere.

A Nantucket visitor of the 1880s described the bathing hour at 'Sconset: "At eleven o'clock straggling down the bank and across the sands to the beach came the bathers . . . in motley suits passing all description." He noted the drawbacks of bathing suits, which to this day inflict torture on men and women, ". . . costumes baggy, short in the extremities, disguising beauty and giving ugliness a new horror—dresses bewitching in the revelation of white arms and fair neck . . ." A Captain Gorham watched over the bathers, ready to rescue the faint. Back then, ocean swimming was a communal activity; some beaches maintained an appointed bathing hour, and at Martha's Vineyard, a band on the cliffs serenaded bathers as radios on the beach do now.

Bathing remains the main event in many places, although old-fashioned notions of concerns for health have washed out to sea. These days we bathe for the pure fun and pleasure of it. (The notion of the sea's curative powers is maintained only by mothers who tell children crying of a cut to soak it in the saltwater, a pleasure that makes them forget their injury.) We continue the play in the water, splashing, chasing, racing, having a game of Marco Polo tag. Polar bear swims, performed in the dead of winter, or at first light, form an integral part of northern lake life. There's a certain hardiness and Spartan prestige to a plunging into cold water before breakfast. Certainly one swim per day hardly suffices. A swim becomes a bath, a cooling practice, a sociable event.

Canoeing

The canoe appeared on the summer landscape during the cottage's golden age. In the late nineteenth century, canoes were all the rage. Victorian canoes reached a pinnacle of elegance in the Rushton canoe. Covered with a striped green canopy, it was a cross between a gondola and a rowboat. Torontonians used to sail to Toronto Island and spend the night in such craft. Removed of the awnings, caned seats and fancy details, canoeing still consumes people all over vacation lakes, as it once did on the rivers of Kennebunkport, Maine. Kennebunkers used to emblazon the names of their canoes along the stern and hold an annual regatta that included an eccentric race. It required the canoeist to run one hundred yards, dive into the river, swim one hundred yards to his or her canoe and then paddle to the finish.

Summer colonies where the canoe reigns as the mode of transport are sanctuaries of nature appreciation. Both transportation and sport, the canoe is the noble craft of summer. The naturalist's instrument, it provides the most peaceful way to move across water. You can travel in a canoe without making any noise, coming close to shore birds without disturbing them. To canoe across water leaves no telling wake, the shallow-keeled craft glides on the water as if it were ice. The canoe answers wilderness dreams and nostalgia for explorers, and expresses solidarity with the native tribes who first used them.

Croquet

Croquet represents the most summery of all summer sports. In North America, it grew up with the summer house as a garden accessory like any gazebo, taking over lawns on one side of the house. William Randolph Hearst's enclave in the northern California woods included a manicured croquet lawn. When introduced about 1870, it was taken very seriously as a sport, and allowed considerable flirtation, as some observers noted. A woman reminiscing about games at Bar Harbor recalls the game was "so exciting that we did not even stop to eat, our lunch being brought to us on trays and sometimes dinner too." The perfect hot-weather game, croquet requires no heavy exertion, and thus no sweating. More important, it's one of the few games during which you can drink—either a beer or gin and tonic, depending on the time of day. A parlor game of the outdoors, croquet encourages conversation, the main topic being the creation, bending and doubting of the arcane and Byzantine rules. Booting balls and other acts of revenge provide more fodder for insults and banter. The game offers an opportunity to express unrepressed hostility toward the other people crammed into the cottage, by nasty bumping and roqueting opponents' balls. Croquet's rules of play are so complex that few who wield a mallet bother to learn, much less understand, them. Yet the extensiveness of regulations doesn't preclude unruly playing.

At the Vermont island where Alexander Woollcott and several others had formed a club, they invented a version of the game full of invective and cruelty—so violent that their shouting alarmed passing boats. Woollcott and his friends, Dorothy Parker, Harpo Marx and others, played on an uneven "lawn" hewn out of virgin forest where roots and rocks cropped up willy-nilly in the path of a ball. This version of dirty croquet, Woollcott said, demanded the guile of a cobra, the inhumanity of a boa constrictor, not to mention the strength of a stevedore. The ball and mallets are only a subtext to a greater game; what really matters is how you play the game, either with a cocktail or a flirtation.

Games played to cocktails, rules as loose as sundresses, cabins named for trees and banquets without tables all compose this twinned culture, creating an atmosphere of leisure that Jimmy Carter consciously captured for that woodsy summit. Diplomats have certainly met at resorts, such as at the Yalta Conference or the Campobello meetings of World War II. But Camp David provided more than just a setting. In between meetings and briefings, the Egyptians and Israelis immersed themselves in summer-house life, as we know it. Inviting the statesmen's wives created a more familial environment. Breaking bread all together in what amounts to a rustic mess hall broke barriers between people. Having the woods of the Catoctin Mountains nearby allowed the participants to renew or refresh themselves in the natural world—an environment psychologists call relaxing. Being crammed together in less than spacious living quarters threw everyone together in a thick stew of people. The gaming atmosphere of sport and leisure added levity to an otherwise deadly serious event. This very private place, dedicated to the private life of public people, allowed three heads of state enough privacy to accomplish what they set out to do.

Carter's alloy turned out successfully, and has held up to various stresses since. When artificial, ritualized, officious protocol collided with the familial, simple and informal atmosphere of the cottage, the result was the beginning of negotiation and, ultimately, an end to hostilities.

le cabanon

7. BUILDING THE SUMMER
HOUSE IDEA

Le Corbusier reinvented the villa in modernist language.
His designs for country residences resembled sculptural ships,
white as ocean liners, floating on the landscape, lifted up by pristine white pilotis. These sophisticated houses, such as the Villa

Savoye and Villa Roissy, have a permanent place in modern architectural history. However, one of the Swiss-born architect's own houses is rarely included in modernist history—it's simply too plain and inconsequential.

After the war, Le Corbusier built himself the simplest summer place in the hills overlooking the Côte d'Azur, France's sunny playground. With log walls and a shed roof, his *cabanon* was the essence of shelter—the lowest common denominator of living space. Like any house in a kit, its pieces were prefabricated elsewhere and assembled on site. Measuring 3.66 square meters (or about twelve feet), Corbusier's *cabanon* included a corner for rest, a corner for work and another corner fitted with a toilet. The furniture was pared down and equally simple. Certainly, the *cabanon* bore no resemblance to his commissioned country houses. The same man who talked of building machines for living built himself a hand tool.

Corbusier's cabin represented anti-architecture; it had no real design in the traditional sense of the word, but fulfilled its functions modestly. What would impel an architect to build himself such a place? When he had a chance to be his own client and build what he wanted, why would he choose a cabin? Was it expense, or if it were, wouldn't he have rebuilt later in his career?

Although a slabsided cabin seems unrelated to Corbusier's usual machines for living, it is related to ideas behind his architecture. He admired the houses of peasants, the shack, things that were modest and on a human scale—things that inspired his notions of ideal proportion he called the Modulor. At about the time he was developing these ideas, he built his summer playhouse and nearby work shed. The dimensions of this square room with two square windows represented the minimal living quarters; basically, Corbusier thought it answered a person's fundamental needs for space. In a way, his *cabanon* was a spatial experiment where he became his own subject of study for the ideal living and vacation unit. It was an idea, as much as it was a place.

Living in that small cabin with his wife, Yvonne, Corbusier retired to his shed to work. The shed answered his need for retreat, and the main cabin enclosed a very intimate form of family life. Really, the architect lived outdoors during the summer, coming under the roof sporadically for shelter. In the glassy Mediterranean light, he indulged his other passion for painting. Sometimes he worked outside: photographs show him sitting at a desk overlooking the glorious blue Mediterranean bay, like a professor addressing an auditorium. And like many creative people, he also created at his place of retreat: in addition to painting, he drew, and even invented the *aéarteur*, a kind of pivoting ventilating door with screens, which he used in other buildings.

Still, the cabin represents a private more than a public creation. Although it may not figure in his lifelong oeuvre, it certainly figured importantly in his life—he spent as much time as he could there. In 1965, he died there of a heart attack while swimming. Like so many others who find their sense of home in the summer, he and his wife were both buried nearby, at the Cap-Martin cemetery.

Although the *cabanon* is excluded from modernist history, the architectural legacy of the summer house is rich. Indeed, its design pedigree could be traced back to Palladio's villas in the Veneto, or the fantastically curved and pointed castles of the Loire whose turrets reappeared in Atlantic coast cottages. Yet the very particular idea of summering in North America engendered a varied architecture of fun and fancy, practicality and purpose, beginning with ornate Victorian gingerbread and ending with unlined cedar boxes pierced with air holes of sliding glass doors.

Summering spread the shingle style of the 1880s and 1890s, with its fringe of shingles covering facade, roof and porch columns. The East Indian bungalow flourished first as recreational residences, before catching on as affordable town housing; the bungalow accommodated both hot-weather and outdoor living. Fusing the Swiss chalet onto the log cabin, the Adirondack style, which began the baring of structural corsets, quickly spread beyond the borders of the park and influenced much of North American resort architecture, from the great lodges of the West's national parks to cottages with unpainted wood walls. With its strict design code, the newly created town of Seaside, Florida, draws on this architectural legacy—and in fact owes its success to the evocation of nineteenth-century summers.

Still, the building tradition of summer is as diverse as the landscapes cottages occupy. A summer house in the forest looks very different from a seaside summer house set high on pilons to escape high tides, which bears no resemblance to a mountain chalet hugging the ground. There has been no Palladio, no manifesto, no reigning style of summer. The sheath for the summer idea takes on many forms. Take your pick from a dizzying buffet: fishermen's shacks, virtuous log cabins, pastel farmhouses, Hampton demi-shingle, Swiss chalets, bettered barns, stork houses on stilts, ready-made ranch, glass-prowed prefab, modernist box with picture window cutouts, and the ignoble, clichéd but practical A-frame.

A summer house may not even be a house, but a windmill, corncrib or boxcar. It is the genre of no genre. No formula or mold dictates its dimensions, decorations or facade. Like the old woman who lived in a shoe, summer folk settle wherever, regardless of building convention and architectural form, so long as the shoe fits. Architects let loose and have fun since no building codes, no rules of style, no close neighbors constrain the architectural imagination. One Florida architect dug beach houses into the sand, and called them dune houses—mounds with sliding-glass doors looking out to sea. On the midwestern prairies, architect Stanley Tigerman created a "hot-dog" house, a country house named for its shape. With imagination, anything can become a summer house. In the San Juan Islands of Washington State, there's even a platform on the beach with only one wall raised against the wind—shelter reduced to a minimum. That floating deck moored on Keuka Lake shows just what an accessible and democratic building a summer house can be.

A dome or tepee shelters the summer experience just as well as a rambling thirty-six-room, shingle-style cottage. When speaking an unwritten language, we make our own metaphors.

Barns make spacious country houses—once emptied of livestock. So do lighthouses and Coast Guard dune shacks along the Cape Coast. There's hardly an empty cow barn in the northeast United States—if cows don't occupy it, then New Yorkers do, or the boards are dismantled and shipped somewhere else to form posts and beams of a barnlike retreat. Taking over unused structures and making them into summer shelter is common practice indeed. Aldo Leopold lived in a rehabilitated chicken shack. Playwright Eugene O'Neill lived in a Coast Guard shack at Provincetown, which measured eleven by nine feet. And Frank Gilbreth, the time-efficiency expert immortalized in *Cheaper by the Dozen*, bought two lighthouses for a summer place to accommodate his twelve children. (As the Coast Guard replaced lighthouse keepers with automated systems, lighthouses all over North American waterways became shells for summer people who, like hermit crabs, adopted them.)

Once the local farmhouse supply dries up, city people use their imagination. In Illinois, a common corncrib became a vacation house, with the grain bins used as sleeping rooms. An article in a 1950s magazine describes a summer compound cleverly composed of four prefabricated garden shacks; though small, they fulfilled their function admirably. As the stock of abandoned farmhouses decreases and second houses rise in price, this tradition of ingenuity continues, and summer people turn boathouses and chicken coops into holiday houses.

Summer houses represent a home-grown building tradition. Of course, there have been several well-known commissions for second houses, such as Frank Lloyd Wright's Fallingwater, but those kinds of highly designed villas are the exception. Indeed, few people call in an architect, but rely on the services of a builder or house catalog to provide them with inessential shelter. Building a cottage doesn't intimidate people the way Architecture does. A vacation house is accessible building; there's even a notion that people can bypass the builder and the architect and construct their own shelter. (If planning anything more architecturally complex than a log cabin or box, they might as well drill their own teeth. When railway magnate Sir William Van Horne designed his model farm in New Brunswick, he ended up with what looked like a summer roof with three dormers, and called architect Edward Maxwell.) With a plan, some power tools, a few friends, anyone can do it. Dozens of books line public library shelves instructing people how to build their own getaway house. Being able to put a roof over your own head is the ultimate in self-reliance.

Back in 1939, Bostonian Charles White built his own place, and wrote a book about it, *Camps and Cottages: How to Build Them.* He recommended the job to everyone: ". . . I honestly think that there is no pleasure more satisfactory than the pleasure of building for yourself some kind of a house." It may be some inborn instinct, says White, who spent seven years building and then building onto his camp, Dunwerken, in New Hampshire—a Jefferson in a poor man's Monticello. White did everything himself, from digging the well to doing the carpentry, of which he said: ". . . the framing and construction of a camp presents no difficulties which the amateur carpenter cannot readily overcome." Although he began with a board-and-batten shanty of the *cabanon*'s grandeur, White eventually added on bedrooms, two porches, a tent platform and a workshop. Doing it all the first year would have taken away the pleasure of letting it grow. Still, White humbly acknowledged the place was "surrounded on every side by the perfection of Nature and the handiwork of the Supreme Builder," which overpowered any human creation. The soul of the craftsman remains in the work, be it nature or cabin.

The Idea of Summer Architecture

If Corbusier's Villa Savoye is architectural couture, his *cabanon* and all the Dunwerkens of this world represent the house dress of building—comfortable, private and not really suitable for display in public. Cottage architecture is more about an idea than about a style. In fact, a retreat is often a deshabille of style, a simple dwelling that doesn't make a design statement. Because of this, few make it into the history books.

Resort architecture answers what architects call a design program vastly different from a normal house, and is usually constrained by a smaller budget. It fulfills different functions, creating a barebones life, reunion with nature, communality and a renewing kind of leisure. "As for me as an architect," said Jon Hobbs in a magazine interview, "I don't believe you should design a cottage the way you design a house . . . It's not really a cottage unless it offers a lifestyle quite different from that of the city house."

The idea behind cottage architecture is to underline that difference, calling attention to it with ornate gingerbread, bark-covered walls or stick-style gazebos, as if to say, This is not a house-house, but a funhouse, a playhouse, a bawdy house, so please don't take me seriously or judge me on my appearance. So thousands of diverse specimens thrive in the fertile field of summer architecture. Yet, while the blossoms may differ, they all rise from the same roots.

Like Corbusier's cabin, which commented on the houses of peasants, the summer house is rooted in simpler shelter. Indeed, many cottages began as tents, as they did at the camps Iron City in Georgian Bay and Rockywold Deephaven in New Hampshire. At the turn of the century, the grand Hotel Coronado in San Diego built a tent city of striped-canvas cloth houses lined in row after row on the sand to house the overflow of visitors, as did some hotels in Muskoka. So, too, families at the revival campgrounds and chautauquas spent their summers living all together in a tent built on a

173

small platform raised above the earth. Their owners gradually replaced the tent with a real wood cottage, yet symbolically these cottages resembled their more nomadic ancestors—their emblematic double arched doors recalling tent flaps left open like lapels. Inside, these tiny cottages echoed the simple spatial arrangement of the tent, with no interior walls to divide the space.

However, not all summer people discarded their tents; these sturdy cloth houses were quite common until the early part of this century. Several hundred families *still* live in summer tents at the Methodist campground Ocean Grove in New Jersey. At summer's end, they roll up the roofs, storing them in wooden rooms behind the tent platform. These white-canvas-covered habitations have little in common with the standard nylon camper's fare. They glow magically when lit from inside, and capture music of soft rain on the cloth roof. Living in a tent is like running away to the circus, a magical world of pleasure and play under the big top.

Tents and summer living continued at Frank Lloyd Wright's Arizona studio, Taliesin West, where he covered the place with the sturdiest of duck. Like the many summer tents that became cottages, though, his desert retreat soon exchanged canvas for the more permanent steel and glass. In the ever inventive California, an odd hybrid of tent and cottage surfaced. *Modern American Homes* of 1913 called them tent houses and noted that "a good type of tent house consists of a wooden floor set on foundation posts, a frame of 2 x 4 studding on which a base of clapboards is nailed with canvas above, and a roof of canvas or shingles, preferably shingles." Canvas or art burlap nailed on wooden frames divided rooms with all the seriousness of a Chinese screen.

One step up shelter's evolutionary ladder from tents sit log houses, shelters built directly from the forest. In a way, all the wood houses of summer refer to the log cabin, the mythic mother house from which all other houses came. All over northern woods—and even in Tennessee—summer houses pay homage to that heritage with circular cut boards, slabsided walls or cedar planks, laid one over another like Lincoln Logs of childhood play. Ironically, the log cabin was adapted to a more sophisticated inhabitant, and inexpensive only for the landowner with plenty of forest and a nearby sawmill. In the late nineteenth century, Montreal architect Edward Maxwell designed several log lodges in the Laurentians for his wealthy clients, with gables and verandas and names such as Château-du-Lac. A log house, even when embellished, announces a certain moral purpose, as it harks back and pays homage to a pioneer heritage, a simpler life.

The cottage has evolved greatly since its tent and cabin beginnings. But even more sophisticated summer villas equipped with modernities recall simpler shelter. Like a tent with its poles and lines apparent, the summer house reveals its structure, baring its bones to all scrutiny. Posts and beams state clearly how the house stands, like a tepee whose poles rise into a concentric vanishing point. The ceiling follows the line of the roof. No niceties of plaster or conventions of wallpaper obscure the structural truth, for summer living is about leaving bark intact and beams exposed. Seeing the mechanics of structure, we no longer blindly trust the calculations of engineers but understand instinctually how and why the place stands up. The roof over our heads is no longer language, but a fact, quickly knowable and readily verifiable.

Simpler in construction and often less sturdy than houses in the city, cottages are subjected to the forces of nature. As waves crash onto the beach, the pilings shake and the entire house vibrates with each roll of the ocean. Rain falling on uninsulated roofs creates a peculiar sort of percussion, revealing the musicality of structure. In high winds of a hurricane the house sways in a kind of back-and-forth dance, as wind bursts through holes in the chinking. The people inside feel the outside, not buffered and protected as they are in more substantial houses.

As no heavy foundations nail it to the ground, a cottage can even be moved from place to place as easily as a tent. If a fire or storm swallows the house, it leaves no grave dug in the landscape but disappears without a trace. It is defined by impermanence. Writer Wendell Berry sensed the vulnerability and ephemeral quality of these shelters at the very border of nature, which respond to natural vibrations. His essay "The Long-Legged House" tells how his camp built on stilts had been washed down the river twice, like a wading heron: "It is a truthful house, not indulging the illusion of the permanance of human things, to be here always is not its hope." The camp, like thousands of others, will eventually disappear back into the landscape, absorbed into the forest floor as quickly as the charred remains of log cabins long since disappeared.

Constructing with Nature

Just as migrants from the city want to reestablish their relationship with nature, so does their summer shelter. Not entirely North American, this intense dynamic between house and nature dates back to sixteenth-century Italy, to Villa Pliniana on the shores of Lake Como.

The villa was a country residence for a family from Piacenza, who came to this lake just as Milanese leave the congestion of their city today for weekends at Como. Faced by an imposing ridge of the Dolomites, the villa sits back against a cliff, down which pours a cataract. Instead of damming or diverting it, the builders welcomed the cascade into the villa itself, letting falling water flow through an arcaded room linking the two wings. It poured down a stone wall, covered in moss and ferns, and eventually into the lake. "The old house is saturated with the freshness and drenched with the flying spray of the caged torrent," wrote Edith Wharton in *Italian Villas and Their Gardens*. Nature raged through the whole house (seemingly unchecked), as if it were a cottage at the base of Niagara. "The bare vaulted rooms reverberate with it, the stone floors are green with its dampness, the air quivers with its cool incessant rush." Wharton called the combination of the wet loggia, its shaded bay, the blue of the lake and the sun-drenched hills "one of the most wonderful effects in *sensation* achieved in the Italian Villa." It was also the coolest villa on the lake, by virtue of its pioneering natural air conditioning.

Villa Pliniana prefigured one of the ultimate houses in nature, Frank Lloyd Wright's Fallingwater, which works in and around its cascade. Wright placed the house over the waterfall where the Kaufmann family used to bathe, over the rocks where the family used to sunbathe when they summered in a wood cabin on the property. Instead of merely looking at the scenery, Fallingwater insinuates itself into the landscape by virtue of complicated engineering.

Rather than bulldozing, flattening or damming whatever gets in the way, a cottage often integrates the natural world; it will embrace cascades and even trees, literally becoming part of nature, or having nature become part of the house. An 1880s photograph of a cottage in the Thousand Islands shows a little sapling in place of a porch column. The sapling rises past a hole cut into the porch roof—scattering a leafy umbrella of shade. The builders accommodated their house to the tree, rather than chopping it into firewood. Eventually, the sapling grew into a tree, the trunk outgrew its hole and was cut down.

Building with trees, not as raw material but intact, as an idea, occurs fairly often in the architecture of summer. As early as the 1830s the Hornby Lodge in upstate New York was constructed around a large oak, with limbs climbing into the rooms and the treetop rising above the roof-top. To all who enter, it says, This shelter is at one with the trees. Another lodge in Yosemite had a cottage built around a huge cedar, its huge bark-covered column in the center of the small room. Called Cedar Cottage, the gimmick was used to lure paying guests. Today, the tradition continues, as summer people cut holes in a new deck, rather than felling the tree already there. When building an idyll of leisure, we display a more accommodating attitude toward nature, one that seems to value trees as much as the house—almost.

Last summer in Georgian Bay, on a jagged island of dark rock and jagged pines, rose a newly built grand shingled affair of Victorian proportions, with turrets, French doors, brass hardware on every hinge and service quarters. In the two-story living room, by the massive stone fireplace, a bit of the Canadian Shield crept into the room, a big black rock hidden in the corner. The architect and his clients had decided not to blast the rock away, but built around it. It was too expensive, and besides, blasting a bit of rock already suffocated by this new building seemed unnecessary, like quashing a bug for no other reason than that it's a bug. They let the rock lie, incorporating it into the decor. (That kind of natural intrusion would never be tolerated in a city house, where different values are at work.) So the rock becomes like the water-smoothed stones people bring inside and display on the windowsill—a piece of nature brought in, like a curio, to be owned and admired. Although merciful with saplings and rocks, human builders still exert control over the landscape, which is merely raw material for their pleasure.

Even without such dramatic landscape features as waterfalls or hulking rocks, most summer houses accommodate nature by embracing a view as unobstructed and panoramic as possible. I don't suppose many people took the task of siting a cottage as seriously as Alexander Graham Bell on his cart. It's an aesthetic decision not a practical one, based on exposing us to nature, rather than protecting us from it. When Chilson Aldrich, who wrote a book on the log cabin, decided to build his own on Lake Superior in the 1940s, his local helper could not understand siting the cabin on the hilltop exposed to the north: he warned his employer it would be a long way when carrying up pails of water. Most so-called locals would probably find boulders in the living room, saplings rising up through the porch, waterfalls running through the house difficult to understand, if not a little daft.

To blend with nature, not to stand out, is the idea—just as a chameleon becomes sand, rock and leaf. The color white, as the country-house maven Andrew Jackson Downing warned in his 1842 book on country cottages, was an affront to the surrounding foliage. He pressed his point by noting that great landscape painters never depicted white houses in picturesque compositions. Perhaps Methodists at the summer campgrounds read his book; old photographs of the religious campgrounds show how the summer pilgrims strung garlands of ivy and flowers on the tents, to camouflage the white canvas in the woods—like leafy branches on metal helmets. About 120 years later, repeating Downing's dictum, architect Charles Moore also forbade the affronting white in the architectural guidelines of the Sea Ranch development in northern California, where houses were covered in weathered wood.

Camouflaging into the landscape starts by using natural, local materials—rather than marble, stucco or brick. Cedar shingles covering beach houses weather into the silver of driftwood washed up on the shore. Northern camps were often covered in sheets of bark peeled off trees and applied as siding. The 1913 book *Modern Homes* proclaimed, "Another demand, which comes from the faculty of the average American to adapt to his surroundings is that the modern country home shall seem a part of the scenery, a requirement which has encouraged the architect and the owner to use local materials . . ." Indeed, the Adirondack camps—and many others—were built of wood logged in nearby forests and the fireplaces made of stones collected from outside.

The earth itself becomes a material: architect Roland Terry built himself a sod-roof house in the San Juan Islands. Grass and wildflowers surround the house and also cover it, blurring the distinction between the built and the natural environment. To a bird overhead, one must look like the other. Inside, Terry used driftwood logs as posts and did not cut down any trees on the property, having "designed it to intrude on the landscape as little as possible." The idea is that architecture should not upstage the natural setting, but rather complement it with a house that's barely distinguishable from the natural environment, no more out of place than a stray boulder. Yet notions of compatibility between structure and environment are relative; Palladio's geometric and stone villas are often said to fit into the landscape.

Still, the Adirondack style was probably the ultimate architecture of nature. Entrepreneur William West Durant is credited with its creation. In the 1880s, he built the first great camps speculatively while trying to develop tourism in the central Adirondacks. Here, the Swiss chalet was fused onto the very American, but extravagant, version of a log cabin. Despite the foreign influence and sometime grandeur, these camps made use of local building style and techniques. At its height, the camp style is characterized by low-pitched roofs, deep eaves, log walls and furniture made directly from the forest itself. Here began the decorative baring of structural corsets, with truss and gables and collar beams left open to view. The basic building material was logs, which were made into trusses, peeled to serve as beams, or exposed their intersecting ends as decoration. Exterior walls were often sheathed in bark, and paint covered none of it. All emphasis was on naturalness, and all effort was made to keep moss on wood, and bark on branches. This rustic design soon spread its influence throughout the continent, to western mountains and Great Lakes and beyond—communicating at first glance a desire for communion with nature, down to the moss and the bark.

Builder William West Durant left moss growing on the stones he stacked into massive fireplaces; the cut sides faced inward, showing the rough contours of rocks and hiding any hint of mortar and human hand. In those New York woods, nineteenth-century campers furnished their cabins using raw material from right outside their doors—in an almost fetishistic manner. The furniture was crafted of twigs and branches. Birchbark supplied butter plates. Toadstools became table centerpieces, and deer hooves were reincarnated as feet for stools or, equally perversely, made into gun racks. The Victorian campers satisfied their love of functionless knickknacks with fungus art, etching designs into fungi that once grew on trunks like bracketed display shelves.

In today's cottages, where pillaging the natural environment for knickknacks would not wash, nature comes indoors by virtue of glass, as big and clear as possible. The view, captured and framed, covers the wall like a landscape painting. Under the glass lies a Claude Lorrain, a Constable, a Thomas Cole or Winslow Homer, framed in wood. Sliding glass doors also help sustain the illusion that we are living out-of-doors, open to breezes or vistas. Or windows become walls, without even a curtain. Vacation houses built after 1950 often bare one entire wall of glass that stretches from the floor to the hackneyed cathedral ceiling, resulting in a gigantic version of the lean-to, entirely glassed on the open side, canted toward the reclining view.

Borrowing Local Traditions

The red-tailed hawk does not collect twigs and bits of fluff to build its own nest but settles into one already made. Summer people do likewise, claiming old nests as their own, and blending unobtrusively into the local scene. Americans have always abandoned their dwellings for something better farther down the road, as Thomas Jefferson remarked, leaving the countryside open for this kind of appropriation. As early as the mid-1800s, Daniel Webster, Julia Ward Howe and William James bought discarded farms for summer pleasure, as many do today. Cheap, practical and convenient, this habitat recycling has long been common. (After leasing land from an iron company back in 1877, the Adirondacks Club pressed abandoned mining buildings into service as its clubhouse and cottage.) Keeping the old nests preserves the spirit of the place, be it Chocorua, New Hampshire, or Prince Edward Island. Mary Gilliatt's *A House in the Country* advises architectural saviors "rehabilitating" an old farmhouse, to "regenerate the simplicity for rural decoration, pare away the inessentials, try to distinguish between the bogus, the fake and the truly traditional and be as honest as you can." Although Gilliatt is discussing English farmhouses, North

Americans display equal reverence to found nests, perpetuating the fantasy of returning to a simpler life.

However, there's never been a large enough supply of farmhouses to go around. So when building anew, summer people often copy their neighbors' shelter, keeping to the local style—like the ersatz Nantucket fishermen's cottages built by a developer in the 1880s. In Newcastle, Maine, a century ago, one summer colonist went to the trouble of dipping roof shingles in oil and lampblack and staining the other woodwork with Venetian red and oil so that the whole place would look a hundred years old. And that was a hundred years ago.

Since clothes and cars and conspicuous leisure mark a summer person, local building customs offer some disguise, like taking on the accent. English Canadians or Americans in Murray Bay often respected the architectural conventions of rural Quebec, keeping the curved roofline and farmhouse dormers in the designs for their *maisons de plaisance*. Country houses all over New England hide behind barn red. Copies of the fisherman's shingled cottage crowd the Atlantic shore. The log cabin of Michigan and Minnesota settlers reproduce themselves at a frenzied rate in order to accommodate all the summer people. In addition to a desire to fit into the neighborhood, practicality also influenced this leaning toward indigenous building forms: in the 1870s and 1880s, the beginning of the resort era, local carpenters knew *local* carpentry. Even the plan books so popular at the time included no working drawings, so builders relied on nearby examples. (Imagine a Chicagoan explaining Palladio to a northern Michigan farmer who did a little carpentry on the side: it just wouldn't work.)

One of the summer's original architectural forms, the shingle style, also borrowed from indigenous tradition. A hybrid of influences, these buildings were inspired by an interest in the colonial revival in the 1870s when architects looked to Massachusetts colonial houses on Cape Cod, Gloucester, Martha's Vineyard and Nantucket. Originally, cedar shingles had been used on the northeastern seacoast. The poor man's weatherproofing covered fishing huts, lobster shacks and modest houses. Easier to import than clapboard to islands such as Nantucket, weathered single shingles could be replaced rather than redoing the entire wall. Like thatch, they also allowed for sculptural shapes. Shingle-style cottages, these horizontal masses crawled low on the ground, like a big rock covered in cedar shake. The shingle style, as practiced by Stanford White, among others, flourished for the last two decades of the nineteenth century and resurfaced less than a century later as designers such as Robert Stern and Charles Gwathmey reinterpreted the look in East Coast holiday towns, and the shingle style was reborn as an architecture of ultimate leisure.

Not leaving well enough alone, many summer colonists add fancier fluff to the found nests or embellish the local style with architectural elements from afar. In 1919, W. D. Howells described the typical coastal Maine house as a "picturesque structure of colonial pattern," shingled to the ground and stained by either paint or real weather. The summer cottages in town existed in "earlier mutation from the fisherman's and farmer's houses which formed their germ." Eventually, the natives caught on to the colonists' interpretation of their buildings, and began building houses to suit an outsider's vision of what a Maine house should look like, and rented them to tourists. Since then, those interpretations have probably been accepted as the local style.

Yet dressing up the local style in more formal attire often results in incongruous disaster. Sculptor Auguste Saint-Gaudens, who created the famed Lincoln Monument, transformed his Cornish New Hampshire house by slapping on a few European elements—some Doric columns and an Italianate pergola. One of his friends described the renovation as "some austere and recalcitrant New England old maid struggling in the arms of a Greek faun." It amounted to molesting the idiom.

Summer houses use local slang, but their accent invariably stands out. Even when they're painted barn red, sheathed in clapboard or cedar shake, something gives them away, a carefree way of speaking with hammocks, gliders and chairs poised for lying around. What else betrays the outsiders? Lot of porches and verandas that would keep sun from warming the house in cold weather or huge expanses of glass that would be too chilly in winter. Summer houses lack the hardiness and practicality of their full-time neighbors, as hardiness and practicality don't suit castles in the air.

Building Fantasies

Once upon a time, in a dark, deep forest, enchanted and enchanting, there lived a powerful prince—for a few months a year anyway. William Randolph Hearst's Wyntoon, located on the bend of the McCloud River in northern California, was a fairy tale come to life. This getaway duplicated a Bavarian village, buried deep in the heart of a fifty-thousand-acre property, which, had it been in Europe, would have equaled a principality. Hearst seemed to build fantasies more than houses, indulging them as only a fantastically rich person can: his first building project was the grand, gilt, extravagant San Simeon. Before San Simeon was completed, he began to rebuild his mother's river retreat after the original stone castle designed by Bernard Maybeck succumbed to fire.

So Hearst commissioned San Simeon's architect, Julia Morgan (who had also done several projects for his mother), to replace the castle with a collection of some half-dozen houses, and hired guilds of craftsmen to hand-forge the details in an Old World sort of way. The result was a turreted and gabled village of half timber, sited around a central green and lined up along the winding banks of the cold McCloud. Wyntoon was as large as a little German village, and could accommodate between sixty and one hundred people. It also housed Hearst's Germanic art collection. Besides the houses, Wyntoon encompassed an airstrip, croquet court, switchboard headquarters and office from which Hearst could rule his journalistic fiefdom.

The village was composed of several guesthouses named Cinderella, Snow White–Rose Red and Sleeping Beauty. Murals depicting scenes from *Grimms' Fairy Tales* decorated two of the houses, painted by a Hungarian émigré who did Hollywood sets.

Here, in a storybook setting, the houses actually tell stories of make-believe that seem real, and perfectly possible. On the walls of Snow White–Rose Red, the prince, emerging from his enchantment as a bear, thanks to the lovely princess, is said to resemble Hearst himself—star of his own woodsy fairy tale. Hearst found refuge in a fantasy world of his own making. But he was not the first or last to build a fantasy to escape to. In a way, all houses of leisure are about fantasy, a fact often embodied in their physical form.

Form follows fantasy in the architecture of leisure. Imagine a country house built to resemble the base of a fluted Doric column. Such a fancy was actually built by a French chevalier in the 1780s. Back in the New World, even the stern Methodists allowed fancy to creep into their religious retreats. Over a hundred years ago, the ornate gingerbread houses of the Martha's Vineyard campground, with their odd scale and matching painted trim, were forever compared to fairyland. The builders of these exuberant houses used forty-five different decorative patterns in the gingerbread—loading up each facade with plenty of froufrous, like a hat covered in lace, feathers, silk fruits and birds. Certainly, those cottages would seem frivolous and out of place in staid Boston and Hartford, which referred so heroically to a Federal past. Yet in this religious resort, that kind of fantasy just reinforced the otherworldiness of the place.

In the Harbor Counties that give refuge to fleeing Chicagoans, architect Ken Schroeder designed a "boxcar" house for his retreat a few years ago. He was inspired not by Palladian villas, Georgian buildings or even the morally superior log cabin, but by train cars used as stopgap shelter during the Depression. To reinforce this downwardly mobile fantasy, the boxcar house slums with its materials. Mundane asphalt tiles sheath the house, and culvert pipes serve as columns. Why? Because, as the architect explained, "being in the woods, you can build almost anything." It's allowed.

At the masquerade balls of architecture, we can express hidden desires, as though adopting a different architectural persona creates a different reality. I know a group of women who live in a rigorously modernist neighborhood in Virginia where the walls are windows and the furniture is black leather and chrome. During the summer, they all move to a little coastal town in Maine, happily exchanging rigid modernist standards of decor for traditional clapboard houses with low-ceilinged small rooms and wraparound porches. There, they indulge themselves in floral chintz and country antiques that would smother a true modernist heart. It's amazing to see what people want to dress up as during their summer flings. Down at one of the West Virginia springs, someone once created the "watermelon" cabin, whose logs were painted dark green, with light green chinking and melon red splashed on the ends of the logs. Somehow a fruit so emblematic of summer seems an entirely appropriate shell for the summer experience.

Conventions of Summer

The Villa Pliniana; a *cabanon* of ideal proportions; a millionaire's Bavarian fantasy castle; Fallingwater—these houses are exceptions to the architecture of leisure. For all the modernist and postmodern glories of the Hamptons, for every grand, architecturally significant summer house, there are dozens of modest bungalows, simple prefabs or owner-built shacks and shanties where people live out the summering idea, unsung and without pretension.

Like their rich relations, these houses, too, relate to their natural surroundings, mirror indigenous forms and indulge in fantasy, but on a more modest scale. And the summering idea has developed several building conventions of its own: porches, decks, patios; a collection of structures; open plans; sleeping lofts; house kits.

There's an architectural slang at work, an informal way of speaking.

No one has ever compiled a text explaining how to assemble the ideal summer house, yet somehow people figure out they'll need a loft for the grandchildren, a porch to keep bugs out, one room for many functions, and hence an architecture of leisure is born. You can tell a pleasure house from a serious house by how it incorporates these elements. You wouldn't really remark on its design, at first glance, but after living there in absolute leisure for a few days, you soon realize how clearly it fulfills its function.

Living Outdoors

More important than the interior rooms are those attached to the outside of the summer house—porches and decks, patios and balconies. Sort of vestibules to the out-of-doors, they form a link to nature. Indeed, the word *porch* comes from the word *portico*, or entry; porches began as shelter above a doorway and evolved into a thoroughly North American institution. The Victorians called them piazzas and verandas, adding the romance of faraway places to a very backyard kind of place. In *Cottage Residences* of 1842, which became the bible of domesticity for generations of housebuilders and homeowners, Andrew Jackson Downing wrote, "In all countries like ours, where there are hot summers, a veranda, piazza or colonnade is a necessary and delightful appendage to a dwelling house, and in fact, during a considerable part of the year frequently becomes the lounging apartment of the family." So verandas, piazzas and colonnades attached themselves like remoras to the country house. Victorian hotels adopted the veranda wholeheartedly. The piazza at the United States Hotel at Saratoga was as tall as a cathedral. The Grand Hotel at Mackinac, Michigan, boasted the longest, measuring some six hundred feet. Visitors used the porch as a concourse for walks, counting laps like runners on a track. They socialized in its shade, as Italian villagers meet in the village piazza. At an Iowa summer village called the Outing Club, a porch snakes around the property following the contours of Clear Lake. Built in 1895, this white-railed artery actually joins the twenty-one cottages to one another, and ultimately to the club's heart, the central dining hall.

As much as Victorians embraced the porch, modernists scorned it—especially the screened porch, which distorts a structure's features like a stocking flattened onto a face. Yet the *New York Times* reported in 1989 that porches have made a comeback, partly because Seaside, Florida, has embraced the institution. The revival is shaded by nostalgia: more than just a place to sit, porches represent a more neighborly way of life when people actually watched the world outside and talked to strolling passersby. The ring of gingerbread porches decorating the Martha's Vineyard campground cottages, so close that one's neighbor is literally within arm's reach, says one resident, is "a literal manifestation of a network"—a sort of orange juice–can communication system that symbolizes neighborliness.

Porches, verandas, decks and patios are the parlors of summer. After all, living outdoors is the ultimate goal of summer life. These exterior spaces form a demilitarized zone, partly inside, partly outside—partly culture, partly nature. The perfect summer room, the porch is shaded by its roof, and keeps sun from heating up the house. Breezes sashay around this room without walls. Providing shelter from the elements is the job of any house, and screened porches offer shelter from the insect element; they protect us from bugs, blackflies and mosquitoes.

Besides being a headquarters for lounging, the porch serves as a locus for *all* activities: eating, reading, parlor games, pea-shelling, sleeping. Some porches specialize in function. In the Adirondacks, among other places, what is called the outdoor dining room is just another version of a porch, but one with a limited function. In grander cottages about the turn of the century, at Marblehead, Massachusetts, even the servants had a porch to call their own, albeit at the back of the bus, far from the view or breeze. Once tubercular treatments of fresh air created a fashion for sleeping outdoors in the early part of this century, cottages incorporated sleeping porches upstairs, for sleeping, and a living porch downstairs for living.

But the porch is just the beginning of the expanding genre of outdoor rooms, which includes patios, terraces, decks, gazebos and loggias for those who like a taste of the foreign. We make parlors outside, somehow unable to just sit on the ground without enclosing it or making a smooth surface of rough ground. Decks are a very twentieth-century take on the porch—stripped of its shade for a generation that likes a good dose of sunshine. Tinged with the acidic hue of treated lumber, decks sit propped outside houses, to the front, back or side, extending interior rooms outdoors with the magic of sliding-glass doors. Even lakeside docks become salons alfresco, once a table and chairs gather in a circle of sociability, and cottagers spend cocktail hours on their water-bordered living room. The porch even climbs on top of the roof. Of course, widow's walks have always graced Cape Cod rooftops like crows' nests, yet modern houses built after the era of whaling widows often incorporate this lookout. The owners of one Florida house called the widow's walk "Granddaddy's playpen," and successfully flew kites from its height, unobstructed by any trees or wires. Nantucket hosts throw cocktail parties on their rooftop porch, where revelers devour the 360-degree view and wash it down with gin and tonics, surrounded by sea air on four sides.

The popularity of porches, decks and widow's walks represents our intention to live in the out-of-doors, succumbing to the comfort of roof and walls only to sleep. Living outdoors is like living in nature, and lends poetry to otherwise banal daily tasks.

So, too, bathing takes on more ritualistic overtones when performed outside. The outdoor shower appears only in summer shelter—mostly by the sea. The origin of these showers was probably more utilitarian than romantic; a shower near the beach allowed bathers to rinse off sand before bringing any inside. And it didn't require any drains or complicated plumbing, as water just drenched back into the sand. Somehow, this shower acquired more sybaritic undertones and became part of summer life for many people. Even the English architectural theorist Leon Krier, who assisted in the planning of the new town of Seaside, Florida, and who probably knew little about American summer houses, knew enough to build an outdoor spray into his sophisticated beach house there. The outdoor shower stall offers the illusion of bathing in nature—standing in the spray of a waterfall. Air on the skin, followed by a chaser of fresh water, makes one of the most exhilarating epidermal cocktails. Bathing suits are stripped off and hung on the shower's walls to dry, stuffed between the slats or else thrown onto nearby bushes to air, as the towel-clad bathers run back into the house, dripping onto wooden floors. The indoors is reduced to a closet, a dressing room quickly visited before returning to life outdoors.

Outbuildings

Instead of building one summer house, architect Richard Hobbs built three. Hobbs constructed a cabin, a guesthouse and a bathhouse, without cutting down a single tree on his tall-treed land on Washington's San Juan Island. As he explained, his divided building scheme makes for a diversity of views, and lets the buildings blend into the landscape and fishing village vernacular. As Hobbs discovered, several buildings hide among the trees better than a single massive structure, preserving the illusion of undisturbed nature; by distributing their weight, they sit lightly on the landscape.

Actually, the summer house has long been dissected into parts. In the days when fires provided heat for warmth and cooking, fires burning out of control threatened every house, be it summer or winter. So separating a house into various outbuildings was an early version of fireproofing. In hot climates, kitchens often sat apart from the main house, and the tradition continued. In an 1870s camp in Quebec's Gatineau Hills, the kitchen was enclosed by a lean-to separate from the house, as it was at a summer house in Harbor Springs, Michigan.

However, constructing several outbuildings rather than one large structure was inspired by early camps in the Adirondacks. It is the Stokes place on Birch Island that is credited with beginning this summer building tradition. Back in the 1880s, when camping in the Adirondacks meant living in tents, the Stokeses built wooden store-rooms behind their tent platforms where they stowed furniture and the tents themselves during the winter. According to the story, Mrs. Stokes simply built over the fifteen-odd tent platforms, replacing canvas walls with logs, making the tents more permanent without embarking on the construction of one large structure. Separating the buildings from one another protected against total loss of a building in a place where any construction posed practical problems; Mrs. Stokes's cabin once burned down while she was in another cabin. The idea of many little houses caught on so fires wouldn't. (Some Adirondack camps later added covered wooden passageways between the gaggle of cabins, which spread fire as quickly as dynamite's fuse.)

As tents turned into cabins, these camps resembled a veritable village in the woods, like Indian encampments. At the great camps of the rich, the number of structures equaled a small city, complete with separate bowling alleys, casinos (for game-playing), dining rooms and blacksmiths' shops. Each of the Vanderbilt children had a cabin at the grand camp Sagamore. And there, as at many of the great camps, each building had its own function: root cellars dug into the hillside kept food cool; icehouses, with double-paned glass or no windows at all, stored frozen blocks under mounds of sawdust; boathouses kept canoes, yachts and launches downstairs on fresh water bedding, and contained apartments for people above.

A collection of icehouses and casinos may not have survived the era of great camps, but the tradition of separate buildings has. Last summer I visited an island where a cooking shed and two small sleeping cabins, furnished with only a bed and wall hooks for clothes, surrounded a central tepee, which rises from the rocks like a cone of fire. Here, among these cabins, it's like life in the village, the smallest increment of organized civilization where conviviality outweighs privacy.

Living in the Open

Like the tents, cabins and barns from which it descends, the summer house consists of open space, like common grazing land. Of course, this spaciousness invites ventilating breezes, but also cultivates a more communal life—one without fences. We call it the open plan, a house without walls, and it evolved with the architecture of summer, well before the modernists erased interior walls from their plans. The nineteenth-century home was divided into many rooms in order to segregate the sexes, separate formal and informal space and banish dull practicalities of housekeeping from view, as well as cooking odors. Yet the Victorian summer house removed some dividers. In *The Architect and the Country House*, Mark Alan Hewitt observes that among monied Americans in the late nineteenth century, "A new, more open house type reflected a life-style based on leisure and greater informality." The great hall, so popular at the time and so reminiscent of grand English castles, opened up to living and dining rooms. At Edith Wharton's house, the Mount, formal by today's standards, one chamber flowed into another unimpeded, as Wharton insisted it should. Even at the humble campground cottages that measured some eleven by nineteen feet, the upstairs and downstairs remained open space; downstairs was living space, upstairs sleeping space.

In today's summer house, the great hall concept has melded into what's called L-D-K on plans, open to the ceiling, brazenly baring the pitch of the roof. The action happens in one room; no parlors, studies, dens, living rooms, breakfast rooms or dining rooms separate one activity from another. Of course, blending living, dining and cooking functions saves space and thus cost, yet the open plan has deeper meaning. When renovating cozy old farmhouses into vacation idylls, summer people remove interrupting walls, so that all these functions join together. Thus we return to a more medieval—or primitive—concept of domestic space.

Even when inhabiting large shingled beach houses, we live, dine and cook there like Inuit in an igloo, like Mongols in a yurt, like Bedouins in a tent—communally. It seems that as the cottage's role in preserving family life increased, so did this notion of creating open, communal space. In *Recherches sur l'architecture des loisirs*, architect Georges Candilis writes, here roughly translated: "The holiday home, place of family liberty, thus extends into communal facilities, place of social life." (Not only does this great room encourage a more communal life, it also allows women saddled with chores to remain within the group, even if chains of habit tie them to the kitchen.)

Living in houses scarcely more sophisticated than a yurt or tent, a family marvels at how it fits into a bungalow without bursting, or imploding with the infallible gunpowder of sibling rivalry. Just as public space takes precedence over private space, communal life absorbs the individual. We gladly renounce our accustomed privacy to experience this gathering of the clan. Solitude, refuge and privacy are found in an expansive landscape instead. Indeed, summer bedrooms are more like bunkrooms. In the 1950s, *Holiday* magazine proclaimed sleeping arrangements should resemble dormitories. The summer house engendered a new kind of bedroom, as tied to communal life as a kitchen without walls.

The Loft

A bedroom opening onto the open plan, the sleeping loft belongs to the architecture of summer. Lacking any doors, and indeed walls, the loft possesses none of the privacy essential to a conventional bedroom. Not even a room, it is a balcony overlooking the circus of family life. It adds sleeping to the living, dining, cooking functions of the great room, making one big spatial mélange. The line between public and private space blurs happily—unless those in the loft sleep later than the early-risers who clank kettles and shuffle newspapers in the great room below.

Although lofts seem quite modern, a product of city art studios, summer houses have long fitted in a platform under their roofs. Winslow Homer's brother built a loft at the first house in the Homer compound at Prout's Neck, Maine, well over a hundred years ago. Cottage and bungalow plan books from the turn of the century show sleeping areas in the crawl space above the first floor, where guests presumably set up cots or sleeping bags.

Since then, these sleeping chambers have squeezed the most out of unused square footage under the roof to accommodate the overflow; they're a frugal solution to the demands of entertaining that come with owning a getaway house. The balcony bedroom is usually reserved for guests, as a bed of last resort. Before the advent of guesthouses, hotels and bed-and-breakfasts, a loft was standard country hospitality. It recalls the most basic form of hospitality when a farmer offered to let travelers sleep in the hayloft. Redolent of sweet green grass, it represented a field's essence reduced to its cured cubic form. Sleeping in a loft is still an adventure for children who climb up the steep ladder to an aerie.

A House in a Box

A house that comes in a kit is cheap and as easy to assemble as a Christmas toy. With plans and a few thousand nails, anyone can do it—from the island carpenter to determined do-it-yourselfers. The rise of prefabricated housing and vacation houses meets in a dovetail joint, and both date back to the mid-nineteenth century. As early as the 1850s, Martha's Vineyard campground cottages were made in Edgartown and shipped a few miles up island to Oak Bluffs, where they were assembled for a cost of $150 to $600. Later, at New York's Chautauqua, an early house was made elsewhere and put together at the lake. Eventually, the common sense practice of building parts of a house in town, and shipping them up island or upstate, turned into a business, as companies constructed an entire product line of different models. In *The Comfortable House*, Alan Gowans asserts that "such transient structures were among the prefabricators' first offerings."

Buying a precut or prefabricated house solved many practical problems of cottage construction in inaccessible areas where materials and labor were scarce, and where the building trades were less than expert, if available at all. It neutered a difficult process, creating architecture by numbers. And a prefab saved money. A 1910 Aladdin catalog stresses affordability, describing "a big summer cottage at a small price." The dimensions of Aladdin's models were equally small; bedrooms typically measured eight by eight feet, and living rooms were not much larger. Without any decoration or fancy details, these summer cottages were basically four walls and a porch, either screened or open; the "hunter's lodge" model came without lath or plaster. In the 1930s, Eaton's catalog for cottage living advertised a "lined" sectional house with four rooms that cost only $950.

These houses helped democratize the summer house, by mass producing the villa and making the rich person's country house affordable. It made the bucolic idyll into an industrialized product that emanated from the assembly line rather than the poet's pen. In the 1950s and 1960s, as second-home ownership became the *second stage of the American Dream*, ready-made-building companies flourished. Houses in boxes made the dream accessible to more and more people. In 1957 the popular houses designed by architect Howard Koch cost between $2,500 and $6,500, which, according to a magazine of the time, equaled the price of a summer rental, and fitted onto one truck.

Many different companies created and sold these houses, yet the prefabricated industry gradually framed its own architecture of democratic leisure. The genre has become more complex than Aladdin's four-sided boxes with attached porch; now house shoppers can choose octagons on stilts, Swiss-derived A-frames, suburban split levels, log homes, cedar cottages or the common prow-shaped facade, piloted toward the view. Houses built from kits are easy to spot; whatever the shape, they exude practicality and simplicity of construction, sheathed in a skin of planks or logs. Typically, a wall of glass covers one side of the wooden box, whose small bedrooms face inland. Inside, the perennial open plan reveals posts, beams and trusses, and walls of tongue and groove. Cedar, with its wonderful weathering into driftwood color, has become one of the prefabricators' favored materials. The choice of that wood lends magic to an otherwise plain building as the redolence of cedar inside preserves family summers as intact as wool sweaters in a cedar chest.

Furnishing Summer

A different idea of shelter needs a different idea of furniture. So summer furniture developed inside the cottage, answering specific needs for comfort, relaxation and natural materials—and declaring independence from everyday life. Of course, the universal cottage decor is carefully composed of leftovers—forgotten chairs, tables and beds. Long abandoned to a netherworld of a garage, they are resurrected for a second life where no one notices their datedness. Old sofas and armchairs live out their last years in respectable retirement down in the country—just like well-worn clothes. Whatever furniture first filled the cottage, be it a hundred or ten years ago, remains in a changeless state of interior decoration. House and contents are not readily separable. When summer houses sell or pass down to the next generation, the furniture is included, as vital to the whole as bodily organs. Still, certain totems of decoration bespeak the summer experience: wicker furniture, rustic furniture, the Muskoka-Adirondack chair and, of course, the hammock. The look of this furniture is not as important as what it represents: a life of leisure in—or close to—the outdoors.

Wicker was one of the first materials to speak this hot weather language. Although we now associate it with casual living—with lounging in sun rooms, porches or countrified apartments—wicker initially caught on as summer furniture. Hollows between the twined willow allowed air to circulate, unlike heavy furniture of the Victorian era. As far back as 1851, a book on the rural home favored so-called cane furniture for its strength, lightness and low cost. Besides praising its coolness, wicker's advocates noted how easily it moved from sunshine to shade. Artisans deftly braided wicker into chairs, planters, chaise longues, cradles, trays, side tables and rocking chairs, all of which sat on the porch, protected from rain but open to breezes. Left unpainted, wicker resembled a wren's nest, brown sticks woven together into a cozy basket of incubation. The material reached its leisurely apotheosis in the armchair with side pocket. A halved basket attached to the chair's side, the pocket held magazines, books, glasses, knitting or whatever else the lounger needed. On the other side, a wicker shelf supported the weight of a teacup, mint julep or sandwich. Not merely a chair for sitting and talking, the wicker armchair, with its deep cushions, accommodated both refreshments and entertainment. It offered a place to stay put for a long while—truly, a center of leisure.

Made with the roots and twigs of trees, often with bark intact, rustic furniture flourished inside the architecture of summer. The Chinese first created these arboreal seats centuries ago for gardens. In the eighteenth century when the Landscape was the fashion, the English placed these rustic seats woven of rough limbs in gardens and grottos, as divans of divine nature. Willow twigs were bent into a sort of rough bentwood, or branches were grafted into arboreal armchairs. In North American country houses, these rustic confections stayed outside in summer houses, porches and arbors until woodsy camps of the late nineteenth century brought twig furniture into the living room to symbolize life in nature. This woodsy furniture filled rough fishing camps in New Brunswick, as well as the ornate great camps of the Adirondacks. For once, the hand of the craftsman was entirely overshadowed by the hand of nature, blessedly unable to make straight lines.

Artisans even used tree roots, sawed off perfectly evenly, as table bases. At the height of its popularity, this woodsy furniture became quite elaborate, with mosaic tabletops composed of twigs or birchbark veneers applied to furnishings as sophisticated as sideboards and secretaries—a far cry from the simple twig bent chair. Made of the very woods, rustic furniture represented the presence, the veneration of those woods. Rustic pieces are more than just furniture, as an artisan's advertisement reveals: "Each piece is imbued with the free soul of the wild forest from which it came and is a never-ending statement proclaiming the sacredness of our earth's endangered forests."

The Muskoka chair may not have come from Muskoka or the Adirondacks. Indeed, "The Adirondack chair has not yet proven to have originated in the Adirondacks," states Craig Gilborn, director of the Adirondack Museum, in his definitive work *Adirondack Furniture and the Rustic Tradition*. It may well have come from the Muskoka lakes region. In any case, the Muskoka-Adirondack chair seems homemade; the slats curving into its back could well have been thrown together from old orange crates. The chair may descend from the Westport chair, a piece similar in design, but made of solid wood planks instead of the Adirondack's thin slats. At philosopher John Dewey's old camp, someone showed me one and called it the original Adirondack chair. (Westport chairs have clear beginnings; made in Westport, New York, during this century's first few decades, the originals were patented, the long number stamped onto their backs.)

Whatever the provenance, the wooden armchair with its exaggerated splayed arms sits on motel lawns and wooden decks all over the continent from seashore to seashore, and has become an icon of summer. It bears an uncanny resemblance to the Rietveld chair of the 1920s, a wide, low, multicolored chair created by a Dutch designer, which features in more modern art museums than cottages. Why has the Muskoka-Adirondack chair escaped the museums? Somehow, without padding or upholstery, the sloping angle tilts the pelvis into a comfortable position. And of course the wide arm, recalling an oar, holds a drink, with binoculars or a book on the other side. Unlike wicker, the Muskoka, or Adirondack, chair doesn't move easily, but is anchored to one spot that's pleasant at various times of the day. It's a place to sit for a while, and a while longer. Emblematic of nothing-doing, the gracefully awkward chair is not for sleep, or lounging, but just for sitting around and taking in the surroundings.

Casting its net into a sea of idleness, the hammock is the most important furnishing of the summer house. It is the universal symbol of summer life, from Florida to British Columbia to Sweden and beyond. Called a *hangmatte* in Sweden, or "hanging carpet," it is essential to holidaying decor at Baltic coast houses. It's not surprising that this beach accessory traveled all the way to Sweden, since hammocks came from South America to Africa with the exploring Portuguese, where early European voyagers used them as litters, or as stretchers for the sick.

Sailors seem to have introduced these sleeping nets to North America: a South Carolina riverboat pilot made himself the first Pawley Island hammock for hot nights on his boat back in the 1860s. Now that handwoven rope version is the standard all over, anything else seems like an imitation hammock. The Gloucester hammock comes from that Massachusetts seafaring town, and is sewn from heavy duck, as sturdy as the sails of Gloucester schooners. The Gloucester hammock resembles a long porch swing, rather than the open net, and is a sort of upholstered chair swing, long enough to accommodate naps—the primary purpose of any hammock.

The hammock belongs at summer houses just as jelly goes with peanut butter. Photographs of cottages back in the 1870s show these nets cast between two porch pillars, a shady place where they remain today. Or tied between two tree trunks, the hammock is a shrine to solitude and quiet, a center for siestas. These pieces of rope, or heavy jute string, woven together in a net, symbolize total escape. Advertisements for resorts frequently use an enticing languid image of a bed swinging from the trees, as naturally as a chimp. As idle, hot-weather furnishings, hammocks seldom find homes in city gardens on patios; they just don't fit. You have to be on vacation to loll about in a hammock. It's impossible not to be relaxed while lying in one; its forced recumbency makes working impossible. Furthermore, the hammock conspicuously lacks the right angles of Western civilization. Although Brazilians and Mexicans may spend the night in one, sleep isn't really possible either: the standard version's rope presses itself into expanses of flesh and keeps the lounger slightly awake. The hammock is a place of conscious rest. Breezes can travel right from the ocean to the body. Although fairly wide, hammocks only fit one comfortably and discourage socializing. Since there's usually only one hammock at every summer place, everyone fights to get there first, or takes turns every siesta.

As essential as they are to a summer house, hammocks, wicker, porches and sleeping lofts are but tools with which we shape the experience of summer. Summer gets built differently to remind us where we are, to reinforce the change. Nevertheless, the summer house transcends architecture and its physical form. Like the *cabanon*, the summer house is more often concerned with ideas than with its appearance; cottage architecture is no more than a shell, built to contain the experience of summer.

8. REAPING A HARVEST OF EXPERIENCE

Winter and summer, cold and heat, town and country,
force and freedom, marked two modes of life and thought
balanced like lobes of the brain.

— The Education of Henry Adams

The road to the cottage is known to all. Forty minutes of city traffic, endless prairies of suburban shopping malls paved over pasture, exchanges, beltways and then the highway. The car knows the path: fifty miles north, twenty miles northwest, eleven miles east and then two miles down a dirt road. After skirting cities that throw a yellowish glow into the sky, the car swerves down a curved ramp and turns off onto a two-lane road.

Suddenly, the scale changes: things become smaller and buildings come closer to the road, daring to approach now that cars no longer fly by as fast as jets. The car slows down, as if paying attention to its path like a horse descending a familiar but steep hill. Every few miles a town appears on the road. The same landmarks lead the way, reassuring travelers of their directions—the abandoned gas station, the town with its lights blaring, the roadside diner in the middle of nowhere, with trucks lined up out front for sustenance like puppies on a row of teats.

The halfway mark calls out like a beacon, a lighthouse leading travelers away from the city's shoals. Once you're past that point of no return, the tensions of leaving, packing and getting off on time melt away. Every twist and bump of the road presses itself into the braille of memory: even when riding in the back seat, eyes closed, you would know where you were by the swerve of the road.

So familiar, that voyage becomes a personal unit of measure. When a quarter of his jail sentence was finished, Czech playwright and later president Vaclav Havel, in a letter to his wife, Olga, compared his prison sentence to the voyage to his country house. "If it were a journey from Hrádaček to Prague, I'd be somewhere just outside of Jičín." The treacherous hills and curves now lay behind him; he looked only down a straight road, the destination well within sight.

As the horizon opens up to water, the car is exchanged for a fast boat or slow ferry. The Iron City history describes the journey to the family camp on Lake Huron: "But there is still something magical about leaving your car and cares behind and heading up the bay toward the open water . . ." The possibilities of summer open up and spread out one by one onto the horizon. That water crossing punctuates the transition from the heavy world of responsibility to the fanciful world of summer. Somehow, a ferry crossing is the most thrilling trip, possessing the size and ceremony of a seagoing voyage, yet ruthlessly edited so that only the pleasures of embarking and disembarking remain. We leave the confines of a car, to stand at the prow of the ferry, right behind the heavy chain that discourages cars from crossing its boundary. These are front-row seats for the opening gala, where deep swells send up a spray of mist to the orchestra. (No one ever stands at the stern, except for the return voyage.) After passing slowly through the channel, the ferry enters open water, the island appears on the horizon, a little to the left, a spot of green and white. The island reveals more and then a bit more of itself as the boat approaches, and the final vision takes your breath away. As the island comes into focus, the passengers point out their houses, picking out from scrubby trees one little dot among many.

Finally, the vessel collides into its berth, metal against metal— the rare crash that inspires a positive excitement. Cars rumble off the ferry in a maddeningly preordained sequence; the tires roll with a rugged boom, boom, boom onto the dock. They head off with the certainty of the homing instinct, and that urgency to get to a county house the Roman writer Lucretius compared to colts being driven to save a burning house. This is the home stretch, painfully prolonged by roads, unmaintained and bumpy as a washboard, vibrating and shaking. So close now, the anticipation builds to a feverish pitch: almost there, almost there, almost there—like a dog straining at the leash, pulling and pulling as it nears the park, then let loose, bounding off into wide-open space.

This open space is a different world, without street signs, corner stores or sidewalks. The roads have no names, the houses, set well off the road, have no numbers. Entrances go unmarked, barely noticeable, except for a break in the row of trees, or a flat spot where no dune grasses grow. Traveling into the landscape of summer means navigating by natural landmarks, finding the way by ponds, boulders, hills and trees. Naming the roads, numbering the cottages would put them on the map, taking away the anonymity of hiding places. So just after the marsh, you turn onto the little road, and keep going until just past the boulder and there at the top of the little hill lies the house, shuttered and deep in its sleep.

When seen for the first time, the vision is one inspiring desire, or love. After pushing, encouraging and prodding a mule over-loaded with possessions to the top of a Provençal hill, Maurice Pagnol looked upon the valley of Auban for the first time: ". . . and so the holiday began, and I sensed a love grow that would last all my life." The love was for the chalk hills of the Provençal landscape, painted by Cézanne and versified by Plutarch. It was a love that inspired him always, resulting in books about Manon and her spring, and his own childhood memoirs, *My Father's Glory*. For those who have already fallen in love, that view at the top of the hill is a reunion with a lover, with the excitement of rediscovery and the comfort of familiarity.

Before unpacking, or opening up the house, formalities must be observed, which means saying hello to the place, looking things over and comparing the view against the memory that has been collecting dust. When going back to the place of her childhood summers, a woman tells me that she runs frantically about the place, checking the dock and paths to make sure nothing has changed. Usually nothing has; perhaps a tree collapsed in a storm, the dunes have shifted and some boards loosened here and there in integral spots, but the place is what it was. It's as constant and obvious as Orion in the night sky.

That first look confirms the place stayed just as memory left it, because little changes in the landscape of summer. There is immense virtue in that immutability; that changelessness renders everything familiar. Every detail is as easy to retrace as one's own signature: the sound wind makes in the screens, the humid feel of sea air, how the door sticks in the heat.

Returning to the pocket of Maine where he holidayed as a boy, E. B. White wrote, "This seemed an utterly enchanted sea, this lake you could come back to, and find that it had not stirred, this constant and trustworthy body of water." Trees and houses may come and go; the lake itself remains.

Those bonds made with a landscape are as resistant to change as the landscape itself. That promise of changelessness is as appealing as the pleasure about to be had. Her grandmother's house, says one friend, is a time capsule from the 1960s—the furniture, the dishes, everything remains the same. Any attempt to alter the smallest detail would be shouted down, voted out by the family members now running the cottage. Summer places archive a family's past, undisturbed by the changes of real life. A grandmother's playing cards, worn down at the edges by endless evenings of canasta, outlive their owner and will be there always.

To William James, this homecoming into summers past contained an odd mixture of sadness and delight: "The sadness of *things*—things every one of which was done either by our hand, or by our planning, old furniture renovated, there isn't an object in the house that isn't asociated with past life, old summers, dead people, people who will never come again," he wrote, "and the way it catches you round the heart when you first come and open the house from its long winter sleep is most extraordinary." It catches you with all those associations—associations that gather as thickly as the layers of dust and spiderwebs accumulated over the winter. What James saw in his closed-up house was not objects of the past, but past *experiences* risen up at him. Just as the notion of home transcends the house, so a summer home transcends its physicality.

A summer house is more than a house. It provides more than togetherness and a well-worn tan. What the cabin or cottage or camp offers is *experience*. No matter how closely a second house may rival a first—with dishwashers, cushions, television, neighbors and all the rest—nevertheless, its walls shape a different way of life. Living in another house, far from real life, closer to the natural world, engenders a very specific experience. Different it may be, yet the experience is eternal and unchanging. Centuries ago, Pliny the Younger described it in part.

> For besides the attractions which I have mentioned, the greatest is the relaxation and carefree luxury of the place—there is no need for a toga, the neighbors do not come to call, it is always quiet and peaceful—advantages as great as the healthful situation and limpid air. I always feel energetic and fit for anything at my Tuscan villa, both mentally and physically. I exercise my mind by study, my body by hunting. My household too flourishes better here than elsewhere . . .

Epistles V.vi.45

What is the experience of the summer? It's life out-of-doors, an elemental life with water to drench in, fire to barbecue with and untainted air to sip and drink deep into the lungs. It's direct and engages each of the senses. Every day presents an overwhelming richness of things to do, and there's an appetite for it all. It starts with a carnival atmosphere, a feeling of celebration that swells up as soon as the sweat and worry of packing are miles behind.

When first visiting the town of Castine, Maine, Katharine Butler Hathaway felt this atmosphere of mirth, and suspected a powerful invisible intoxicating presence at work—the genius of the place: ". . . under its influence the behavior of hitherto conventional, cautious summer visitors can be completely disrupted and can give way to a mood of unprecedented personal allurement and joyous abandon which they generally lose again after those two or three weeks are over." It's as though a primitive aphrodisiac suddenly made brittle and conventional people succumb, says Hathaway, to "boldness and gaiety." Most summer places produce the same magical effect. Like champagne at a party, the place itself promises celebrations and celebrating. All of life is so gaily decorated that even daily chores seem fun; I've heard many people compare life at the cottage to "playing house," going about the ordinarily tedious tasks of life, cooking, getting wood and doing repairs with the delight of a child moving imaginary people around a dollhouse.

The Sensual Bath

Every summer, when we opened up our family beach house, the smell of baked cedar overcame me at the doorway, pouring out like smoke. The combination of sun hitting the roof, closed shutters and precut cedar planks cooked into this heady, aromatic confection. That cedar smell symbolized the beginning of summer, powerfully recalling summers past and awakening all the senses. Along with the cedar perfuming the house, there was the sweet taste of brackish water that washed off the stickiness of dried saltwater, like a chaser after a shot of Scotch. Even sheets felt different at the cottage. On certain days—what would have been laundry days in town had water been unlimited—the sheets were aired out in the sun. I slipped in between two crisp pieces of cloth, like a bookmark between two pages. To this day, cedar casts a spell over me, even though the house was sold to another family and our snapshots have faded, turning the blue sea green.

Apparently odor and memory are powerfully connected in some nether region of the brain, as smells evoke the most powerful emotional memories, transporting us clearly and uncannily into the past. And when people reminisce about their retreats, they talk about the smell of the place: the sea air, the pine woods, the hay from surrounding farms. Women who frequented Adirondack camps once made balsam pillows to send to friends, importing the smell of summer into the city.

Leaving the city takes you into the realm of the senses—the kingdom children inhabit until they've suffered years of stifling classrooms and even more years of television, until they no longer seek to know an object by tasting it. Surviving in the city requires that the natural sharpness of our senses—so crucial to surviving in the wild—be dulled like an old knife. To open your senses in the city is to be assaulted. Screeching sirens or sparring neighbors cloud concentration. Black belches of truck exhaust and foul clouds hovering over metropolitan areas discourage any savoring of the air. The jostling of other bodies in elevators, on crowded streets, goes unfelt, unnoticed. With skin swaddled in layers of cloth and feet bound in leather, you're protected from the environment. According to Rhonda and Robert Rapoport in *Leisure and the Family Life-cyle*, the mania for second houses stems from a need for "sensory gratification."

Constantly starved, all five senses are hungry, and feast in the summer banquet. Describing Nantucket life of the 1880s in *'Sconset Cottage Life*, Judd Northrup wrote, "All the senses are lulled to luxurious rest, and we would be content to sail on under the summer sky on an endless day like this . . . We gaze and dream and drink the air, and hear the gentle whispers of the sea; while ever and anon, we peer into the distance along the horizon where sea and sky mingle." Not merely a vision, the landscape is experienced in all its dimensions, devoured with a lusty appetite. In a letter, William James explained how he tired of the vacuous excitements of civilization, and craved the sensorial excitement of his camp in the Adirondacks: "the smell of spruce, the feel of the moss, the sound of the cataract, the bath in its waters, the divine outlook from the cliff . . ." Escaping the urban environment turns the spigot to our bottled-up senses. And the senses open up a whole new world of experience: the faint song of far-off tree frogs, the smell of warming sap, the taste of rain. Those sensations provide texture to which memories can adhere, clinging for years.

Summer is about bathing in sensations; bathing in light, bathing in the sun, bathing in the water. Although we call it swimming, most of us merely bathe—without thoughts of laps or speed.

We float, buoyed by the salt water, traveling where the current goes. This kind of swimming is not exercising, but rather *experiencing* the very qualities of water itself. Water, salt or sweet, lulls the skin into feelings of well-being. Without a swimsuit, the body feels as fluid as the water itself. All the drag is gone, and it seems we could slide through the water like a smooth-skinned porpoise. At poet Edna St. Vincent Millay's place, Ragged Island, poetic policy dictated that neither residents nor guests submit to the restriction of bathing costumes, tightly wrapped bandages that keep sun, air and sea from the skin and otherwise covered parts of the body. (Humans seem to be the only animals who appreciate water for how it makes them feel. Birds dip and drink at baths, horses will swim a river, if prodded. Certainly, dogs jump in a stream on a hot day, or chase a stick thrown into the ocean. But how many gently bob up and down in the waves for the pure pleasure of it?) Water isn't just something to drink, or wash with, or cross, but deserves to be savored for its very own qualities, and so it is savored during the morning, afternoon and late afternoon swim. Each type of water creates a different bathing experience. Cold seas grab and squeeze your heart, in a wet kind of strangulation, until the body adjusts to the chill. Swimming in lakes or rivers washed with the sediment of mineral rock leaves a taste in your mouth, of sweet iron, or of chalky lime. Each type of water dries on the skin differently, as the sun evaporates it.

After that, we bathe in the sun, the summer's glory. To sunbathe is to experience the sensations of the sun itself, letting it warm the marrow deep inside your bones. There is no purpose apart from the experience itself. Sunbathing is for summers spent at the cottage, tanning is for quick weekends at holiday hotels. In contrast to this cursory scaring of the skin, sunbathing is a slow boil, where the heat spreads gently and evenly into every pore. It feels just as good when you're covered head to toe in caftan and hat, or through a window that permits the sun's warmth to penetrate—like a self-made sauna. For sunbathing is actually about warmth. Even a dog, on a sunny day, will choose the sunny spot shaped by the window frame to lie down in and warm itself. It's a natural craving, a mysterious version of photosynthesis. It might be the state of perfect rest.

Active Rest

On holidays, the mind goes on vacation and the body gets to work. The body that usually supports the brain with no greater purpose than a stand displaying a bronze bust now awakens, propels us forward. Mildred Phelps Stokes Hooker described a typical day's activities in her Adirondack memoir: ". . . tennis most of the morning; swimming before lunch; sailing in the afternoon; tea at 4:30 or 5:00; supper at 6:30; canoeing until 10:00; refreshments and talk in the dining room until 11:00; then bed." Unfortunately, she was limited in her swimming time as the TB doctor down the lake convinced her mother that spending more than twenty minutes in the water was deleterious to one's health—perhaps simply bringing on the prune effect. Although she was describing the sporty days in the 1880s, her descendants probably keep to the same athletic schedule. Sports connect us to the outdoors; they are an active form of nature worship and a disguised training of survival skills. And sometimes people make a sport of labor itself.

This practice of physical leisure reaches its apotheosis when the industrious actually build their own summer house, as did Witold Rybczynski. Architect Rybczynski set out to build a boathouse, where he planned to conduct the business of building a boat. Eventually, he abandoned boat building and redesigned the house for weekend living, and immortalized it in his book *The Most Beautiful House in the World*. It remained "the Boathouse" in name, in spite of embracing a less constructive function.

Even when it's already built, owning a summer house inspires much physical activity: repairing docks, pulling down dead trees, bush-hogging meadows, tending the vegetable patch, building fences or repairing whatever else falls apart. For some reason, people who abhor and evade chores at home relish them at the cottage. Somehow dreary maintenance is transformed into something that evokes the life of the woodsman and pioneer.

In Czechoslovakia, where a large percentage of the population spends time at country places, pottering and tinkering have practically become the national sport. In Czech, they call it "active rest." Experiencing this active rest in his garden outside Hartford, Connecticut, Charles Dudley Warner wrote, "In half an hour, I can hoe myself right away from this world, as we commonly see it, into a large place where there are no obstacles. What an occupation it is for thought! The mind broods like a hen on eggs. The trouble is you are not thinking about anything, but are really vegetating like the plants around you." Exerting the body becomes relaxation for the mind.

At his country house, Winston Churchill practiced the art of bricklaying and constructed small outbuildings with his own mortar and hand. He pursued this hobby so ardently that the bricklayers' union gave him a card entitling him to membership. Unlike much repetitive, abstract work of town, the projects and putterings of summer yield immediate, physical and tangible results: a house, a wall, a squash. The Benedictine monks even thought labor to be a kind of prayer that transports the worker to holier realms. So it is, at a monastery or a weekend garden.

This physicality of life changes everything. Hunger works on its own clock and sleep comes easily, lullabied with fresh air, salt air, mountain air. Gardening, hunting or fishing delivers a double joy of movement, as the body becomes a life-sustaining tool, a functional rather than a decorative object, even if only for a day or two. Back in town, aches resonate in hitherto ignored parts of the body, and somehow it's not unpleasant to be reminded of the wonderful complexity of the musculature. Ever aware of the varieties of experience, William James described the physicality of life at his farm: ". . . exercising my arms as well as my legs several hours a day, and already feeling that bodily and spiritual freshness that come of health and of which no other good on earth is worthy to unlatch the shoe . . ."

There's a directness of life at the summer house. We *experience* firsthand and for ourselves the world and our place in it. This is not the case in the city, where we consume experience rather than create it—scanning newspapers and watching television, reading books and listening to the radio. In other words, we ingest and digest other people's experience. Even vacations spent touring cathedrals and castles represent another form of spectatorship; travelers take pictures, buy postcards and watch Parisians or Patagonians go about their daily business, in the manner of a sideshow. With its sports and projects, sensory baths and view into the natural world, a summer house encourages first-person experience. We act. We do. We are. The trip we take is from the passive to the active voice, choosing among a bounty of verbs to fill the day. I fished, I swam, I walked, I slept, I birded, I golfed, I cut wood, I lived to tell the tale. We make sentences giving "I" top billing and giving experience reality for ourselves. The circus of birds that performs outside is more compelling than any televised nature special, regardless of errors in behavioral interpretation. As we sit on the porch at night, a chorus of tree frogs and crickets fills the night air, rather than some composer's impression of the world—and an orchestra's interpretation of that impression. There is already music there. Often, summer houses with the richest experience are those without media since mediums get in the middle.

Camped Out in a Natural State

From the high porch, the woods pitching down to the lake are more than a known and loved place. They are a habitat we were once fully adapted to, a sort of Peaceable Kingdom where species such as ours might evolve unchallenged and find their step of the staircase of being.

— Wallace Stegner, *Crossing to Safety*

Although roofed and walled, the summer house, by bringing us closer to nature, encourages us to become more natural beings, and therein lies its compelling attraction. "I suspect that many of us are, after all, really camping temporarily in civilized conditions; and that going into the wilderness is an escape longed for, into our natural and preferred state," said Charles Dudley Warner. In Warner's time, people may have lived in flimsy tents during their escape into the Adirondacks, as opposed to our comfortable cottages, yet our desire for a preferred natural state remains the same. Biologist and environmental thinker René Dubos said that spending time in the wilderness lets people revert to the state of Paleolithic man. Part of existing in that more natural state is experiencing nature itself. So we escape to diluted wilderness and live a little more directly—experiencing a more natural life.

The day itself keeps its natural rhythm and we live out the full cycle of the day. Shadows glide, as on a giant sundial, from one side to another, and each day has a beginning, middle and end. And night falls like an alarm going off. The highlights of the daily cycle become events in themselves, transcending any human activity, influencing and dictating it. Sunrise and sunset are observed like rituals. Sunsets, changing as often as the soup du jour, remain one of the most spellbinding natural events, their glory doubled over water. W. D. Howells remembers how they used the river for watching sunsets. On Michigan's peninsula, cottagers used to leave smaller inland lakes and drive over to watch sunsets on Lake Michigan, where the peeled-back horizon soaked up the entire reflection. Dozens of cars parked alongside the beach's de facto theater, as families watched the quick, brilliant red path of the sun. Of course, sunsets happen every day, but there's rarely the space or time to notice them. On vacation, however, they become an event, a daily ritual to observe. There is time to appreciate the sun's pirouette.

Camping in this natural state demands no activity. Although he could not throw a fly, Dwight Sedgwick tells of fishing trips in the woods near Murray Bay. "The pleasure was to get up at daybreak, take a quick bath in the lake, drink morning coffee, sit complacently in the flat-bottomed fishing boat, forget the rod, and watch the glory of the rosy clouds at their matins, magnifying the Lord, and at sunset (while the golden light upon the lake passed into silver, and the first put off their greenery and stood solemn for their evening prayers) to listen to the frogs and to fish jumping everywhere except within reach of my rod, and see the stars come out one by one." The surroundings themselves become entertainment, something to observe as intently as a painting or a culture under a microscope.

Observing becomes itself a pleasure. In the country quiet, you notice the slightest rustling of leaves, and the small lizards who cause it. With senses tuned as delicately as the four strings on a violin, you can see in detail. There's a sense of wonder at the smallest things, even a mosquito crawling on your skin before making its strike. The comings and goings of the humblest creatures become worthy of study. It's a soft and passive observation that leads to an almost hypnotic state. Binoculars bring things closer; a bird on the wing looks inches away, as each feather reveals a particular pattern of coloration.

When we live closer to the outdoors, not hermetically sealed away in airtight buildings, weather matters. Part of living closer to the outdoors means we are more affected by weather's mercurial changes. In cities, the daily pattern continues as usual, regardless of rain, snow or winds outside; at a summer house, weather determines the order of the day. Suddenly, weather and the quality of life are intensely linked. A rainy day needs a good book. The day after a storm yields a bounty of shells washed onto the beach, waiting for greedy beachcombers. A windy day sends sailors on the water and keeps canoeists on land. When paid attention to, weather affects us. Judd Northrup wrote, "These days of storm seemed to impress the entire summer population of 'Sconset with awe. They forgot to be witty and jocose and went about as if a tragedy of some kind had occured in the midst . . ." At the sign of a storm, picnickers and hikers rush back to their den, their shelter, their cottage, scurrying with the same sense of urgency displayed by birds floating to cover.

Thunderstorms, with all their inherent drama, are summer entertainment. Blue light flashes on the walls, the house shakes, the glass rattles and lightning pierces the sky, as the audience huddled inside counts the seconds between each jagged sliver of light. The lights are turned off or blown out, and the house sits down for the show.

The temperature itself decides whether the day is active or indolent. Weather is so vital to the quality of the day that houses are often equipped with the tools of atmospheric prediction: barometers, thermometers, wind socks. Part of knowing a place is learning its weather, observing the patterns and atmospheric happenings; no book reveals this meterological fortune-telling. It's a skill of people living closer to the land. After several summers, sailors learn to read the amazing combination of cloud, wind, waves, activity of fish and gulls, until they tell the story of perfect wind conditions of fast tacking into the wind.

Sometimes just surviving the weather becomes the day's activity—downing endless icy glasses, taking swims whenever the cooling effects of the last have worn off. When visiting his friend Edith Wharton, Henry James became undone by the heat wave that lingered like malevolent cloud over the Massachusetts Berkshires, accustomed as he was to tepid English summers when strawberries ripen in late June. Wharton had recently acquired an automobile, and delighted in taking visitors for drives. She soon discovered that only motoring relieved her friend and mentor of the oppressive temperature, as the auto was open on all four sides, as all were at the time. So the two literary figures spent several days sailing through the countryside in her new motor, with the wind in their faces. They visited villages in the vicinity, stopping occasionally to get the novelist something cooling at a soda fountain, and continued this mobile air conditioning until James returned to temperate England.

The Directness of Food

Fishing, berry-picking, hunting, clamming, mushrooming—in the farm of summer, a perpetual harvest offers itself to those who seek it. Even if refrigerators brim over with delicacies brought from town, we work at feeding ourselves and go berrying or fishing anyway. It's simply one of the things to do. We can hunt and gather; sustenance is there for the taking. Food gathering itself becomes an experience to savor as much as the taste itself: nibbling berries off the bush like birds or raking the sand for hidden clams. I know a woman who steps outside her house into the woods for an early morning walk, collecting berries in a little plastic sack as she goes, and brings them back for what she considers the ultimate breakfast. The proliferation of "pick-your-own" farms proves the universality of this thrill: not going to the store, choosing, paying for, unwrapping and finally eating berries, but picking them directly off the plant, grazing like animals.

There's a wonderful sense of satisfaction in getting your own food, and a confrontation with one of the central facts of life. In recalling her childhood days at Newport during its golden age, Edith Wharton says, "From the landing we used to fish for 'scuppers' and 'porgies,' succulent little fish that were grilled or fried for tea . . ." Someone else probably fried her fish, but no matter—the succulence came from the catching of it. Eating a fish of your own catching, a blueberry pie of your own picking, elevates nourishment to narrative, giving it a clear beginning, middle and end.

For once, we're connected and involved in what we eat. Teddy Roosevelt supplied his ranch with game, Mabel Bell boasted of making jam herself. Even barbecuing, the summer method of cooking, answers this need to get a little closer to food, as we watch meat cook under our very own eyes, not shut out from the process by an oven door. Cooking becomes a communual, ritual act, as diners and chef stand over the fire, and the process of cooking transcends the food itself.

The Directness of Doing

Pumps break, and mend with duct tape. Docks miraculously hold together with slapdash engineering. There is a self-reliant atmosphere of making do at a summer house. Away from the city, many revel in that sense of getting along and making do. Life presents certain challenges; no service people are nearby and no city government takes care of things. If you want water, you have to get it. If something needs fixing, you fix it. Our innate ingenuity is challenged, and it often triumphs. Down in Nova Scotia years and years ago, a city businessman devised an ingenious water pump system, using a waterwheel, which finally delivered water into his little cottage. Problems are no longer abstract but need real solutions: a boulder blocking an addition, supplies that are too heavy to be carried up the hill. In the Echo Lake newsletter, a man tells the story of moving a 1,900-pound boulder from the site where he wanted to build. Although it happened over a decade ago, it's a story worth repeating, of a man's struggle with granite's nature. He tells of putting a line on a tree, chains around the rock, planks under it and using a hand winch and a prodding crowbar to move the huge rock twenty-five feet away from his house. On a Georgian Bay island, another man devised his own three-horsepower railroad; five little freight cars chugged his supplies up the steep fifty-foot rise. The solutions, just as real as the problems, give tangible proof of self-sufficiency.

Many people—and especially men—relish this sense that they have only themselves to rely on. "If you get hurt up at the cabin, you're not going to get medical attention anytime soon," a Californian who sometimes travels to his cabin 7,600 feet above sea level by snowshoes explained to me. "If there's a fire, you're not going to see the fire department for two or three hours. You *have* to be self-reliant." Not about surviving, living at the cottage is, rather, about getting by.

A Necklace of Sundays

Henry James once said the words *summer afternoon* were among the most beautiful in the English language. A summer afternoon speaks of total contentment and leisure, for unlike nature, we rest during the summer. The morning's work—or play—is done, a lunch eaten lustily out-of-doors has sated all hunger. Only the siesta and the rest of the long afternoon stretch out before you. Even the afternoons of summer are themselves languid, lasting until nine or ten in the evening. A summer afternon is the ultimate leisure.

Leisure is really about freedom. *Leisure*, after all, means "freedom"—with its roots in the Latin word *licere*, "to be allowed." Houses dedicated to leisure are about freedom. No rules bind. The atmosphere promises freedom from expectations and routines. Freed from social conventions and social pretensions (at more relaxed summer colonies), you don't even have to mow the lawn if there is one. You can wear your oldest clothes or go to bed at any hour. It's the one place where a body is free to do what it wants—after scrounging two or three meals a day. Suddenly, we're allowed to do what we please. "It's awfully peaceful to sit here without the news blaring, to watch the sunset and those mountains and make dinner when you darn well *feel like it*," says one woman who summers in the Adirondacks.

This attitude is not new. "What's left undone today can be done to-morrow," promised a nineteenth-century article on Nantucket, "and the nervous man of affairs from the bustling city who is in the habit of doing everything on the jump learns amid these restful surroundings, to take things leisurely." Writing about her place on Lake Superior, Frances Hutchinson says, "The simple fact of awakening in the morning at no especial time, with no appointments is in itself so pleasing a feature of country life that I should think it would commend itself to all city folk. The utter ignoring of time, the scorn of man's invention, the obliteration of the passing moment, does it not bring us to a keener realization of the eternal."

With the freedom of leisure comes the freedom from the conventions of time.

And watches get put away in a drawer. "I always say about Nantucket that after a day you can throw away your watch, and after a week your calendar," said that island's champion and Svengali, Walter Beinecke. What's true for Nantucket applies to other summer places that exist in the universal time zone of leisure, where watches are banished. Days are not marked by hours, but are stretched out to their full length. You can tell the time of day by the sun's position or by the tides. In the Sierras, the day officially begins for a family when the sun slants into their sleeping porch in midmorning—certainly the quietest kind of prodding by any alarm. A woman who spent childhood summers at the top of the St. Lawrence River remembers staying in the water for a full cycle of the tide. The water's coming in signaled her day was over. The chef who works as an olive grower for a few weeks a year says, "It seems like the clock has stopped because no one's rushing you, olives take their own time to ripen. You can't rush them." Olives ripen once they've drunk their fill of sun, and that moment is abritary, unknowable.

Summer-house time is a continuum; days of the week blur one into the other, a necklace of Sundays strung together. Time passes differently away from newspapers and calendars. What day of the week, what day of the month doesn't matter as much as the quality of the day. Time's passage is marked by natural events, rather than by goings-on in the greater world. The summer of the eclipse stands out more than the winter of the election. Summer-house time represents a voyage into the calendar of a more natural being. Years are marked by hurricanes, like Agnes from the graduating class of 1973 who claimed hundreds of miles of southeastern beaches.

Outside the FM frequencies of cities, quiet is the only station on the dial. No human sounds cloud the reception. No engines, no cries, no highway, no horns, no lawn mowers. Getting away from people means escaping from their noise; on Nantucket, there was once a village constable whose job was to keep the place quiet. Yet, this quiet is not silence—the total absence of sound, which exists only in the cruelest tanks of sensory deprivation. The quiet of retreats is the quiet of the natural world, gentle sounds like the flight of hummingbirds, the lapping of a lake on the shore, the wind ruffling the feathers of the trees, the furious clucking of a ruffed grouse.

People leave the city to escape its noise, and exchange it for country quiet—a quiet so mesmerizing that machines duplicate it for insomniacs. It's a silence that satiates. In that quiet, you can hear the sound made by the machine of the world, a cranking of the cogs and wheels inside the earth. At this moment, I hear crows and the high-pitched whir and buzz of heat bugs—they're called June bugs even in July. The crows eventually stop their clatter, but the buzz abates and rises at undetermined intervals, reassuring that everything is as it was, constant as breath itself. I hear no car, no echo from the pounding of a hammer on some fence in the valley. Only planes roaring overhead ruin the illusion of an Edenic world. Despite the crows and June bugs, this is quiet, the kind of quiet that erases the outside world. It's a quiet to soak in, it pours over you like water. This orchestra and chorus is the music of the cottage, the lullaby of reverie and dreaming.

All along the verandas of the East and West coasts, and throughout the middle, too, rocking chairs form an assembly line of idleness. Rocking, or swinging in the hammock, glider or porch swing is a way to seem active while doing nothing. Yet doing nothing is a perfectly acceptable summer activity. After all, it first caught on with the aristocratic classes who did nothing all year round. Now during allotted vacation time, we play at aristocratic idleness. The Italians have a name for this kind of summertime sloth; they call it *il dolce far niente*, "the sweetness of doing nothing." Idleness is really the dessert of life, the reward that digests a winter of labor. I call it lying around, and it's a noble occupation.

Strangely, we travel to a separate house to feel that we are allowed this nothingness, absolving ourselves of the ever-present duty of work. A cottage releases us from the terrible cold-weather compulsion to do something—with the afternoon or with the rest of our short lives. Over and over again, people have told me, "I don't feel guilty about doing nothing." So the busy, achieving class of society works harder and saves money in order to buy houses where there is no room for busyness or achieving. Even idleness has a point. It is actually *good* for us, as healthful as mineral baths or upland resinous air. The authors of *Time Off* say that "*doing nothing is an integral part of self renewal*, it provides the breathing space needed by everyone's scolding inner voice that can make us feel we're wasting time." It's okay not to work while on vacation, and at a vacation house. The lounge ethic replaces the work ethic; chaise longues and hammocks call out to all passersby, sirens of loafing. Finally, indolence and idleness are permitted, although, of course, they are clothed in the respectability of rest.

The siesta is just such an institutionalized form of nothingness, when people don't necessarily sleep but shut down the system for brief hibernation. A siesta means lying down somewhere, eyes open or closed, with thoughts turned inward or outward onto the nature scene before you. One Victorian brochure for seaside cottages put it this way: "Laziness drifts into sleep and sleep awakens into laziness; so gradual is the change it is hard to tell where one ends and the other begins," promising a state of altered conciousness. Indeed, the atmosphere is meditative—turning off the awareness of everyday reality and opening up to another. The view becomes a visual mantra, stared at blindly for hours, the horizon a focus point where all attentiveness rests. Life itself seems to take a deep breath and doing decelerates into being.

The cottage experience is really a fantasy, a few weeks of life with the barbs removed. The senses are teased into wakefulness and then gently put to rest; the heart is warmed by the summertime hearth and the people around it; the body accepts and meets its own challenges; the soul has room to run in any direction. Arabic has a charming word to describe this, *mazag*. The ablest translation is "all desires are answered." There's nothing more to wish for, when blessed with gaudy sunset, fresh fish on the table, a breeze that tickles faintly as a feather, family and friends gathered. Some people call this simply the sensation of being alive.

To really live, to experience the pleasures of life acutely—this is what we experience at the summer house. It's living for the very moment, concentrating and reveling in it. Pliny felt energetic, fit for anything. At his farm, William James experienced a feeling to which no other could compare to "unlatch the shoe." Reuniting with his place of past summers, the protagonist of Wallace Stegner's novel *Crossing to Safety* muses, "I wonder if I've ever felt more alive, more competent in my mind and more at ease with myself and my world, than I feel for a few minutes on the shoulder of that known hill while I watch the sun climb powerfully and confidently and see below me the unchanged village, the lake like a pool of mercury . . ."

Taking Leave

As nightfall descends earlier, the summer comes to an end, and the summer house returns to its winter hibernation. The rocks and sticks scattered around the house are packed in boxes to come back to the city, where they become paperweights or simply fill the closet. Sometimes, these souvenirs are repatriated: one woman in Maine takes all the amazingly colored and sculpted stones that guests had brought to the cottage as gifts, and brings them back to the beach.

So the house is packed up, cleaned out, defrosted and emptied of all the water halfway through the pipes. The beds are stripped, the cupboard emptied of food. Screens are stored under the house, and shutters cover the picture window, the eye of the cyclops. Embalmed in cleaning smells, the house becomes a lifeless, barren shell.

After the house is shuttered and closed, there's one last task, to say good-bye to the place and pay last respects to the view. The parting is a calm and quiet observance, rather like a moment of silence. A long, hard look exposes everything onto the film of memory. Even before you leave, homesickness sets in, a sad missing of the place. Months later, you may need to summon that image of a lake, to imagine the freedom, to remember how quiet really sounds, to summon the pleasures of idleness. Those stored feelings are dipped into, to cure the restlessness of sleepless nights. Whenever she is troubled, a woman I know imagines herself sitting on the dock at her cottage, dipping her feet in the water—mimicking the calm of that water. Those feelings and sensations are banked and saved like pennies. When hot and feverish with toil, wrinkles and worries, Adirondack travel-guide writer Reverend Murray wrote that he would throw down his book and fancy himself once more upon that bank: "Blessed be the recollection, which it allows the ills and cares of life to fade away, enables us to carry all our pleasures and joys forever with us as we journey along." Mildred Phelps Stokes Hooker described how, as a child, just the thought of the place would make her happy, as she'd repeat the incantation, "Never mind, we're going to the Adirondacks." Summer is the reward, and planning for the next one starts as soon as you've made the trip home.

As much as the trip there is feverish and frantic, the return is slower, thoughtful, with the taking of last looks while there's still something to look at. It seems entirely unnecessary to leave. A country house book from 1865 described this leavetaking: "They returned to town in the early days of September, with many a backward glance, longing look at the attractions and delights from which they reluctantly tore themselves away . . ."

Getting away and coming home. We talk about both with the greatest anticipation. The call of the wild gets drowned out by the allure of city lights. At the end of one summer, W. D. Howells faulted those who had returned to town, but confessed, "I myself sniff the asphalt afar; the roar of the street calls to me with the magic that the voice of the sea is losing." Getting away promises excitement, adventure, escape. And coming home promises warmth, familiarity and finding things just as they were left. Without a homecoming, going away would hold no pleasure but would equal banishment, exile. After spending time at a second home, the first home welcomes you back, and you wonder what made you want to leave. Stacked to the sky with libraries, people, ideas and culture—all miraculous gifts of civilization—the city seems a rich and wondrous place and all its shortcomings temporarily forgiven.

Funnily, one of the finest things about going away is coming home. A woman who travels from Ontario to her family cottage in the Maritimes explained it this way: "I'm always so happy to go to Nova Scotia, but then a few weeks later, I'm just as happy to come back." In the physics of summer houses, they are equal and opposite attractions.

AFTERWORD:
GOING AWAY AND COMING HOME

Whatever road to progress he takes man will reach a desirable destination only if he is guided by the direct perception of his senses, and by the yearning for elemental modes
of life.

— René Dubos, *A God Within*

T own and country are equally enticing and yet opposite in
their attractions. And a summer house gives us residency in both
worlds. Otherwise, we'd have no rights in one, no responsibilities
for the other. It reconciles the civilized and wilder aspects of our
nature, so that we may be half-cultivated—pruned garden and
untamed forest. Most of us want dual citizenship, without having to
swear allegiance to only one world. That means moving fluidly from
one to the other, conversant in two languages—from hailing cabs to
knowing when berries will be at their sweetest. But if one world
were to become like the other, blend into the other, if the dunes

should be flattened, the woods cleared, there would be no reason to leave town. The herons, the dunes, the woods provide the contrast from the city, bringing out the rest in high relief.

With nature in short supply, the privilege of enjoying it comes with responsibility. Taking a bite out of a place makes us responsible, answerable, and the relationship becomes reciprocal. As long as a house stands, its inhabitants are implicated in the landscape. Not floating high above the land, our weight sits on top. No longer separate, we become part of it—tied to a place by the very act of sheltering ourselves from it. Rather than letting the house's footprint sink deeper and deeper, we can try to make that footprint, and our own steps, lighter. And so, many summer people have become rangers assigned to their own park.

The innumerable and growing lake-resident associations formed by a quorum of part-time inhabitants are attempts to help preserve and protect a place, as it was, as it's remembered. Sensing the frailty of the difference that brings life out in high relief, these people are nursing it. It starts as a selfish desire to keep things just as they are. Feeling it's home, even for only a few weeks, we want to protect the place, for our own enjoyment of course, but also for the sake of the place. As people who enjoy it, we have a stake in its future, and want to preserve it until the next visit. Land trusts, easements slapped onto deeds, these legal devices are about keeping things pristine, valuing views over profits, preserving habitats rather than adding houses. When these measures move into the future, easements continuing into perpetuity, those actions go even beyond selfish concerns for unblemished views and water that's swimmingly clean, and represent a sincere feeling for the place, its goodness and the need to leave it be—for no other purpose but itself.

Beyond maintaining the landscape outside the summer house, we need to maintain the values inside—which transcend real estate. Those values, misplaced during the other seasons, have built the summer house. And if they go missing, the meaning of the place itself is lost—its difference papered over.

Unfortunately, as the phrase *second house* has become more common, so, too, the one is coming to resemble the other. The distinctions between first and second are attenuating, the difference fading. Civilization inches closer to summer colonies and the colonies themselves inch toward civilization. Electricity and water systems have followed the cabin into its previously undisturbed clearing. The telephone has come, too, not to be left out in case of emergencies, problems at the office or snakebites in the field. I'm not saying voltage, municipal water or phones are a bad thing, but as they arrive, certain things go. Gone are nights by the fireside. Gone is the taste of springwater, and the challenge of fixing the pump house. Gone are notes left for the neighbors, tucked in between the screen and the door. Gone are days uninterrupted by bells.

It's not just a question of doing without, but doing with. What do you do with whole days all to yourself? What do you do with a fortnight of evenings spent with your closest family without parties, movies, meetings to keep you apart? What do you do with a mile of beach in the quiet of first morning? If we leave the city to live as we do in the city, merely changing the views, we might as well stay at home. The summer house should preserve difference, maintain and underline it with big strokes. It's a place to take the long way round in all things—for the view, for the fun, for the good of it.

Rarely will summer houses set the scene for international peace agreements, yet they are places for another kind of peace whose accord goes unwritten. Nor will many contribute masterpieces of naturalism, seascapes hanging in museums, documents of cowboy life or an example of ideal architectural proportions. Yet as Leopold did at the shack, we forge a partnership with place. We feast on the quiet and isolation of places like Poplar Forest, which nourish beyond words. As at Beinn Bhreagh, families can gather and tie themselves together with bonds of shared summers. And like Roosevelt, we can discover a life as unobstructed as the prairies. There, we can live a little closer to the ground we walk on, feeding and sating all the senses. And when leaving we can bring a few of those values back with us.

As I write this in deep midwinter, it is gray in the morning, gray in the afternoon, so that only a clock tells when to wake, when to lunch; there are no cues from the sun—no lines cutting across the room at certain times of day. And I think about going back to the studio. For four months I've stayed away, caged indoors in town, and have a famine for the place—my thirst goes unquenched. From this upright chair, straight as a schoolmarm's, I think about the old wicker chaise longue, where I might stay for the length of a day.

By the time I get there, the ground will just be starting to thaw, with an oddly heady, intoxicating smell, powerful with the promise of softer weather. And I think about days without hours, walks without destinations, led only by the instincts of the dog, a dowser pointing to an unseeable layer of the landscape. There, the days have a clear and definable beginning, middle and end.

Living by the rhythm of light, shivering instinctively when brush wolves howl in their hunting relays, all these things about life at summer places reveal that we, too, are part of that system of biology we call nature, not above or separate from it, but connected with a few weakened, frayed ties.

BIBLIOGRAPHY

Below is a list of books that inspired and informed my text, or that I drew upon often during my discussion. Also included are a few titles that would be worthwhile to explore for those desiring to do more reading on summer houses. What is not listed here is derived from interviews.

Ackerman, James S. *The Villa: Form and Ideology of Country Houses*. Princeton: Princeton University Press, 1985.

Amory, Cleveland. *The Last Resorts*. New York: Harper & Brothers, 1951.

Berry, Wendell. *Recollected Essays*. San Francisco: North Point Press, 1981.

Bode, Carl, ed. *The Portable Thoreau*. New York: Penguin, 1984.

Bovie, Smith Palmer. *The Satires and Epistles of Horace*. Chicago: University of Chicago Press, 1959.

Corbin, Patricia. *Summer Cottages and Castles: Scenes from the Good Life*. New York: E. P. Dutton, 1983.

Dubos, René. *Wooing of the Earth*. New York: Charles Scribner's Sons, 1974.

Gill, Brendan. *Summer Places*. Toronto: McClelland and Stewart, 1978.

Hathaway, Katharine Butler. *The Little Locksmith*. New York: Arno Press, 1980 (first published 1943).

Howells, W. D. *Literature and Life: Studies*. Port Washington, N.Y.: Kennikat Press, Inc., 1968 (first published 1902).

James, Henry. "New England: An Autumn Impression" and "The Sense of Newport." Chapters 1 and 6 in *The American Scene*. New York: Harper Brothers, 1907.

Leopold, Aldo. *A Sand County Almanac*. New York: Oxford University Press, 1989 (first published 1949).

Niesewand, Nonie. *Holiday Homes*. New York: Henry Holt, 1987.

Shi, Donald. *The Simple Life: Plain Living and High Thinking in American Culture*. New York: Oxford University Press, 1985.

Stegner, Wallace. *Crossing to Safety*. New York: Random House, 1987.

Tuan, Yi-Fu. *Topophilia: A Study of Environmental Perception Attitudes and Values*. Englewood Cliffs, N.J.: Prentice-Hall, 1974.

Walker, Lester. *Tiny Houses*. New York: The Overlook Press, 1987.

Warner, Charles Dudley. "In the Wilderness." In *The Complete Writings of Charles Dudley Warner*. Hartford: The American Publishing Company, 1904.

White, E. B. "Once More to the Lake." In *One Man's Meat*. New York: Harper & Row, 1978.

1. The Idea of the Idyll

Anderson, Dorothy M. *The Era of the Summer Estates: Swampscott, Massachusetts, 1870/1940*. Canaan, N.H.: Phoenix Publishing, 1985.

Barry, James P. *Georgian Bay: The Sixth Great Lake*. Toronto: Clarke, Irwin & Co., 1978.

Battiata, Mary. "Czechoslovaks' Cottages Are Their Castles." *Washington Post*, 30 July 1990, A13.

Boyer, Barbaranne. *Muskoka's Grand Hotels*. Erin, Ont.: Boston Mills Press, 1987.

Brissenden, Constance. "Cottage Fever." *Western Living*, June 1989, 27-30.

Building in Canada. Summer Cottages Edition. Toronto: Whittemore Publications, July 1937.

Campan, Jeanne Louise Henriette. *Memoirs of the Private Life of Marie-Antoinette to Which Are Added Personal Recollections Illustrative of the Reigns of Louis XIV, XV, XVI*. Vol. 2. New York: Brentano's, 1930.

Coombe, Geraldine. *Muskoka Past and Present*. Toronto: McGraw-Hill Ryerson, 1976.

Coppock, J. T., ed. *Second Homes: Curse or Blessing?* New York: Pergamon Press, 1977.

Curry, David Park. *Childe Hassam. An Island Garden Revisited*. New York: W. W. Norton, 1990.

Curtis, George William. *Lotus Eating: A Summer Book*. New York: Dix, Edwards & Co., 1856.

Guide to Summer Resorts in Wisconsin, Minnesota, Michigan, etc. Rand McNally & Co., 1874.

Kaufman, Edgar and Bruno Zevi. *Frank Lloyd Wright's Fallingwater*. Milan: Etas Kompas, 1965.

Lakes and Resorts of the Northwest. Chicago: Chicago and Northwestern Railway, 1915.

Langley, Joan. *Yesterday's Asheville*. Miami: E. A. Seeman Publishers, 1975.

Leffingwell, Georgia Williams. *Social and Private Life at Rome in the Time of Plautus and Terence*. New York: AMS Press, 1968 (originally published 1918).

McKay, A. G. *Houses, Villas and Palaces in the Roman World*. London: Thames and Hudson, 1975.

Porter, Phil. *View from the Veranda: The History and Architecture of Summer Cottages on Mackinac Island*. Mackinac Island: Mackinac Island State Park Commission, 1981.

Orr, Robert T. *Animals in Migration*. New York: Macmillan, 1980.

Owens, Carole. *The Berkshire Cottages: A Vanishing Era*. Englewood Cliffs, N.J.: Cottage Press, 1984.

Tregaskis, Moana. "The Palaces and Gardens of Chengde." *New York Times*, 20 January 1991.

Wall, James and Joanne. *Fishers Island. A Book of Memories*. Southold, N.Y.: Peninsula Press, 1982.

Walker, Willa. *No Hayfever and a Railway: Summers in St. Andrews, Canada's First Seaside Resort*. Fredericton, N.B.: Goose Lane Editions, 1989.

Wilson, Richard Guy, ed. *Victorian Resorts and Hotels: Essays from a Victorian Society Autumn Symposium*. Published as Nineteenth Century: vol. 8, nos. 1-2. Philadelphia. The Victorian Society in America, 1982.

Wolfe, Roy. I. "The Summer Resorts of Ontario in the Nineteenth Century." *Ontario History*, September 1962, 149–160.

Zweig, Stefan. *Marie Antoinette: The Portrait of an Average Woman*. Toronto: The Macmillan Company of Canada, 1933.

2. Living on the Edge of Nature

Appleton, Jay. *The Experience of Landscape*. New York: Wiley, 1975.

Beam, Philip C, et al. *Winslow Homer in the 1090s: Prout's Neck Observed*. New York: Hudson Hills Press, 1990.

Berger, Frank, ed. *A Sharp Lookout: Selected Nature Writing by John Burroughs*. Washington: Smithsonian Institution Press, 1987.

Callicott, J. Baird, ed. *Companion to A Sand County Almanac: Interpretive and Critical Essays*. Madison: University of Wisconsin Press, 1987.

Fletcher, Katharine. *Historical Walks: the Gatineau Park Story*, Ottawa: Chesley House Publications, 1988.

Godley, Margaret. *Historic Tybee Island*. Savannah Beach: Savannah Beach Chamber of Commerce, 1958.

Gould, Jean. *Winslow Homer: A Portrait*. New York: Dodd, Mead & Co., 1962.

Helfrich, G. W. and Gladys O'Neil. *Lost Bar Harbor*. Camden: Down East Books, 1978.

Howe, Julia Ward. *Reminiscences 1819–1899*. New York: Negro University Press, 1879.

Hutchinson, Frances Kinsley. *Wychwood: The History of an Idea in Three Parts Our Country Home, Our Country Life, Our Final Aim*. Chicago: The Lakeside Press, 1928.

Huth, Hans. *Nature and the American: Three Centuries of Changing Attitudes*. Berkeley and Los Angeles: University of California Press, 1957.

Johnson, Madelcine, C. *Fire Island 1650s–1980s*. Mountainside, N.J.: Shoreland Press, 1983.

Krakauer, John. "In the San Juan Islands: Driftwood and Sod Shape a Seattle Architect's Residence." *Architectural Digest*, June 1989, 190–93.

Lowell, James Russell. *Poems*. Vol. 3. Boston: Houghton, Mifflin, 1890.

Meine, Curt. *Aldo Leopold: His Life and Work*. Madison: University of Wisconsin Press, 1988.

Murray, William H. H. *Adventures in the Wilderness; or Camp-Life in the Adirondacks*. Boston: Fields, Osgood & Co., 1869.

Nash, Roderick. *Wilderness and the American Mind*. New Haven: Yale University Press, 1984.

Northrup, A. Judd. *Camps and Tramps in the Adirondacks*. Syracuse: Davis Bardenn & Co., 1880.

Reed, William. *My Nantucket Summer: Extracts from the Diary of William M. Reed II*. Nantucket: Reprinted from the *Inquirer and Mirror*, 1939.

Tanzer, Helen. *The Villas of Pliny the Younger*. New York: Columbia University Press, 1924.

Town of Summerville, miscellaneous pages from the Town Hall and Archives.

Woodward, George. *Woodward's Country Homes*. New York: Geo. E. Woodward, 1865.

3. Sojourns in a Simpler Life

Ahlbrandt, Patricia. *Beaumaris*. Erin, Ont.: Boston Mills Press, 1989.

Aslet, Clive. "The Adirondacks." Chapter 12 in *The American Country House*. New Haven: Yale University Press, 1991.

Bishop, Joseph Bucklin. *Theodore Roosevelt and His Time Shown in His Own Letters*. 2 vols. New York: Scribner, 1929.

Blake, William Hume. *Brown Waters*. Toronto: Macmillan Canada, 1940.

Brechin, Gray. "Echo Lake: Paradise Leased." *Countryside*, Spring 1991.

Brine, Jenny. *Home, School and Leisure in the Soviet Union*. Boston: George Allen & Unwin, 1980.

Brower, David. *For Earth's Sake: The Life and Times of David Brower*. Salt Lake City: Peregrine Smith Books, 1990.

Dubé, Philippe. *Charlevoix: Two Centuries at Murray Bay*. Montreal: McGill University Press, 1990.

Freud, Sigmund. Letter in the collection of the Adirondack Museum, Blue Mountain, N.Y.

Gilbreth, Frank B., Jr., and Ernestine Carey. *Cheaper by the Dozen*. New York: Harper & Row, 1963.

Gilliatt, Mary. *A House in the Country*. London: Hutchinson, 1973.

Helfrich, G. W., and Gladys O'Neil. *Lost Bar Harbor*. Camden: Down East Books, 1978.

Herlemann, Horst. *Quality of Life in the Soviet Union*. Boulder, Colo.: Westview Press, 1982.

Hooker, Mildred Phelps Stokes. *Camp Chronicles*. Blue Mountain Lake, N.Y.: Adirondack Museum, 1964.

Hoyt, Edwin. Chapter 12 in *The Life of an Island*. Brattelboro, Vt.: Stephen Greene Press, 1978.

Kaiser, Harvey. *Great Camps of the Adirondacks*. Boston: D. R. Godine, 1982.

Kaplan, Robert D. "Robert Frost's Vermont: In the Green Mountain National Forest, scenes from the Poems." *New York Times*, 1 September 1991.

Little Echoes: Echo Lakes Newsletter, vol. 4, nos. 1–4., 1991.

Long, Charles. "Stopping Time in Algonquin." *Cottage Life*. September/October 1983.

McCullough, David. *Mornings on Horseback*. New York: Simon & Schuster, 1981.

Meinecke, Conrad. *Your Cabin in the Woods: A Compilation of Cabin Plans and Philosophy for Discovering Life in the Great Out Doors*. Buffalo: Foster & Stewart, 1945.

Naisbett John and Patricia Aburdene. "West by Southwest: A Telluride Log House with Mining Camp Roots." *Architectural Digest*, June 1989, 206–212.

Pearson, Haydn S. "Week-end Farming." *American Home*, July 1941.

Roosevelt, Theodore. *Ranch Life and the Hunting-Trail*. Ann Arbor: University Microfilms, Inc., 1974.

Roosevelt, Theodore. *Theodore Roosevelt: An Autobiography*. New York: The Macmillan Company, 1914.

Scully, Vincent. *The Shingle Style Today: or the Historian's Revenge*. New York: George Braziller, 1974.

Sedgwick, Henry Dwight. *Memoirs of an Epicurean*. New York: The Bobbs-Merrill Company Publishers, 1942.

Shi, Donald. *The Simple Life: Plain Living and High Thinking in American Culture*. New York: Oxford University Press, 1985.

Smith, H. Perry. *The Modern Babes in the Woods or Summerings in the Wilderness*. Hartford: Columbian Book Company, 1872.

Tevlin, Jon. "A Taste of the Rural Life: Finding Peace of Mind on a Midwest Farm." *Travel Holiday*, September 1988, 32–35.

Thomas, George E. and Carl Doebly. *Cape May: Queen of the Seaside Resorts*. Philadelphia: Philadelphia Art Alliance Press, 1976.

Town of Summerville. Miscellaneous papers from the Town Hall and Archives. 1248–45.

Van Court, Robert H. "Vacation Homes in the Woods." *The Independent*, 1912.

Wah Wash Kesh: The Early Years. The Wah Wash Kesh Conservation Association, 1986.

White, Stewart Edward. *The Cabin*. New York: Grosset & Dunlap, 1911.

4. Retreating from the World

Conover, Jewel Helen. *Nineteenth-Century Houses in Western New York*. Albany: The Research Foundation of State University of New York, Albany, 1966.

Curtis, George William. *Lotus Eating: A Summer Book*. New York: Dix, Edwards & Co., 1856.

Dullea, Georgia. "In Tents by the Sea, an Annual Revival of the Spirit." *New York Times*, 6 July 1989, C1.

Engel, J. Ronald. *Sacred Sands: The Struggle for Community in the Indiana Dunes.* Middleton, Ct.: Wesleyan University Press, 1983.

Fitts, Dudley. *Sixty Poems of Martial in Translation.* New York, Harcourt, Brace & World, 1967.

Fryer, Mary Elinor. *Pictorial History of the Thousand Islands of the St. Lawrence.* Brockville, Ont.: Besancourt Publishers, 1977.

Gorham, B. W. *Camp Meeting Manual, A Practical Book for the Camp Ground.* Boston: H. V. Degen, 1854.

Harris, Neil. "On Vacation." In *Resorts of the Catskills.* New York: St. Martin's Press, 1979.

Juvenal, translated by Peter Green. *Sixteen Satires.* New York: Penguin, 1974.

Lovejoy, J. Frederick. "The Isle of Rest, A Pen and Camera Picture of Nantucket," *The Four Track News,* July 1904, 39–41.

McEwan, Barbara. *Thomas Jefferson's Poplar Forest.* Lynchburg Va.: Warwick House Publishing, 1987.

Millay, Edna St. Vincent. "Ragged Island." *Harper's Magazine,* November 1946.

Mills, Barriss. *Epigrams from Martial: A Verse Translation.* Lafayette, Ind.: Purdue University Studies, 1969.

Morrison, Theodore. *Chautauqua: A Center for Education, Religion, and the Arts in America.* Chicago: University of Chicago Press, 1974.

Murray, William H. H. *Adventures in the Wilderness; or Camp-Life in the Adirondacks.* Boston: Fields, Osgood & Co., 1869.

Ricketson, Anna and Walton, eds. *Daniel Ricketson and His Friends: Letters Poems, Sketches, etc.* Boston: Houghton, Mifflin and Cambridge: The Riverside Press, 1902.

Rothery, Agnes. *Houses Virginians Have Loved.* New York: Bonanza Books, 1969.

Soames, Mary. *Winston Churchill: His Life As a Painter.* Toronto: Viking Penguin Canada, 1990.

Stern, Robert A. M. *Pride of Place: Building the American Dream.* Boston: Houghton Mifflin and New York: American Heritage, 1986.

Sweet, William Warren. *Religion on the American Frontier. Vol. 2, The Presbyterians.* New York: Cooper Square, 1964.

Thompson, Shawn. *River Rats: The People of the Thousand Islands.* Burnstown, Ont.: The General Store Publishing House, 1989.

Townsend, Reginald. *God Packed My Picnic Basket.* New York: New England Society in the City of New York, Inc., 1970.

Turcotte, Dorothy. *Greetings from Grimsby Park: The Chautauqua of Canada.* Grimsby: Grimsby Historical Society, 1985.

Victoria Point, Lake Simcoe. Orillia, Ont.: Clark's Land Agency, circa 1914.

Walker, Lester. *Tiny Houses.* New York: The Overlook Press, 1987.

Weiss, Ellen. *City in the Woods: The Life and Design of an American Camp Meeting on Martha's Vineyard.* New York: Oxford University Press, 1987.

Wiley, Harvey W. "A Day's Vacation Once a Week Is What Every Housewife Needs." *Good Housekeeping,* July 1927, 26.

5. Coming Home to the Family

Beinn Bhreagh Recorder. Issues from 1909, 1910, 1915.

Beyer, Bill. "The Outing Club: An Iowa Heirloom." *Architecture Minnesota*, July/August 1989, 34–35.

Blue Hill Library. Miscellaneous papers.

Bruce, Robert V. *Bell: Alexander Graham Bell and the Conquest of Solitude*. Ithaca: Cornell University Press, 1973.

Eber, Dorothy. *Genius at Work: Images of Alexander Graham Bell*. New York: Viking, 1982.

Evers, Alf, et al. *Resorts of the Catskills*. New York: St. Martin's Press, 1979.

Greene, Francis. *History of Boothbay, Southport and Boothbay Harbor*. Somersworth, Me.: New England History Press, 1984.

Iron City Fishing Club. Published by Iron City Fishing Club, 1981.

Ishwara K., ed. *Family and Marriage: Cross Cultural Perspectives*. Toronto: Wall & Thompson, 1989.

Johnson, Madeleine, C. *Fire Island 1650s–1980s*. Mountainside, N.J.: Shoreland Press, 1983.

Northrup, A. Judd. *'Sconset Cottage Life: A Summer on Nantucket Island*. Syracuse: C. W. Bardeen Publisher, 1901 (first published 1881).

Our Spirit's Home: Rockywold-Deephaven Camps, founded 1897, A Chronicle. Holderness, N.H., 1985 (material assembled by Franklin Perkins).

Rath, Sara. "Summer People Summer Places," *Wisconsin Trails Magazine*, March/April 1987, 16–23.

Waite, Helen Elmira. *Make a Joyful Sound: The Romance of Mabel Hubbard and Alexander Graham Bell*. Philadelphia: McCrae Smith Co., 1961.

Wharton, Edith. *A Backward Glance*. New York: Charles Scribner's Sons, 1962 (first published 1933).

Wister, Fanny Kemble, ed. *That I May Tell You: Journals and Letters of the Owen Wister Family*. Wayne, Pa.: Haverford House, 1979.

6. Cottage Culture

Adams, Samuel Hopkins. *A. Woollcott: His Life and His World*. Salem, N.H.: Ayer Co, 1972.

Atwood, Margaret. *Wilderness Tips*. Toronto: McClelland and Stewart, 1991.

Bourgeault, Cynthia. "Swan's Island, Maine." *Yankee*, May 1991, 54–60, 110–112.

Butler, Joyce. *Kennebunk Scrapbook*. Vol 1. Kennebunk, Maine: Thomas Murphy Publisher, 1977.

"Camp David—and After," *U.S. News and World Report*, 18 September 1978, 16–19.

Carter, Jimmy. *Keeping Faith*. New York: Bantam Books, 1982.

Carter, Rosalynn. *First Lady from Plains*. Boston: Houghton Mifflin, 1984.

Collier, Sargent F. Mt. Desert Island and Acadia National Park: An Informal History. Camden: Down East Publications, 1978.

Coombe, Geraldine. Muskoka Past and Present. Toronto: McGraw-Hill Ryerson, 1976.

Dubé, Philippe. Charlevoix: Two Centuries at Murray Bay. Montreal: McGill University Press, 1990.

Dulles, John Foster. America Learns to Play. New York: P. Smith, 1952.

L'Espace et son double: de la résidence secondaire aux autres formes secondaires. Paris: Editions du Champs urbain, 1978.

Evers, Alf. A History of the Catskills. New York: St. Martin's Press. 1979.

Finland: Land of the Midnight Sun. Helsinki: Oy Valitut Palat–Reader's Digest, 1980.

Gill, Brendan. "View from Hoover Hall." Architectural Digest, June 1991, 156–63.

Hurwitt, Jannika. "Let the Lanterns Be Lit!" Yankee, August 1983, 156–7.

"Inside Camp David." Newsweek, 2 October 1978, 39–40.

Kanfer, Stefan. A Summer World. New York: Farrar Straus and Giroux, 1990.

Kazanjian, Dodie. "The Bushes of Kennebunkport." House and Garden, June 1989, 140–45.

Konya, Allan. Finnish Sauna. London: The Architectural Press, 1987.

Lee, Edwin. Watering Places of England. London: Churchill, 1853.

Northrup, A. Judd. 'Sconset Cottage Life: A Summer on Nantucket Island. Syracuse: C. W. Bardeen Publisher, 1901 (first published 1881).

Peabody, Marian. "Old Bar Harbor Days." Down East, July 1965, 34–37.

Percival, Reniers. The Springs of Virginia. Charlotte, N.C.: University of North Carolina Press, 1955.

Sargent, Shirley. Yosemite's Rustic Outpost: Foresta, Big Meadow. Yosemite: Flying Spur Press, 1983.

Sedgwick, Henry Dwight. Memoirs of an Epicurean. New York: The Bobbs-Merrill Company Publishers, 1942.

Sloane, Florence Adele. Maverick in Mauve: The Diary of a Romantic Age. Garden City, N.Y: Doubleday, 1983.

Townsend, Reginald. God Packed My Picnic Basket. New York: New England Society in the City of New York, Inc., 1970.

Wheeler, George Augustus. Castine Past and Present. Boston: Rockwell and Churchill Press, 1893.

7. Building the Summer House Idea

Aldrich, Chilson. "I Build A Log Cabin." In 130 Summer Homes. Craft Publishers, 13 July 1942.

Boutell, Sara Holmes. Julia Morgan, Architect. New York: Abbeville Press, 1987.

Brown, Patricia Leigh. "Chicago's Getaway: Not the Hamptons. No Way." New York Times, 16 August 1990, C1.

Building in Canada, Summer Cottages. Toronto: Walkers Publishing, 1942.

Candilis, Georges. Recherches sur l'architecture des loisirs. Paris: Editions Eyrolles, 1973.

Comstock, William Phillips. *Bungalows, Camps and Mountain Houses*. Washington, D.C.: The American Insititute of Architects Press, 1990 (originally published 1915).

Curtis, William J. R. *Le Corbusier: Ideas and Forms*. New York: Rizzoli, 1986.

Downing, Andrew Jackson. *Victorian Cottage Residences*. New York: Dover Publications, 1981 (originally published 1842).

"The Extra House," *Look*, 10 August 1957, 69,70.

Gagnon-Pratte, Françoise. *Country Houses for Montrealers 1892–1924: The Architecture of E. and W. S. Maxwell*. Montreal: Meridien Press, 1987.

Gardiner, Stephen. *Le Corbusier*. New York: The Viking Press, 1974.

Gilborn, Craig. *Adirondack Furniture and the Rustic Tradition*. New York: Harry N. Abrams, 1987.

Goldberger, Paul. "The Hamptons: Architectural Vigor of the Summer Enclave." *Architectural Digest*, June 1987, 74–75.

Gowans, Alan. *The Comfortable House: North American Suburban Architecture 1890–1930*. Cambridge: The MIT Press, 1986.

Grow, Lawrence, ed. *The Old House Book of Outdoor Living Spaces*. New York: Warner Books, 1981.

Hamilton, William L. "The Architecture of Leisure." *Metropolitan Home*, July 1989, 67–72.

Harbor Springs: A Collection of Essays. Harbor Springs, Mich.: Harbor Springs Historical Commission, 1981.

Hewitt, Mark Alan. *The Architect and the American Country House 1890–1940*. New Yaven: Yale University Press, 1990.

Kaiser, Harvey. *Great Camps of the Adirondacks*. Boston: D. R. Godine, 1982.

Kay, Jane Holtz. "The Return of a Native: The Porch." *New York Times*, 8 June 1989, C1.

Lewis, Arnold. *American Country Houses of the Gilded Age* (Sheldon's "Artistic Country-Seats"). New York: Dover Publications, 1982.

Lindbloom, K. G. "The Use of the Hammock in Africa." Stockholm: Broderna Lagerstrom, boktryckare) Swedish Ethnographic Library, 1928.

Long, Charles. "The Catchacoma Connection." *Cottage Life*, May/June 1991, 38–42, 90.

Menz, Katherine B. "Wicker the Vacation Furniture." In *Victorian Resorts and Hotels*. Philadelphia: The Victorian Society of America, 1982.

Murphy, Jim. "A Gate at Seaside." *Progressive Architecture*, vol. 70, December 1989, 66–73.

Newton, Roger Hale. "Our Summer Resort Architecture—An American Phenomenon and Social Document," *The Art Quarterly* 4, no. 4. Detroit: (Autumn 1941) 297–318.

The Pawleys Island Story. Pawleys Island, S.C.: Pawleys Island Hammock Company, 1991.

Ragot, Gilles and Mathilde Dion. *Le Corbusier en France: Réalisations et projets*. Paris: Electa Moniteur, 1981.

Saint-Gaudens, Augustus. Adapted from a lecture. Cornish, N.H: Saint-Gaudens Memorial, 1927.

Scully, Vincent. *The Shingle Style*. New Haven: Yale University Press, 1955.

Scully, *The Shingle Style Today*.

Tatum, Rita. *The Alternative House. A Complete Guide to Building and Buying*. Los Angeles: Reed Books, 1978.

Van Holst, H. V. *Modern American Homes*. New York: Dover Publications, 1982 (originally published 1912).

Wharton, Edith. *Italian Villas and Their Gardens*. New York: The Century Co., 1904.

White, Charles D. *Camps and Cottage: How to Build Them*. New York: Thomas Y. Crowell Co., 1939.

Wolgensinger, Bernard. *Vacation Houses of Europe*. Paris: Office du Livre, 1968.

Woodbridge, Sally B. and Tim Street-Porter. "Historic Architecture: Julia Morgan's Woodland Creation for William Randolph Hearst." *Architectural Digest*, January 1988, 98.

8. Reaping a Harvest of Experience

Adams, Henry. *The Education of Henry Adams: An Autobiography*. Boston: Houghton Mifflin Company and Cambridge: The Riverside Press. 1961.

Dubos, René. *A God Within*. New York: Charles Scribner's Sons, 1972.

Gould, Jean. *The Poet and Her Book*. New York: Dodd Mead, 1962.

Havel, Vaclav, translated by Paul Wilson. *Letters to Olga*. New York: Alfred A. Knopf, 1988.

Hooker, Mildred Phelps Stokes. *Camp Chronicles*. Blue Mountain Lake, New York: Adirondack Museum, 1964.

Hutchinson, Frances Kinsley. *Our Country Life*. Chicago: A. C. McClurg & Co., 1912.

James, Henry, ed. *The Letters of William James*. New York: Kraus Reprint Co., 1969.

Lovejoy, J. Frederick. "The Isle of Rest, A Pen and Camera Picture of Nantucket." *The Four Track News*, July 1904, 39–41.

Northrup, A. Judd. *'Sconset Cottage Life: A Summer on Nantucket Island*. Syracuse: C. W. Bardeen Publisher, 1901 (first published 1881).

Pagnol, Marcel. *La Gloire de mon père*. Paris: Editions Pastorelly, 1957.

Rapoport, Rhona, and Robert N. Rapoport. *Leisure and the Family Lifecycle*. Boston: Routledge & Kegan, 1975.

Sedgwick, Henry Dwight. *Memoirs of an Epicurean*. New York: The Bobbs-Merrill Company Publishers, 1942.

Shapiro, Stephen and Alan J. Tuckman. *Time Off: A Psychological Guide to Vacations*. New York: Anchor Press/Doubleday, 1987.

Wharton, Edith. *A Backward Glance*. New York: C. Scribner's Sons, 1933.